LIFE AND CULTURE
OF POLAND

> *Litwo! Ojczyzno moja! ty jesteś*
> *jak zdrowie;*
> *Ile cię trzeba cenić, ten tylko się*
> *dowie,*
> *Kto cię stracił.*
>
> Adam Mickiewicz,
> *Pan Tadeusz,* I, 1-3.

LIFE AND CULTURE

OF

POLAND

As reflected in Polish Literature

by

WACLAW LEDNICKI

ROY PUBLISHERS   NEW YORK

PRINTED IN THE UNITED STATES OF AMERICA

ACKNOWLEDGMENT

I WISH to record my indebtedness to Mr. Leon Lipson, a former student in my Slavic courses at Harvard University who generously helped in preparing my English text. These lectures were given in the fall of 1943 at the Lowell Institute.

Contents

Contents

Preface

POLES are generally known as indulging in either national pride or in self-criticism. The rich and brilliant achievements of their national culture and at the same time their inability to preserve their political existence at the end of the eighteenth century developed in modern Poles these two conflicting tendencies.

While self-criticism represents the attitude of the Pole when he speaks before a Polish forum, the emphasis is on national pride in his attitude toward the outside world, each time he feels that the outside world is unjust toward Poland. This unfortunately has happened only too often. It came about as a result of the fact that Poland is situated historically and geographically on great crossroads, the meeting ground of mighty powers which for centuries have been rivaling for domination. Poland always seemed to stand in the way of somebody's ruling ambitions and therefore was always an object of denunciation. And so also, the very fact that Poland did not exist politically during the whole nineteenth century (and even longer) created in the historical consciousness of the outside world a sort of emptiness, a horrible vacuum, as far as Poland was concerned. Because of this lack of information and of curiosity about the cultural and political attainments of the Polish nation, anti-Polish propaganda has been able to achieve considerable success and triumph. Consequently, the Pole finds himself in a situation which obliges him to take a defensive attitude.

This book, written by a native Pole, naturally reflects both of these tendencies of the Polish mind. It is a picture in which shadows and lights are mixed, in which the truth is to be found behind the emotional approach to Polish life, to Polish culture and to Polish history. This life is shown here partly as revealed in Polish literature, as the author himself is in the first place a historian of literature. Polish literature has very often been particularly severe to the nation, but it was a severity guided by a very deep, strong attachment to the Motherland; it was guided by didactic purposes of a higher order. This is the reason why some pages of this book will perhaps give the reader an impression which might appear as too dark, too pessimistic, especially if one forgets the story of so many other nations in which one may find sometimes much deeper and darker shadows. Some other pages, on the contrary, might give the impression of national self-glorification, simply because they emphasize the indubitable and yet so little-known achievements of Polish culture.

In other words, this is the true story of Poland. It is, in the first place, an attempt to give an essentially human story. I have not tried to present here any abstract formulas. My speculations are connected with Polish life as revealed by Polish human nature in its historical development. This book is a sort of intellectual novel, the chief hero of which is the Polish nation. I think this method has some advantage, especially where the aim is to give to the foreign reader a general impression of the main characteristics of an unknown national soul. It is not a book of mere factual information—it is an interpretative discourse about the most salient traits of the Polish nation and most important tendencies of its historical evolution.

It is a personal synthesis, given in the form of public lectures.

It is a personal synthesis of the dynamic movement, of the constant effort toward evolution so deeply characteristic of the Polish nation.

This book represents an attempt to seize the movement, to give not so much a definition of it, as a feeling of it, an impression, the aim of which is to show the human truth of the inexhaustible Polish will to live and to create—to create personal and collective human happiness, in spite of all inhuman powers of history and nature mobilized for centuries against this so profoundly unfortunate nation. Poles, like every nation, like every human community, knew errors and sins, downfall and weaknesses in their common and individual life—but there is one trait very particular to them: they were and still are great when facing misfortune. This irrational, religious power of resistance, this boundless Polish enthusiasm, this Polish longing for greatness represents an undeniable justification of the existence of the Polish nation. These faculties of moral exaltation are the best guarantees of its survival and regeneration, as the law of regeneration has become its law. And this is the essential law of life . . .

LIFE AND CULTURE
OF POLAND

I

Interpretations of Polish History

WHEN our great poet Krasiński read in Lamartine's *History of the Girondists* certain passages devoted to Poland, he took his pen and wrote the French poet a wonderful letter. I wish I could quote it in full, but unfortunately I cannot. I must reduce my quotation to the first page:

"I know nothing more poignant than perceiving a speck in the middle of a radiant expanse of light. You who are more familiar than anyone with the mysterious ways of art, ought also to understand better than anyone else the effect produced upon the human heart by anything which, cast across a masterpiece, has the sad effect of blemishing its perfect beauty."

"Imagine Francesca da Rimini in the depths of the Inferno suddenly breaking off her sublime plaint to relate one of Aesop's Fables; and Dante, who was about to swoon with pity, forced to come back to life by dint of an involuntary smile which, brought in spite of him onto his lips, stops up the tears in his eyes and, by profaning it, kills the emotion in his heart. Imagine that, Monsieur, or anything similar, and you will have the impression I experienced when, after I had, seized with admiration, passed through that gallery of statues carved with the chisel of Phidias

3

to which you have given the name of the *History of the Girond-ists,* I reached the place where you describe, may I say with name-less levity, the condition of Poland at the moment of Dumouriez's expedition . . ."[1]

This case is not an isolated one. We Poles have constantly to defend ourselves against such "Aesop's Fables," and there are many reasons for this.

In the historical development of Poland compared with that of other European countries there is a sort of disharmony. Al-though on one hand closely bound to Western European civiliza-tion, and representing on the other hand a transition between West and East, Poland has frequently found herself in a sort of contradiction with the historical evolution of the countries of both Eastern and Western Europe. When, in the East, the power of the Muscovite State was growing and developing under the quite irreducible principle of the unlimited despotism of the Muscovite Czars, while in the West the absolutism of Kings and Emperors was emerging from the period of feudalism as a powerful and creative political factor, Poland established a re-publican style of life in which the monarchical power was reduced to the status of a servant of the freedom of the Polish citizens.[2] At the time when all Europe was absorbed by the most

[1] Zygmunt Krasiński, *Pisma,* Wydanie Jubileuszowe, Kraków, Gebethner i Spółka, 1912, V-VII, p. 219.
[2] Field Marshal von Moltke, comparing the destinies of Russian Poland, stressed this characteristic of Poland's political development in his book, which is a very important one even for the present time: *Darstellung der Inneren Verhaeltnisse und des Gesellschaftlichen Zustandes in Polen* (1832). "At an early period the inde-pendence of the (Russian) people was lost in serfdom, that of the nobles in the absolute power of the princes. The will of the individual was lost to sight more and more in the will of the State, or rather in that of the head of the State, who united in his person the highest civil and ecclesiastic power, in a manner unknown in any other part of Europe. Hence the unity and strength manifested in the enterprises of the (Russian) State, and its quick development, for despotism is the best govern-ment for barbarians. The Polish annals are thus the histories of great men, the Russian annals the history of a great State. In the former, we see the virtues of the individual contending with the faults of the community; in the latter, a line of princes with hereditary power who force a nation to assume a higher civilization."

savage religious wars and shaken by the most violent religious and racial persecutions, Poland herself enjoyed, and offered to everybody else, the most peaceful existence, based on respect for the rights of the individual and tolerance for religious faith. Then as Europe, in the seventeenth and eighteenth centuries, entered upon the period of free thought and rational criticism, Poland followed the line of political and religious reaction. Later, at the end of the eighteenth century, after Poland, in trying to save herself from that perilous road, had by a great spiritual effort elaborated reforms that aimed toward progress and democratic evolution, the reactionary forces of Europe mobilized against her as a source of dangerous political liberalism and liquidated Poland for more than a hundred years. Later, when all the active powers of Europe were bound together in a coalition against Napoleon, Poland fought for him everywhere until his finish.

The nineteenth century, which for the whole of Europe was an age of industrialization and the creation of great quantities of material goods, was for Poland—in spite of her domination by Russia, Austria, and Prussia—an age of a much more astonishing development of her spiritual creative powers and genius than of her material prosperity.

Poland belongs to the Slavic family of nations. Among these nations there developed at the end of the eighteenth but especially in the middle and later nineteenth centuries a strong movement, created by the so-called Slavophile doctrine. This doctrine had many adepts in Russia, in Serbia, in Bulgaria, and especially in

(Moltke, *Vermischte Schriften*, ii., p. 121—quoted by Charles Sarolea: *Letters on Polish Affairs*, Edinburgh, Oliver and Boyd, 1922, pp. 76-77.) "No Polish noble," says Moltke further, "was the vassal of a superior lord—the meanest of them appeared at the diet in the full enjoyment of a power which belonged to all without distinction. It is here that we find the fundamental difference between the Polish constitution and the Feudal States of the West and the despotism of the East (see Sarolea, *op. cit.*, p. 77).

Bohemia. There were some sympathizers with this historical and political conception in Poland—but very few. The whole nation, the whole thinking intellectual élite of Poland, has always been against it. Again, Poland found herself in a peculiar and isolated situation.

In the field of social structure, we see in Western Europe in modern times—that is, in the eighteenth and nineteenth centuries —a constant and persistent development of the bourgeoisie, the so-called middle class. This middle stratum of society created the spiritual culture of Western Europe and until very recent times assumed responsibility for Europe's political fate. The middle class, from which the so-called intelligentsia everywhere emerged, was distinctly separated from other classes of society. In Poland, we see that the ancient Polish-Lithuanian-Ruthenian Commonwealth was built by the nobility and that it was the nobility which lost it. We see, further, that it was to a great extent the nobility which later fought for the reconquest of former independence— in the insurrection of Kościuszko, in the insurrection of 1830-31, and in the insurrection of 1863. We see a great number of Polish nobles in all the revolutionary and socialist movements of the latter part of the nineteenth century and the beginning of the twentieth. We see finally that in the Polish middle class and in the Polish intelligentsia a very considerable part, if not the majority, originate from the nobility or the gentry. And this social phenomenon is followed by another—the role which the gentry's customs, manners, and general way of living played in the life of the whole nation. The Polish peasant, the Polish worker, and the Polish bourgeois—all of these classes adopted the style of life of the Polish gentry. This sort of special social unification has no other example, save possibly in Spain. Among the Slavic nations, Poland is from this point of view very exceptional.

These are, in broad lines and in short words, the most characteristic traits of Polish historical and cultural development. But such phenomena are rather signs than facts, and the average Pole as such is not very conscious of them. He feels only one thing: that his world-outlook, in spite of his deep attachment to Western civilization, differs from that of the Western European, and that his opinion of his country, her past and present, is very unlike the opinion held by the non-Pole. Here we face a very peculiar phenomenon—the immense disparity between the Polish interpretation of Poland and the non-Polish interpretation. And here we must deal not only with the present and with the character of the Polish nation, but with the past. The most important fact in that past, which absorbed the attention of Polish historiography as well as Polish literature, was, of course, the Polish catastrophe, the disappearance of Poland from the map of Europe—in other words, the partitions of Poland.

Before touching this question I should like to tarry an instant at one capital fact in the history of Poland. This is that, although at the end of the eighteenth century Poland had reached the end of her power, she had still in the seventeenth been one of the mightiest and at the same time one of the vastest, states in Europe. Suffice it to say that her frontiers advanced in the east to Smolensk, in the southeast to the Black Sea, in the north to the Baltic Sea. In the west, her neighbors were Bohemia and the German Empire. It was in the sixteenth century that Poland attained the pinnacle of her power.

But that is not all. The Polish state—this immense empire— was a free union, a federation of Poland, Lithuania, and Ruthenia, with Prussia as vassal-country and Livonia as well under Poland's wardship. The hereditary monarchy of Poland was little by little transformed into a republic with an elective king at the head.

In some respects, therefore, it recalled England, in some—the Republican Rome. The lower class, that of the peasants, did not participate in the government. "As to that," says one of our authors justly, "all the criticisms of our enemies, who strive to represent the oppression of the peasants as peculiar to Poland, are based on ignorance or malice. Nothing essentially distinguishes Poland, in this regard, from the rest of Europe."[3] What does distinguish her is that Poland preceded all the nations of Europe (save England) in the success of political organizations inspired by the ideas of liberty and equality before the law— ideas which became the mottoes of the French Revolution. By the end of the fifteenth century Poland had already solidly established a regime which guaranteed citizens individual liberty: the law, *"Neminem captivabimus nisi jure victum,"* was published in 1433. If, to these national and individual guarantees, to these principles of federation with neighboring peoples and of civil liberty, we add the astonishing religious toleration and the marvelous blossoming of literature, art, and science in Poland with Copernicus at the head, we must acknowledge that at this period of her history Poland had attained the level of a truly brilliant civilization.[4]

But this civilization had its defects. It was too hasty; it had been too quickly and too easily elaborated, its territorial expansion had been accomplished with too little effort, the nobility had too easily made its liberal conquests, the diminution of the royal power had been too rapid; the principles of liberty and equality began too much to contradict and counter one another; national

[3] See Eugène Starczewski, *L'Europe et la Pologne*, Paris, Perrin et Cie, 1913, pp. 8-9.

"The (Polish) peasant," says Moltke, "did not belong to the lord, he could not be sold. The estate might pass into other hands, but the peasant was not obligated to leave his farm. The fact that he could possess land prevented him from ever becoming a mere serf . . . the peasant was well off; he could raise money on his property and had regular tribunals . . . He enjoyed the possession of home and land . . . The Polish peasant enjoyed these privileges at a time when villein-age existed in all the rest of Europe . . ." (See Sarolea, *op. cit.*, p. 82.)

[4] Moltke says: "Poland was already in the fifteenth century one of the most civilized states in Europe—" (see Sarolea, *op. cit.*, p. 83).

activity tended no longer toward the struggle with the neighboring enemy but toward internal civil evolution—an evolution which was too rapid, as I have already said. It led to the Polish paradox, which was that the least of the country squires could say in Poland, *"L'Etat c'est moi."*

Slightly better oriented in the general situation of historical Poland, we may, after this preamble, enter upon the essential subject of our research. The essential problem which Polish political and historical thought has been striving, and is still striving today, to resolve is the problem of the Partitions—the catastrophe of 1772 and that of 1795, and the problem of responsibility for them.[5]

In his now classic book, *The Eastern Question in the Eighteenth Century*, the illustrious French historian, Albert Sorel, established a thesis that no one, in the fifty years since his book appeared, has been able to refute:

"By signing this partition (of Poland) the monarchies of divine right themselves shook the edifice of their power . . . The authors of the partition were, without suspecting it, the precursors of a revolution, and this revolution, in order to overturn their thrones and overthrow their empires, needed only to turn against them their own conduct and imitate their examples. The partition, which was an iniquitous job, was at the same time an impolitic job. The historian must judge it as severely as the philosopher . . ."[6]

Some time before Sorel, Zygmunt Krasiński said the same thing in his *Memorial to Pope Pius IX:*

". . . The divine order that presides over human affairs was violated by the trustees of this very order. The three sovereigns

---

[5] The best source of information: Robert Howard Lord, *The Second Partition of Poland*, Cambridge, Harvard University Press, 1915.

[6] Albert Sorel, *La Question d'orient au XVIII siècle*, 2ème éd., Paris, 1889, pp. 274-275.

who, like vile conspirators, stealthily undermined the edifice of the republic of Poland and who later, throwing off the mask, revealed themselves to her as her executioners . . . have by that very act committed an apostasy and a revolt against the word of Christ . . ."[7]

We may find the same opinion, quoted by R. H. Lord, in a book by an old French author: "It was the kings themselves who, on the eve of the insurrection of peoples, taught them that no right existed for them except that of the strongest, and that when they invoked liberty, it was an ignoble sacrilege; they taught them that they were not to be believed even when they spoke of the public tranquillity, and of the respect due to the hereditary power of princes; for these same monarchs who constituted themselves the defenders of monarchy in France, dismembered Poland while appealing to the most anarchical liberty! In short, there was only one law for them, only one principle, that of interest and the glory of their dynasties. The peoples have profited by the lesson."[8]

But here again is another characteristic of this historical fact. This is the commentary of an Englishman—Lord Eversley, who demonstrated that the victory of Valmy, and the victory of the Revolution, must be explained not by "the miracle of the Revolutionary faith—the true explanation is to be sought not in the forest of Argonne, but in the plains of Eastern Europe." England's allies were busy in Poland, and Prussia had spent the money, furnished it by England, for the Partitions of Poland, not for the war against the French Revolution.

"The French Revolution was saved not mainly because of the heroism of the Sans-Culottes, but because at a critical moment

[7] Zygmunt Krasiński, *op. cit.*, p. 244.
[8] F. Laurent, *Études sur l'histoire de l'humanité*, Paris, 1865, quoted by R. H. Lord, *op. cit.*, pp. 504-505.

Poland diverted the main forces of the enemies of liberty. Not for the first time nor for the last, Poland was sacrificed to the cause of liberty."[9]

The act of the Partitions, which Sorel judged so severely, produced no indignation in European public opinion. There were two reasons for this. The first was propaganda, and well-paid propaganda. Catherine II appears in the guise of "Catherine the Great," and Frederick II likewise as the "Great Frederick" of d'Alembert, Diderot, Grimm, Voltaire—all the Encyclopedists—those clerks of their time, who, with all their might, explain, justify, admire the "enlightened despots" "who were inspired with the loftiest motives" in "partaking of the Eucharistic body of Poland."

The other reason is the political tradition, customs, skeptical and amoral spirit—above all in politics—of the "Age of Enlightenment." The partition of Poland had by no means opened a new page in the history of international relations in Europe; on the contrary, this act of brigandage was connected with a secular tradition. No difficulty at all for the co-partitioners to find excuses and justifications for their "operation"—the age offered them precedents to their taste, and quite ancient ones, too. Already Pascal had sighed sadly in his *Pensées, "Ne pouvant fortifier la justice, on a justifié la force."* "When justice is lacking in force, force is the only justice." And Richelieu: "He who has force is often right in a matter of state; and he who is weak can with difficulty exempt himself from being in the wrong in the judgement of the greater part of the world."

Machiavelli had firmly established the principles of "Realpolitik": "It is perfectly natural and ordinary to desire to extend

[9] Cited by Charles Sarolea, *Letters on Polish Affairs*, Edinburgh, Oliver and Boyd, 1922, p. 64.

and widen one's boundaries, and when men can do it and undertake it, they are greatly praised for it, or at least are not
reproved."

The law of the stronger would appear to be the better. Men
admired conquest, and even Montesquieu, speaking in the eighteenth century about law and conquest, could say: "A law unfortunate but necessary and therefore legitimate." The spirit of
relativism and skepticism had completely demolished all the
ideological bases of international law: "Time, occasion, usage,
prescription, force, make all laws," says Voltaire. To be sure,
as we know, Bossuet, Montesquieu, and even Rabelais had attempted to "condition" the "right of the stronger," but the European practice followed the tradition established from Machiavelli to Voltaire. Hence the sovereigns who had dismembered
Poland did not have to bother about the reactions of European
public opinion.[10]

But for Poland it was different. It was different not only because Poland had to play the sad part of victim of this "law" of
conquest, but because this "operation" was absolutely contrary to
the practice as well as to the theory of Polish political tradition.
At the very moment of the catastrophe, as well as immediately
after it—given all the great events which followed that catastrophe: the Napoleonic Wars, the creation of a Duchy of Warsaw,
the Congress of Vienna, the Polish insurrections—it was difficult
for the Poles to take up, under such conditions, studies of a
"historiosophic" character.

This does not mean that in the eighteenth century there were no
Polish historians who dwelt upon the study of the causes of Po-
land's decadence and weakness. Quite the contrary—we see the
Bishop of Smolensk, Naruszewicz, father of our modern his-

---

[10] See K. Waliszewski, *Poland the Unknown*, London, William Heinemann, 1919.
Also R. H. Lord, *op. cit.* See also Stanislaw Kot, *Rzeczpospolita Polska w Literaturze
Politycznej Zachodu*, Kraków, 1919.

toriography, advancing the opinion—to be developed further— that the essential cause of the fall of Poland is the state of anarchy in which the Republic lay, that anarchy being the resultant of the weakness of monarchical power in Poland. This opinion prevailed even among the Polish "progressives" of the eighteenth century, such as Kołłątaj and Staszyc, admirers of Rousseau, Franklin, and Washington. This theory was later, after the insurrection of 1830-31, developed in Paris in those circles which were grouped around Prince Czartoryski.

On the other hand, there existed also the republican current, represented by Wielhorski—collaborator of Rousseau—and carried later into the nineteenth century, above all after 1830 (at Paris and Brussels) by Lelewel. Anarchy had brought Poland to its fall—but it was the kings, magnates, and nobility who were responsible for Polish disorder, because they had introduced into Poland alien elements of usurpation which had caused her to deviate from republican principles, principles of general equality and liberty. This democracy of Lelewel, his attacks on the Polish nobility, this liberalism, in the broad sense, were to become the point of departure for the school of Warsaw, representing the optimism of Polish historiography. The thirties of the last century, then, can be considered the moment when Polish thought made a particularly great effort to exalt the national misfortune. It did this despite the fact that fate had hounded Poland and had never granted it peace—be it only leisure to think. But nations of vigorous and resistant spirit bear political suffering with Stoicism, just as human beings of rich moral resources adapt themselves to physical ills. Between the insurrection of 1830 and that of 1863, and then between 1863 and the First World War, the poetry and prose of Polish belles-lettres as well as historiography continued to be absorbed by the problem of the nation's catastrophe and the nation's future.

One must, however, keep in mind the painful, tragic conditions in which Polish thought was obliged to accomplish this great task —conditions not only morally painful, but dangerous. They were painful because they forced Polish creative thought to confine itself to national problems and sacrifice all attempts that spoke of broader, universal horizons. Only the greatest Polish geniuses succeeded in wedding the national and the universal, in finding formulae of a general order for the very essence of Polish unhappiness. The conditions were dangerous because every criticism of the Polish past, every attempt at the heroic act of making Poland herself responsible for even a *part* of the causes that had led her to catastrophe, was immediately exploited by her enemies, tireless in justifying the Partitions.[11]

For over a century this secret conspiracy of German and Russian historiography has promoted in the memory and imagination of the whole world several "truths" about Poland which we even today strive vainly to combat, for this conspiracy has not ceased to exist, and the adherents of Stalin and those of Hitler, and many others, persevere in using the same old arguments against us. For, in spite of the fact that Poland was in ruins and the nation in three coffins, Polish thought continued to defend itself. It was on the defensive. And the defensive is never advantageous, as we all know without being strategists.

I think that Wacław Sobieski, one of our greatest contemporary historians—former professor of the University of Cracow—has given the best, and most penetrating explanation of the shades and tendencies of modern Polish historical thought, as well as the conditions that have determined them. By way of introduction to his study, *Optimism and Pessimism in Polish Historiography* (which appeared in 1912), Sobieski recalls the example of Taine,

---

[11] See the brilliant book by Robert Howard Lord, *The Second Partition of Poland*, Cambridge, Harvard University Press, 1915.

studying the French catastrophe of 1871. Taine—the objective
scholar par excellence, implacable defender of the principles of
positivism, "ascetically" impartial historian—felt a mortal wound
at the sight of the terrible devastations wrought in France by the
Commune: "The heart is dead in my breast," he confessed. The
historian is no machine; the historian has a heart, and Taine's
heart bled as he feverishly pursued the studies whose end was to
seek out the genesis of unhappiness! As a result of this suffering
comes the pessimism of Taine and his "school," which at last
finds the causes of disaster in the interior of the nation, above all
in its character. As we know, France later underwent a reaction
against this pessimism, and the French Revolution was justified
in French historical works by the fact of Prussian aggression—
that is, *external* causes.

If a single defeat, a single catastrophe, could produce such
sudden perturbation in the general interpretation of the *entire*
past of a glorious nation, which had, besides, the privilege of
continuing a quite peaceful existence after the catastrophe—it is
not astonishing that to this day the historiography of Poland has
not been able to stop floundering in the grasp of the struggle between pessimism and optimism. That is why we find in our literature a permanent dualism, a continual contradiction, an incessant
struggle of antinomic opinions. Our great Romantics exemplify
it. Słowacki—"the poet-historiographer" of Poland—wrote once
that Poland is "the Winkelried of nations," the people angelic
and Christian in the very essence of its soul, "the elected of the
nations"—and at another time, in a moment of ill-humor, flung
the reproach that we ourselves repeat in moments of gall and
rancor against ourselves, that "Poland is the fawn and parrot of
the nations," and that there are no limits to its megalomania.
Mickiewicz will attack the vices and faults of his compatriots to
console them later with his doctrine of "the Christ of nations"—

that theory which has done as much harm as good to Poland. Krasiński—the deepest and best-balanced among them, the most penetrating, and possessed of a particularly open mind—will develop, just the same, that doctrine of Polish Messianism—for all of which, no one before him and almost no one since has had the courage to advance, in regard to Poland, such bitter and annihilating criticisms as are to be found in some of the great poet's letters.

Yet it is striking, as Sobieski observes, that it should be in Paris, in the Polish emigration after the Insurrection of 1830-31, that the optimistic doctrines were founded and elaborated. It is striking, but it is comprehensible; it was a quite legitimate and natural effort by Polish thought, the purpose of which was to give the nation powers of resistance, console it for the catastrophe, by assuring it of a justification of a superior order—namely, religious. For the very essence of this optimism lies precisely in the religious character of these speculations on the "Christ of the Nations." The suffering of the Polish people—in the doctrine of our Romantics—received a religious sanction, it became an expiatory suffering which was in a certain way gratuitous, it became a theodicy of the historical existence of Poland. Poland was expiating its own faults, but also the faults of other nations, and its future resurrection was to inaugurate a new era, the era of Christianized international politics. This doctrine conformed, as we shall see later, to the conceptions of the Polish political writers of the sixteenth century—that is why it must be considered deeply national and traditional. On the other hand, despite its somewhat exceptional character and the aberrations of its phraseology, it contained elements of common sense and realism: it was clear that there was no possibility of the restoration of Poland so long as that European political system should endure which had permitted the Partitions of Poland. A new world, a new universal order must be established for Poland to emerge from its tomb. In this sense our poets, with all the visionary fervor of their romantic temperaments, represented an idealism which ought not to be ridiculed and abused;[12] the current war puts us face to face with problems which are in truth of absolutely the same nature. But insofar as the optimism of our Romantics as they envisage the future of the world and of Poland appears to us today defensible—the War of 1914-18 justified it—their optimism adapted to Poland's past was indefensible, in the same degree; the Poland of the past, seen from the banks of the Seine in 1830-50, seemed to them "more beautiful, rich, and powerful" (I am quoting Sobieski) "than it had ever been in reality."[13]

Nothing disquieted this optimism, not even the year 1846, which was particularly grievous for Poland. This was the year of the subjugation of Cracow, which had theretofore been a "free city," and the massacre of Galicia. Metternich's government had successfully accomplished these two undertakings. What is really astonishing is that it is at this same Cracow, and immediately after the catastrophes of 1846, that a current of optimism de-

[12] This doctrine is not exclusively a Polish one—I tried to give its genealogy in my study *Poland and the Slavophile idea*, published in *The Slavonic Review*, London, 1928-29. Milton speaks about England as about a nation elected by God; Puritans call the British "the Lord's people," and even Lord Curzon considers the English Empire as an "instrument of Providence." I need not quote here representatives of Russian messianism, beginning in the fifteenth century with the theory of "Moscow the third Rome" and reappearing, after all the Russian Slavophiles and Panslavists, in the messianic theories of the Third International. In France, Ganneau, as well as Hugo, calls the French *grand—Christ-peuple*. I have not to cite Germans—the German people are not "the elected of God," but simply "people—God" (like Dostoevski's Russian *narod bogonosetz*)—*"nicht das auserwaehlte Volk Gottes, sondern das Gottvolk."* Polish messianism begins in the fifteenth century and develops later the conception of *antemurale Christianitatis*, certainly connected, like all messianic theories, with the chief source of messianism of every sort—Hebrew messianism. We may find elements of messianic character already in Długosz, Ostroróg, later in Skarga, Potocki, Starowolski, Kochanowski—the defense of religion is always connected with the defense of the state. Brodziński was the first (and after him our great Romantics) who advanced the comparison between the sacrifice of Poland and the death of Christ on Golgotha. (Comp. J. Bystroń—*Megalomanja Narodowa*, Warsaw, 1935.)

[13] Wacław Sobieski, *Studya Historyczne*, Lwów, 1912, p. 30.

veloped in Polish historiography! This time, as Sobieski justly
points out, the current was due to Metternich's agents! Exactly as
at present, as in this painful hour for us when a new dismemberment of Poland is in preparation, Metternich's agents hurled and
spread the slogan: "Down with historic Poland—it was a hell for
the people, for Poland and serfdom are one and the same!"[14]

This propaganda, the end of which was to provoke class-struggle
in order to disintegrate Poland socially and nationally, became
especially intense later on—after the Insurrection of 1863, when
the Russian Government and Russian journalism, aided too by the
agents of Bismarck, seized this instrument of destruction and
annihilation. All the writings of Russian Slavophiles and Panslavists, as well as those of German scholars, repeat the same
argument: throughout its existence the Polish Republic was a hell
for the peasants. That argument envisaged two goals: one, we have
just defined, was a matter of sowing social discord in Poland
and weakening the cultivated classes of the country, the classes
representing national consciousness, and the other was to justify
the Partitions. Catherine II was to appear as a liberator of the
Polish people, she "freed it from the yoke under which the Polish
nobility had held it for centuries." Parenthetically, I should like
to call it to mind that the lot of the Russian peasant had been
for centuries, and perhaps is still today, the hardest in the world,
and that Russia never did anything essential for the lot of the
peasants of Poland.

Reacting to these currents, hostile to the Polish historical past
and deforming that past and that history, a movement of optimism
arose at Cracow. Head of this movement was a celebrated historian
—Kalinka, who in 1848 published a study, *Poland as She Was in
the Past,* the aim of which was to convince the Polish peasant that

---

[14] *Op. cit.,* p. 32.

his lot in old Poland had been better than under the German and Austrian regimes.

In other publications appearing somewhat later Kalinka, subjecting the "stunted" generation of his time to mordant criticism, opposed to it the grandly shining image of the old nobility, full of generosity and heroism. To those who dared to disapprove of and find fault with the past, Kalinka replied by telling them that they were distorting and deforming the past: "Instead of giving your children a sun-bathed image (of the past) you write on foul dishclouts the history of the pathology of your own heart, and your slovenly mouths have destroyed all the charm of the past."[15]

These violent words of accusation and defense were long engraved in Polish hearts. They were repelled after a time, but they continued, ever recurring to memory; they returned at a decisive moment of the evolution of Polish historical thought to inspire it with unique power.

Kalinka's studies had their effect at the very moment of their appearance; the poet Wincenty Pol followed them closely in his stories about the Polish squires.

But very quickly Kalinka had a change of heart himself, for everything was changed, above all in Cracow. In 1850 Cracow fell into a period of decadence, and this "free city," this lively "republic," this center of optimism became, for who knew how long-forever!—"the center of the spirit of criticism, of rancor toward the past . . ." Yes, all had changed . . . The population of the city lessened alarmingly in a few years. The Austrians destroyed everything in Cracow that they *could* destroy—the Wawel, that magnificent Polish Westminster Abbey, that Acropolis of Poland, was emptied, befouled, looted, defiled; the Italian Castle of the Kings was transformed into barracks, the wainscot-

[15] Cited by Sobieski, *op. cit.*, p. 34.

ing and frescoes of the sixteenth and seventeenth centuries were plastered over an ancient tomb, a cemetery—such had Cracow become. And Kalinka thinks of Jerusalem—he compares his cherished city to the cemetery of Constantinople, lamenting how she that was "princess among the provinces" is become "as a widow."[16]

Sobieski would seem to be correct in claiming that the atmosphere of Cracow had been of some account in the fact that it was Cracow in which Polish revisionism took birth, and that at the head of the famous historical school of Cracow were three men all of whom were sons of Cracow: Kalinka, Szujski, and Bobrzyński.

Yes . . . Kalinka! The apologist for the past becomes its condemner: it is not the enemies of Poland who are guilty, the responsibility for the Partitions falls on the Poles themselves, "The Poles themselves were the authors of their catastrophe."[17]

What a terrible avowal, what distress resounds in this confession of an ardent and passionate historian who loved his country with all the strength of his heart and his soul . . .

At the University of Cracow appeared the great, illustrious Szujski, rector of this five-hundred-year-old university, the Szujski whom we used to be able to admire in his ermine-covered scarlet rector's toga in Matejko's magnificent painting in the State Hall of the University . . . Szujski, author of scores of volumes, poet, playwright, novelist . . . great master of the history of Poland. He, too, feels himself "slave of the tombs" and calls Cracow "the most wretched Lazarus in the world." It is at the Wawel that he hears the piercing cry of Kościuszko at the battle of Maciejowice: "*Finis Poloniæ.*"[18]

Here occurs the disaster of the Insurrection of 1863. One more insurrection, a third, a fourth . . . Once more Polish blood flows

[16] See Sobieski, *op. cit.*, p. 36.
[17] *Ibid.*, p. 35.
[18] *Ibid.*, p. 39.

desperately . . . once more in vain . . . There re-echoes the terrible hymn of that revolution—"with the streaming blood of our brothers, with the smoke of the conflagrations." Russian atrocities have no limits; in Lithuania Muravyev, "The Hangman," gulps down the "streaming blood"; in Warsaw the Cossacks butcher children, sack the houses, loot from top to bottom, destroy collections of art, libraries, put the torch to manuscripts—this in the marvelous palace of Zamoyski, established in the sixteenth century—throw through the window a cradle and child, precious porcelains . . . and Chopin's piano, which, cast on the sidewalk, utters one last cry of distress . . . A terrible silence extends over the country. Europe, as always, does not budge, faithful to its policy of neutrality, adopted since the Partitions, since the Insurrection of 1830 . . . Napoleon III had promised, as Napoleon I had promised, but neither kept his word. Bismarck and Alexander II sign a military convention guaranteeing the Czar the aid of the Prussian armies in case the insurrection should take on too considerable proportions . . . Bismarck even meditates an occupation of the kingdom of Poland—for the King of Prussia—if Russia should be repulsed . . . Despite all the steps taken by sympathizers with the Polish cause in France and England, the governments do not move, in spite of the Russo-German convention . . . It is then that Ruskin will say, in his course at the Manchester School in 1864—which, exceptionally, represented the doctrine of nonintervention: "Alas! It is the narrowness, selfishness, minuteness, of your sensation that you have to deplore in England at this day; sensation which spends itself in bouquets and speeches; in revellings and junketings, in sham fights and gay puppet shows, while you can look on and see noble nations murdered, man by man, without an effort or tear."[19]

[19] John Ruskin, *Works* (the works of . . .), Library Ed., London, 1905, Vol. 18, p. 81.

At the same moment, a bit after April 24, 1864, Pope Pius IX made a speech at once severe and dignified, protesting against the Russian persecutions and atrocities in Poland. At the occasion of the Christmas holidays, in 1865, Baron de Meyendorff, Russia's chargé d'affaires for the Holy See, was received by the Pope in official audience. He permits himself certain reproaches—Pius, indignant, shows him the door.[20]

On the other side, in 1863, at the very moment of the insurrection, P. J. Proudhon flung his famous brochure, *Whether the Treaties of 1815 Have Ceased to Exist,* in which, addressing himself to the Poles, he told them: "What you want, today as before, as always, for you are nobles, is to exploit, to rule . . . I protest against this treason toward the peoples. After the example of your ancestors, I oppose to you my *veto* as French citizen: Poles, the past, the present, the future; liberty, progress, right, the Revolution, and the Treaties, all condemn you. Your only glory henceforth is to accept your condemnation. To hesitate would be unworthy of you . . ."[21] So communism had stretched forth its hand to the Russian Government of the Czar . . . to the government of Bismarck . . .

In Russia appeared the articles of Katkov, abusing Poland, *The History of the Fall of Poland* by Solovyev, anti-Polish novels of the Russian writers; in Germany, Hueppe's book, presenting a disastrous interpretation of the history of Poland and accompanied by a series of publications of the same kind.

On the other hand, do not forget the teachings of the positivism of Auguste Comte, of the school of determinism of Taine, of Buckle in England and of the Polish positivists in Poland—who set themselves to preaching reason, common sense, to demonstrating the futility of the sacrifices imposed on the nation by the

[20] Edmond Privat, *L'Europe et l'Odyssée de la Pologne au XIXe siècle,* Lausanne, 1918, p. 322.

[21] Cited by Privat, *op. cit.,* p. 316.

insurrections, and who propagated "organic work" and resignation, collaboration with the co-partitioning regimes in order to save Polish life and civilization.

So it is in these terrible conditions, after a new national catastrophe, in the turmoil of ideas and opinions facing historians hostile to Poland and at the same time seeking historic truth, that the Polish historians—working generally as *Privatgelehrte*, since Polish education had been reduced to the minimum all over Poland by the oppressor—undertook the heavy task of a new interpretation of Poland's past.

Now let me turn to the School of Cracow and to Szujski. One need not insist that in such conditions it was not easy to keep one's balance and follow a straight, direct line.

Szujski[22] is defending liberal Polish institutions when he replies to Huppe, but he becomes pessimistic when he speaks to Poles. It was not external factors that determined our fall, but internal ones. It was not heterogeneous violence, but homogeneous weakness, that brought Poland to catastrophe.

In the first place, the prolonged immutability of economic conditions kept Poland at a very low economic level up to its very last days. In the second place, its premature parliamentarism disaggregated and decimated the monarchical power, thus taking away from the nation, from the state, its guide and leader in the domain of foreign policy and bringing it to internal disorder. "This anarchy is become gangrene, wasting the whole body of the nation."

Poland's expansion into Eastern Europe, Poland's colonizing mission in the Ukraine and Lithuania—the civilizing beauty and grandeur of that grandiose enterprise notwithstanding—was a mission which to his mind exceeded the forces of the nation; the

[22] See Józef Szujski, *Dzieła*, Wydanie Zbiorowe, Serya II, t.t. V-VI, Kraków, 1885 and t.t. VII-VIII, Kraków, 1888.

best, most active and creative elements of the nation were lost, absorbed by the immense territories united to the Republic, and the Republic was gutted. Humanism and the Reformation likewise weakened Poland, having decimated the homogeneous force, principles, and organization, of Catholicism. In accomplishing its civilizing mission in the East, Poland gradually lost or at least attenuated its occidental characteristics; it underwent the contagion of oriental and Muscovite barbarity.

However, Szujski was a vacillating and inconstant man, and his pessimism did not reach the utmost limits. The man who pushed criticism to this utmost limit was the celebrated Michael Bobrzyński, Professor at the University of Cracow, Viceroy (at the start of our century) of Galicia, illustrious Polish statesman. His book, *History of Poland*,[23] was written, and appeared, after the Franco-Prussian War, after the defeat of France. This defeat, like Poland's in 1863, gave him an example of the power wielded by a state whose bases rest on a discipline and an organization of iron. His criticism of Poland-before-the-Partitions attacked above all the problem of executive power, the problem of the formation of a strong, potent, solidly organized bureaucracy and the problem of the role of great individuals in the history of nations. Taking these premises as a point of departure, he completely disowned Poland's historical past, even from the sixteenth century on. He accuses the Polish nobility of having produced no men sufficiently ardent and powerful, passionate and decisive, to have the courage to push history into drama, into great conflicts of passions and of political ideas. Polish toleration seemed to him a proof of weakness, not strength, and the struggle against powerful and resolute monarchical power appeared to him one of Poland's greatest historical sins.

[23] Michał Bobrzyński, *Dzieje Polski w Zarysie*, Vols. I and II, Warszawa, 1887 (III ed.).

Our civil liberties were the source of all our calamities, and the fact that the rights of the individual, of the person, were never sacrificed to the needs of the state led this state to ruin. He hails the influence of Byzantium in the orthodox Slav states where the Church was subjugated to the laic power and hence had never participated in the work of the emancipation of society. In brief, he was the advocate of absolute power and the admirer of great sovereigns who had had the strength to impose their will on the nation. Therefore, Polish parliamentarism, which had been the glory of Poland, becomes under his ferociously brave and bold pen the cause of her annihilation. "Our fall could come only after a whole series of faults, after a long period of violations of the higher laws God assigned to the life and development of nations."

His pessimism is great, and it was immediately exploited by Russian historiography: Kareev, the Russian historian of Poland, paid him homage in 1888 and developed these theories with much enthusiasm in his publications.

But Bobrzyński's book contained also an element of latent optimism. There had already, in his time, been advanced the argument of geography, which had supposedly determined the fall of Poland. This argument appears often even today, and it is perhaps the most fatalistic argument of all those envisaging the justification of the Partitions and annexations executed, or about to be executed, on the body of Poland. To accept this argument means *Finis Poloniae* forever, for nothing will ever change that geography. Besides, it is essentially false. In the first place, Poland existed, along with this geography, for nine centuries. In the second place, Prussia had no better geography, nor did the Muscovy of the fifteenth and sixteenth centuries. The fate of a nation is determined not by its geography but by its vital and moral forces.

Having placed the Polish catastrophe on Polish responsibility,

Bobrzyński gave proof of great courage and moral energy—he
was the interpreter of his nation's courage and energy. His book
provoked polemics which have lasted till now, and the opinions
advanced by his adversaries bring to light some factors of moral
potency and regeneration that have always existed in the Polish
nation and which have allowed it to survive the catastrophes. Only
the truly strong can acknowledge and accept responsibility.
Churchill has told us at Harvard: "The price of greatness is responsibility." Bobrzyński's book contains still another element of
greatness: the nostalgia for strength, the inquiry addressed to
great characters—those who have the courage to dominate, to
dominate first of all their own nation.

One might say that the young scholar—Bobrzyński was thirty
years of age when he wrote his book—was inspired by our great
poet Słowacki, who in his poem, *The King-Spirit,* in which he
develops a sort of mystic historiosophy and a sort of metaphysic
of historical metempsychosis, wrote:

> And yet the great Lord of the heavens
> Robed me in terror and in awe,
> And this awe was somber, it was royal.
> ... And what was strange—the people adored me
> For the power, for the terror, for the torments.
> When I appeared, the people bent their knees—
> The people—sheep that seek and run toward their shepherd.

It was a search for the superior man; Mickiewicz would have
said, *"Hominem non habeo."* Doubtless, we have there one source
upon which Piłsudski drew later. His struggle with the Polish
Parliament between 1920 and 1935 was inspired by Bobrzyński
as well as by his favorite poet, Słowacki. He sought the means
of organizing and consolidating the nation around a principle
of power and around a will ready to accept responsibility. His
struggle against Polish parliamentary parties was a struggle

against the heritage of the seventeenth and eighteenth centuries. As we have said, Bobrzyński's book provoked polemics. Warsaw in particular becomes (along with Lwów) the center of Polish historical optimism, energetically opposed to Cracovian pessimism. At Warsaw,[24] the very heart of Poland, those complexes of inferiority, induced at Cracow by the powerful Germanic civilization before it, did not operate. Warsaw faced a civilization younger and so less ripe, less strong—Russian civilization—and therefore optimistic currents had better conditions for development. It is there, and at Lwów, that two theses were elaborated. Korzon demonstrated all the value and importance that must be attached to the federative and republican institutions of ancient Poland.[25] Rembowski proved in a plan of comparative history that all the "anarchies" and all the risings of the *szlachta*[26] in Poland represented nothing exceptional in Europe. Smoleński gave a detailed description of the moral revolution produced in Poland at the end of the eighteenth century, which had come too late, immediately before the catastrophe, but which had bequeathed to the nation regenerative and renovative principles.

Finally, at Lwów, Askenazy, the most brilliant of all, writing a prose which was elegant but ornate and baroque, devoted himself to the task of demonstrating that the Partitions had been the result of entirely exterior factors. His rich archival researches, his great knowledge of diplomatic documents and persons, his penchant for biography, and his Polish nationalistic spirit facilitated for him the execution of this enterprise. However, it was not very difficult, for obviously it was Russia, Prussia, and Austria who had dismembered Poland, and not Poland herself. But,

---

[24] See Tadeusz Korzon, *Wewnętrzne dzieje Polski za Stanisława Augusta*, 1887; Władysław Smoleński, *Przewrót umysłowy w Polsce wieku XVIII*, Kraków, 1891.

[25] See Tadeusz Korzon, *Listy otwarte, Mowy, Rozprawy, Rozbiory*, Warszawa, 1916. R. Rembowski, *Konfederacya i Rokosz*, etc., Warszawa, 1896.

[26] *Szlachta*—gentry.

also obviously, during the period of her prosperity and power
Poland had been in a position to face that danger, the first fore-
bodings of which could be perceived by the end of the fifteenth
century. The problem, then, is more complex, and it was not
until still later that the ensemble of all the factors that had determined the Polish catastrophe was brought to light.[27]

The optimism of the "Warsaw School" (I have cited here only
a small number of historians) was reinforced by a man whose
glory swiftly passed beyond the Polish world—this man became,
at one given moment, a universally known writer, honored
by the Nobel Prize, and his books were translated into all the
literary languages of the world. He was read and reread in
America as in Europe, several generations of Americans have
admired and loved his novels—excellently translated, incidentally, by a most distinguished Bostonian and Harvardian—
Jeremiah Curtin. You have already, I trust, guessed that I have
in mind Henryk Sienkiewicz. In 1900 his name was so popular
in the United States that when President Gilman of Johns Hop-
kins spoke for the universities of America in Cracow at the ex-
ercises commemorating the five-hundredth anniversary of the
Jagiellonian University, he could say, "America thanks Poland
for three great names: Copernicus, to whom all the world is in
debt; Kościuszko, who spilled his blood for American independence; and Sienkiewicz, whose name is a household word in thousands of American homes, and who has introduced Poland to the
American people."[28]

But in America they had above all read *Quo Vadis*. They had
less generally read the celebrated trilogy—*By Fire and Sword*,

[27] See W. Sobieski, *op. cit.*; Władysław Smoleński, *Szkoły Historyczne w Polsce*,
Warszawa, 1898.

[28] See W. Lednicki, *Poland and the World*, New York, 1943, p. 59. (Reprinted from
the "Bulletin, of the Polish Institute of Arts and Sciences in America," Vol. I, Nos.
1, 2, 3 and 4.)

The Deluge, and *Pan Michael*—and the *Teutonic Knights*, which
Europe knew as well as it knew the *Three Musketeers* of Dumas
and still earlier the novels of Walter Scott and of Victor Hugo.

It does not behoove me here to give you an esthetic analysis of
Sienkiewicz' novels or to establish their literary genealogy. It
will suffice to say that in Poland the historical novel possessed
before Sienkiewicz an honorable tradition, represented toward
the end of the nineteenth century by a very great Polish writer—
Kraszewski, likewise translated (not all—this Polish Walter Scott
had written, like Sir Walter Scott, hundreds of volumes) into
English. But the glory of Kraszewski was immediately eclipsed
when the historical novels of Sienkiewicz appeared. These novels
impassioned Poland, they captivated the hearts, imagination, and
thought of Poles as no book, with the exception of *Pan Tadeusz* of
Mickiewicz, had ever done before.

These novels galvanized Poland, they mobilized her spirit of
resistance, they brought her faith and hope, they brought her an
internal peace, they flattered her dreams of independence and
gave her confidence in herself. Evidently Sienkiewicz' genius
was of some account—his exceptionally powerful and captivating
narrative gift; the plastic richness of his grandiose fresco; his
language, wedding ancient and modern speech; his evocative
talent, which surprised the most sadly humdrum imaginations.
The essential thing was that in this trilogy he had shown a Poland
in distress, a Poland in Cossack wars, Turkish wars, Muscovite
wars, Swedish wars (in the seventeenth century)—assailed, lac-
erated, burnt, wasted, betrayed by her allies and by her own
subjects, but a Poland which, thanks to the heroic efforts of the
whole nation, its chiefs, the mass and individuals, arose, defended
herself, and saved herself. Sienkiewicz showed vices and faults,
but equally he showed virtues—virtues formed by the Polish
family, courage and the faculty of sacrifice, altruism, the spirit

of organization, love of liberty, attachment to the fatherland; virtues formed by Poland's political and social institutions, virtues formed by history, by Poland's civilizing mission. The influence of Sienkiewicz was enormous in Poland and has lasted till our time, despite a movement of revisionism, unleashed some years before this war, in respect to his historical documentation, and despite the fact that Sienkiewicz, as a writer, belongs today only to the history of Polish literature—his vogue in Poland, as in the whole world, having been very much diminished.

This Varsovian current of optimism continued to develop; it reached its apogee at the moment of the World War of 1914-18. At that moment appeared some studies by Polish historians which established two essential theses: first, that the organization of ancient Poland—the rule of the noble republic—compared to the contemporary regimes of other countries, represented positive values, and, second, that while the European West formed its ideal in the psychic concert of the human collectivity and the East saw it in the crowned representative of this collectivity, Poland perceived it and had created it in the person of the free individual, in the conscience of man himself. Poland had therefore produced a superior type of state, a morally superior historic type, preceding other countries in this field, and *there* lay the principal cause of her fall.

In 1917 the Historical Society of Cracow organized a cycle of lectures which were published in 1918 under the general title, *Causes of the Fall of Poland.* This three-hundred-page book can be considered, perhaps, as the expression, the definitive general formula adopted by modern Polish historiography as to the problem which interests us here.

On the eve of the restoration of Poland, exactly on the eve of this restoration, Cracow once more pronounced its verdict. This time we have a synthesis, a synthesis which comprehends, dare we say, all the causes and all the factors that determined the catastrophe. We have a synthesis which embraces the pessimism *and* the optimism of preceding studies, a synthesis which balances these two currents of Polish historiosophic thought, which represents one conclusion.[29]

Everything was included—the evolution of historical ideas, geography (having demonstrated that it was firm and solid), the history of the social and political regime, the history of foreign policy, of economic life, of the social structure, of the spiritual culture of Poland, the elements of weakness and the elements of strength, the negative and the positive—to reach the final conclusion—the *optimistic* conclusion—that it is indeed the nation itself which must be considered responsible for the catastrophe. The motifs of the Partitions represent an external factor: the appetites of the partitioning powers—but the *causa efficiens,* in the last analysis, lay in the weakness of the nation, the inefficacy of the Polish state at that time.

These studies showed that toward the middle of the eighteenth century the economic structure of the country presented the pitiable picture of immense landed states—*latifundia*—belonging to several families of magnates who disposed of the fate of the peasants, the small gentry, and the Jews, representing at this time ten per cent of the population. We note the complete absence of a powerful Polish bourgeoisie and the decadence of commerce, of the careers of the Christian bourgeoisie; a more and more accentuated decadence of the cities; lack of industry, exploitation of the peasant and his gradual degeneration. Beside this still other factors of forfeiture are observable—change in the routes of world commerce, which lost Poland the privileged situation she had possessed before the economic preponderance of Lisbon, Antwerp, and Amsterdam; the overthrow of the balance of power

[29] See also R. H. Lord, *op. cit., Introduction.*

in Europe by the French Revolution. Poland had fifty-five years
of defensive wars which ruined, devastated, fatigued, and exhausted her. The great epidemics of 1652-55 through 1737—ten
or so—took off a large number of citizens. The nobility led a
luxurious life—due above all to the wars which always provoked
too great a scorn for money.

Other factors taken into account include the deplorable condition of the state's finances; the insufficiency of the country's military defense; the fact that the economic interests of the nobility
were not attached to the existence of the country.

In the legal and political field they found lack of unity in the
organization of administrative and executive power, lack of effi-
ciency in the working of this machine; in letters, arts, sciences,
education—decline, leading to an obscurantism, barbarism, and
a profound demoralization, decay of manners and customs; in
the field of foreign policy—lack of an organized policy or instruments for a foreign policy—neither permanent ambassadors nor
ministers; faults and errors signalized previously and belonging
to an anterior epoch—the abandonment of the purely Polish
territories to the West and the colonization of the East, a weak
policy in regard to Prussia, lack of wisdom and perspicacity in
our Russian policy.

The very fact, finally, that the Polish sovereign was an elected
king diminished his prestige in the royal courts of Europe. In an
age when kings all over Europe boasted of reigning by Divine
right, one could not but look down upon a king who reigned by
the vote of nobility.

It is in general true also that some national vices and sins developed during the century that preceded the Partitions, when the
conditions of the Republic's existence were so unfortunate.[30]

But beside so black a picture, beside this historical canvas

[30] However, we must not become victims of exaggeration: England was, in the

painted with a brush which borrowed its colors from the school of Cracow—another picture was created, another canvas was mounted. The lecturers of Cracow all sketched out—each in his field—the admirable, stupefying, pathetic work of Reform that Poland had undertaken on the eve of her catastrophe. It was a period of renaissance, of awakening from the torpor and prostration of the Era of the Saxon Dynasty (end of the seventeenth and beginning of the eighteenth centuries), this period from 1760 to 1795—thirty years of work, struggles, wars against Russia and Prussia, of insurrections; the Constitution of May 3, 1791, with rights granted to peasants and the bourgeoisie, the reforms of King Stanisław-August Poniatowski; the magnificent development of science, letters, the arts, poetry, the theater; the constitution of a ministry of public instruction—first ministry of instruction in Europe; the economic rebirth of the country, its administrative consolidation, the abolition of the *Liberum Veto*—in short, an unbelievable change of the whole national life.

In truth, this period represents one of the most beautiful and grand stages in the history of Poland, and a wonderful proof of the vitality of the nation. It is precisely this renaissance, it is precisely this awakening of the nation to a new life, which determined its loss. Russia and Prussia saw that it was time to act

---

eighteenth century, in a most perilous situation and ripe for catastrophe. France does not represent a different case. "It is possible," writes a distinguished English historian, "that the faults of the Polish gentry were common to all such classes in the eighteenth century. Pride of class, ignorance, faction, fighting were common in France or Germany. The English gentry were just as selfish and corrupt as the *szlachta*. But most countries had a central administration run by a body of experts, whereas in Poland the legislature, run by the general body of gentry, was supreme. This legislature, the *Sejm*, was in reality controlled by the provincial assemblies, *i.e.*, by petty squires quite ignorant of European affairs, of diplomacy or finance. The principle of the *Liberum veto*, by which a member of the *Sejm* bearing a mandate from his province could prevent any measure becoming law, was a democratic safeguard in the society which evolved it. It was a calamity when its abuse became frequent." See *The Survival of Polish Civilization*, by A. Bruce Boswell, *Historical Association Pamphlet*, No. 120, London, 1941, p. 9.

See also K. Waliszewski, *Poland the Unknown*, pp. 120-135.

promptly. The first step was to impose conditions—namely, to stop the reforms; and, when neither the king on whom they counted (Stanisław-August had "deceived" his former mistress, Catherine II), nor the nation they believed to be dead, would lend themselves to accept these conditions, the next step was to proceed to the Partitions. The most important fact about the Partitions is that they occurred at one of the most brilliant moments in the history of the Polish people.[31]

The group of Cracow had done a good job, it had accomplished a courageous task. This appeared especially in the text of the last lecture, which gave a general conclusion to the cycle—a conclusion of a logical, as well as a moral, order. This very beautiful and moving text shows that the intent of all Polish historians, and particularly those of the critical school of Cracow, was to discover the historic truth without regard to whether this truth might always be glorious, to discover the intrinsic forces of the nation which had not only decided its past but were to decide its future.[32] This impressive final lecture was given by a great master of the history of Polish literature, a master who during his seventy-five years of life had formed legions of students of Polish literature. This great and illustrious scholar, Ignacy Chrzanowski, died in 1939 in the concentration camp of Oranienburg, where the Nazis cast one hundred and seventy-five professors of the University of Cracow, and where eighteen died in consequence of the terrible regime under which they existed. Polish historiography had, then, fulfilled its duty—it had well prepared the nation for a new life in a restored Poland. And what had literature and poetry done? Very much, but I shall cite here only one act, only one masterpiece—one drama. This drama moved every Polish conscience as no one since the great Polish Romantics had suc-

[31] See R. H. Lord, *op. cit.*, pp. 56-63 and 491.
[32] See *Przyczyny Upadku Polski, Odczyty*, Nakład Gebethnera i Wolffa, Warszawa, Kraków, 1918.

ceeded in doing. It was performed at Cracow for the first time on March 16, 1901, that is, at the zenith of bourgeois quietism, of the beatific peace which reigned in Europe and which had plunged in sleep not only those who had a right to profit by its benefits but also those who ought not to have slept, who ought to have been awake, waiting the hour when the alarum should be sounded— the Poles.

The play to which I am referring envisaged this "bourgeois" somnolence, and it touched something else, too: the great problem of the union of classes in Poland. I have in mind *The Wedding*, by Stanisław Wyspiański.

The plot of the drama is connected with the following fact: A very popular Polish painter of noble connections had startled his class by marrying a peasant girl and settling in a country cottage in her native village near Cracow. The example had tempted another man of the same group, a poet, to do likewise. Wyspiański's play is concerned with the story of that second unconventional wedding, and strange things happen in it. Writers, journalists, artists, and ladies of the town meet and talk with peasant men and women. This turns their minds to thoughts of Poland's national unity in the past and her degradation in the present, of the great tasks of the future, in which the nation cannot hope to live and regain its freedom except through democracy and union. The dreariness and despondency of Poland's subject and divided existence are contrasted with its noble aims and solid strength in the past, and visions of this earlier glory take the form of ghosts who appear to individual guests and mock their littleness.

"Finally," says Professor Dyboski, whom I am quoting here, "out of all this ferment of reflection the idea emerges that the new spirit of unity created by this wedding between townspeople and peasants should be set to work in a joint armed rising, to set Poland free. This thought is ushered in by another ghost—the

Ukrainian singer and harpist of the eighteenth century, the half-legendary Wernyhora, who foretold both the fall and the resurrection of Poland. The host of the house, the painter, who has long lived among the peasants—is to have the lead . . . The villagers of the neighborhood are to be called together and arm themselves with scythes—as the villagers of Kościuszko's insurrection did in the eighteenth century."

"The peasants are ready, but the appointed leader fails, in dreamy, Hamlet-like irresolution, and the peasant boy sent out by him loses the golden horn whose blast was to be the signal for the great enterprise. The assembled people sink into sleepy indifference, and move in a drowsy wedding-dance to the sound of a straw fiddle played by a man of straw—the winter-covering of a rosebush, here made a living figure, and serving as a symbol of the dullness and futility of the ordinary day-by-day existence."[33]

This was an interpretation of the past and of the present; it was also an appeal for the future . . . The nation understood it . . . Guided by historiography and poetry, Poland was ready for the coming times of her resurrection—and of the independence she had so long desired. The best hope for resurrection lay precisely in the courageous attitude of Polish historical thought, which, in its very acceptance of responsibilities, asserted the creative forces of the nation and taught the great lesson that Poland's fate was still in her own hands. This lesson is the purest flower of Polish spiritual independence.

[33] See Roman Dyboski, *Modern Polish Literature*, Oxford University Press, 1924, pp. 93-94.

II

Political Ideals

PERMIT me to begin today's lecture with a man who is no longer an entire stranger to you and with a text the beginning of which you already know—I mean the letter written by Krasiński to Lamartine. Lamartine had repeated the old, eternal formula, which even now pursues us, that Poland was "an aristocracy without a people." "To say that," wrote Krasiński, "of the single, the only, the most magnificent democracy that ever existed in Europe—but really, that, Monsieur, is puerile. A million voters, each of whom could become deputy, senator, or even king, is that an aristocracy without a people? Where in Europe have you ever seen a million voters, all of them eligible, either in antiquity or since Christ? Everything dreamed of by the Revolution whose efforts you are recounting was already realized in Poland, and that in the sixteenth century; but everything the Revolution accomplished in place of its dreams, that is to say, all the unspeakable crimes that have come to be put between it and its idea, never found a place in Poland. That is the difference. After supernatural prodigies of heroism and unexampled atrocities, whither have you arrived? At two hundred and fifty thousand voters. *There* is your democracy. Compare that with the million I speak

37

of, and do not forget that Poland contained only fourteen million inhabitants, whereas in France you number thirty-six millions today. That is what you call an aristocracy without a people."[1]

As a matter of fact, Krasiński was right. The opinion he advances in this letter was the opinion of foreign observers and political thinkers of the sixteenth century—as well as before and after—on the subject of Poland. We can take the Italians Ruggieri and Lippomano, the Frenchmen Théodore de Bèze, Agrippa d'Aubigné, Guillaume Rossaeus, Bishop of Senlis, and many others, and we shall see that they all considered the regime established in Poland in the fifteenth and sixteenth centuries as a sort of political ideal realized. All these authors, too, share the opinion of the Polish authors of the time—that the Polish Republic represented a mixed government—*genus mixtum, monarchia temperata*. Now, this *genus mixtum* was considered the political ideal of the time.[2]

"In fact, it suffices to leaf through the political writings of the monarchomanes," we read in Professor Kot's study, *The Polish Republic in Western Political Literature*, "to see what a role unknown Poland played in Europe thanks to the particular traits of its political regime. This role was that of helping Europe to formulate liberal political ideas. In an epoch when it needed civic courage to advance the idea of the superiority of the citizens' interests to those of the monarch, the idea of the limitation of the sovereign's power by means of the contract with the citizens, the idea of the dependence of political form upon the will of the people, the idea of the sovereign as (merely) a higher official of the state—in all that, Poland served as an example, by having

[1] See *op. cit.*, pp. 223-224.
[2] See Stanisław Kot, *Rzeczpospolita Polska w Literaturze Politycznej Zachodu*, Kraków, 1919.
See also *Relacye Nuncyuszów Apostolskich i innych osób o Polsce od roku 1548 do 1690*, Wydanie Biblioteki Polskiej w Paryżu, Berlin-Poznań, 1864, Vols. I-II.

realized certain republican and constitutional principles in her institutions, which were known in Europe especially after the election of Henri de Valois."[3]

I had already said it was in the sixteenth century that Poland had attained the pinnacle of its power and civilization. That is true; it is also in the sixteenth century that an extraordinarily rich political literature developed in Poland. This literature studied numerous problems of social and political liberty of the citizen, the problem of the organization of executive power, diplomacy, the problem of the equality of all citizens before the laws, the problem of religious toleration, the fate of the peasants . . .

This astonishing abundance of writings and variety of subjects treated by our writers of the sixteenth century was no accidental phenomenon. Poland had indeed reached a very high level of public life and had established certain traditions, concerning on one side its external policy and on the other its internal policy, which had become the mold wherein the Polish writers elaborated and formed their ideas, their judgments, and their conceptions. On the other hand, of course, they exercised a direct influence on the political life of the country.

Before touching on this literature, I should like to cite certain facts and certain Polish political documents prior to the sixteenth century which might give an idea of what was represented by this Polish political tradition, of which the sixteenth century, that Golden Century in the history of Poland, had become the culminating point.

The first thing that must strike everybody, especially for the age, are the ways of Poland's territorial expansion. Here are some examples. The accord of Casimir the Great, King of Poland, with Hungary, concluded in 1340, obtaining the *complete and*

[3] Kot, *op. cit.*, p. 43.

definitive cession of Red Ruthenia, was an act conceived in the spirit of the Polish tradition. "Without having to shed one drop of blood," writes a French historian, ". . . Casimir was able to obtain the country's voluntary attachment to the state of the Piasts (the first Polish dynasty). It was to stay in her inheritance up to Poland's dismemberment."[4]

Poland did even better. The Act of Horodło, 1413, definitely united Poland with Lithuania, an immense state that extended as far as Vyazma, near Moscow, and as far as the Black and Baltic Seas. This act is one of the most characteristic testimonies to the Polish policy. "It is animated,"—I am quoting the same French historian—"by a spirit of fraternity of which history had nowhere yet given an example."[5]

This is the text of the Act's incomparable preamble: "It is an evident truth that one cannot go to salvation without the aid of charity. This virtue knows not how to commit evil, and it sparkles with the goodness which is its essence. It is that which reconciles disunited hearts, appeases quarrels, dissipates hatreds, smashes ill-will, procures for all men fertile peace . . . Consequently, we, prelates, barons, nobles, and magnates of the Kingdom of Poland, all in the name of all and each in the name of each, signify to all whom it may concern, now and in the future, that they take cognizance of the present act. In order that we may find repose in the shade of the wings of Charity, and live under its dominion according to the aspirations of our religious desires, we have united and mingled, we do unite, join, mingle, and conform, by the tenor of these presents, our houses, our genealogies, our issue, our arms, with the nobles and boyars of the lands of Lithuania, that from this day and perpetually they may possess, use, and have joy of them in the same way that we have received them from our

[4] H. Grappin, *Histoire de la Pologne des origines à 1922,* Paris, 1922, p. 43.
[5] *Ibid.,* p. 55.

fathers and our ancestors, with all the potency of true charity and of a fraternal union, just as if they had received them as a hereditary patrimony. Let Charity unite to us and place on a footing of equality these brothers whom the profession of one same religion and the identity of laws and graces have made our companions. We promise in good faith, of our firm and loyal word, on our honor and under the weight of oath, never to abandon them in any adversities and necessities whatsoever, but on the contrary to lend them our counsel and succor against ambushes and all their enemies."[6]

This policy created around Poland such an atmosphere of jealousy that all the neighboring countries desired to be united with her. We see Hungary and Bohemia on several occasions proposing their thrones to the Jagiellons. The republican cities of Pskov and Novgorod push their desire to be united with Poland so far that the Ivans—Ivan III and Ivan the Terrible—destroy these desires with unutterable atrocities and terror that strings the gallows in rows along the road from Novgorod to Moscow, as one of the greatest Russian historians admits.

I should like to recall here the curious sequel to this story— the fact that Zygmunt-August, on his deathbed, told his courtiers that they should elect the Czar of Muscovy as his successor to the crown of Poland. What is the meaning of this testament? Why should the last of the Jagiellons wish to bequeath his throne to the last important Rurikide—his constant rival and the representative of all that was opposed to his policy of peaceful union? Is it a confession of failure, a dying admission of despair? Or is it, perhaps, the ultimate expression of Zygmunt's political acumen, based on the feeling that here alone was the means for peaceful conquest of Muscovy and on the certainty that even Ivan himself, as King of Poland, must perforce submit to the

[6] *Ibid.*, pp. 56-57.

traditions of liberty and charity that had built up the Polish-Ruthenian-Lithuanian Commonwealth? I am certain that we are justified in accepting the latter explanation.[7]

These acts, this stunning foreign policy, were the work of the Polish nobility—to which, indeed, every merit reverts. Nor did it lose time in domestic matters. Likewise there we see that the same spirit of liberalism reigns, knowing no rival.

In 1433 we have the *Privilege of Cracow*—the Polish Charter —the *Neminem captivabimus*—which antedated many Western statutes: we know that the English *Habeas Corpus* dates from 1679. The Privilege of Cracow proclaimed that, save in case of *in flagrante delicto*, the person of the *Szlachcic* (noble) was inviolable before a judgment in form. Before modern times, then, Poland had received its charter of liberty and civic dignity.

The Privilege of 1454 goes even further: it guaranteed that nothing would be decided in the state without the gentry's being previously convened and consulted. This privilege freed the gentry from aristocratic domination; it gave it the right to elect judges and abolished the jurisdiction of the castellans. Above all, it put political power in the hands of the gentry. The assent of the dietines (local assemblies of the nobility) should henceforth be indispensable for the promulgation of any new law and the general convocation of knighthood (mobilization). This last point is especially important.

By 1493 we already have a general national diet, hence a parliament! And the number of deputies gradually increased: in 1552, 57; in 1569, 119; and after 1569, with the deputies from Lithuania, 158.[8]

The Senate, which constituted the council of the king, com-

[7] See Wacław Sobieski, *Studya Historyczne—Król a Car*, Lwów, 1912, pp. 20-21.
[8] See Aleksander Brückner, *Dzieje Kultury Polskiej*, Kraków, 1931, Vol. II.

prised the bishops, wojewods, castellans, and ministers, and the number of senators rose to one hundred and fifty.

The deputies of the Sejm (Parliament) were elected by the dietines and came to the sessions of the Sejm with *lauda*—instructions from their electors. The President of the Diet was elected by acclamation. The Sejm was dissolved if the minority did not accept the will of the majority—but compromise was usual. (The first case in which compromise was not attained and the principle of the *Liberum Veto* triumphed took place in the Diet of 1652; it is the beginning of the decay of the Polish parliamentary system.)[9] The deliberations of the Senate were public. The deputies delegated by the Sejm likewise attended the Sessions of the Senate. It was the Senate that became the school of Polish political eloquence; it must be admitted that our senators' speeches were really very beautiful, very dignified, typically and highly eloquent. Their one fault was that they were too long.

What must be stressed again is the fact that this spirit of liberalism had also triumphed in the field of the organization of local autonomy: each district possessed not only the privileges of local

[9] A distinguished English historian, Professor A. Bruce Boswell, has this to say about the *Liberum veto* (*The Survival of Polish Civilization*, Historical Association Pamphlet, No. 120, the Paternoster Press, Exeter):

"It was a mandate from his local body which enabled a deputy to oppose a measure in the central parliament. This is the origin of the famous 'liberum veto,' which was an ancient institution that survived into our own times in the Russian village commune and the English jury system. It is the subject of a scholarly work by Professor W. Konopczyński, who points out that this great change from unanimity to the rights of a majority passed unnoticed by chroniclers and historians. In Poland the principle of unanimity was maintained to protect provincial independence; *e.g.*, in the west, Posnania could successfully refuse, through its representatives, to take part in an expedition against Moscow, whereas the gentry of Lithuania or the Ukraine were not concerned about the defense of Pomerania against Brandenburg. The system was criticized by Polish reformers in the sixteenth century, but it worked tolerably well while the *Sejm* was in the hands of an educated class. It was only abused when education and civil ideals declined. The first instance of its abuse occurred in 1652; it became a scandal under the Saxon kings and was abolished in 1791. Under this system of government the country prospered so long as the citizens displayed intelligence and patriotism." See W. Konopczyński, *Le Liberum Veto*, etc.. Paris. 1930.

autonomy but also certain rights as constituents of sovereignty. And these dietines were exceedingly active. Their union was realized in the General Diets. The same federative system, then, which had been the great accomplishment of Poland in the domain of foreign policy, emerged here, in the field of local administration.

These political successes of the nobility (gentry) continued; they must be considered not only as proofs of the constant and systematic aggrandizement of the political role of the gentry but also as testimony to the spirit of law which, in an ever broader and more profound way, was being established in Poland. Gradually Poland attained to the consideration of the community as the one guardian, protector, the sovereign power of the state: *tota communitas*. It was a medieval doctrine that no longer had any hold on Western Europe in the sixteenth century. In Poland the situation was different: one Zaborowski writes in the sixteenth century that the state is identical with the *people*, not the king: *"quid enim regnum nisi populus ei subiectus?"*[10] This community was confined to the nobility; but let us not forget that in the sixteenth century this nobility (gentry) comprised already not less than two hundred thousand men, and that in the eighteenth century it represented ten to twelve or fourteen per cent of the general population of Poland. It was not, therefore, either an aristocracy or a caste. Thence proceeds the very important fact that the law, *neminem captivabimus*, guaranteed immunity to a very great number of Polish citizens—and these citizens were all absolutely equal in their rights.

This conception of the equality of all the gentry was an absolutely original trait; in Western Europe the nobility was divided into two groups—the higher, titled group and the lower group.

[10] See Stanisław Estreicher, *Kultura Prawnicza w Polsce XVI wieku* in Polska Akademja Umiejętności: *Kultura Staropolska*, Kraków, 1932, pp. 89-90.

Polish gentry forbore from titles, and it is only later that the particularly powerful and rich Polish families acquired foreign titles. There were cases where these titles were accorded in the fifteenth and sixteenth centuries by foreign sovereigns or the Emperor to some Polish lords for special merits, or with the object of gaining their *benevolentia;* but these cases were rare, and the *szlachta* was firmly opposed (and remained opposed until the end) to the use of these titles. The principle of equality was jealously defended, and the traditional Polish dictum that "the *szlachcic* in his cottage is equal to the Palatine" expresses it very neatly.

The principle of equality was, in truth, a trait belonging only to Poland: no inequality, whether in the Diet, or in the dietines, or in the elections, or before the tribunal, between a potent lord and his humble farmhand. "Lacking the constituent of feudalism—dependence by the freeman on anyone but the representative of public authority—Poland defends herself against the reception of feudal institutions, she does not permit the assignment of official positions to members of the royal family, she forbids titles. No one shall be 'better' than the Polish citizen."[11]

The concept of equality was reinforced by a sentiment of fraternity. It was not even a mere sentiment; it was an idea, based on another concept, that of the origin of nobiliary privileges. "It was a matter of seizing upon the necessary qualifications in order to profit by those laws having the common good in mind. In Poland recognition had been given, as the element guaranteeing these qualifications and these faculties, to noble origin. It was understood that the brave produced the brave, the honest—the honest. It was believed that the condition of noble blood was the condition of honest blood, that it was the guaranty of superior moral

[11] See Józef Siemieński, *Polska Kultura Polityczna wieku XVI*, in *Kultura Staropolska*, p. 143. See also A. Brückner, *Dzieje Kultury Polskiej*, Vols. I and II.

worth, guaranty of a sentiment of civic responsibility." It was a moral qualification. Here is what a Pole of the sixteenth century wrote on the subject: "It would be unworthy to put in office men of low origin and to consider capable of governing the republic those who pursue profits and devote themselves to mean trades, above all the people, neglectful of public affairs, seeking only personal goals and profits; for it believes that what belongs to everyone belongs to no one . . ."[12]

The concept of noble origin, then, had taken on, in the heads of the Polish nobles, a quasi-mythological and mystical character; at the very base of their idea of the past was the principle of the merits of their ancestors. Let us not forget that new acts of ennoblement were performed by way of affiliating coats of arms —they were therefore acts of brotherly recognition of personal merits.

This same nobility had established the principle of freedom of conscience—an absolute religious tolerance. It was this that from the twelfth century on made Poland the Paradise of the Jews (I am quoting a French author), hounded in every Christian country.[13]

[12] See Siemieński, *op. cit.,* p. 144.

[13] As early as 1264 King Bolesław the Pious conferred on the Jews in the communities of Poznań and Kalisz the privilege known as the Statute of Kalisz. In 1334, by the Statute of Wiślica King Kazimierz the Great confirmed the application of the above-mentioned privileges to all the countries subject to the then King of Poland. Since then it is known as the Jewish Statute, and it became part of the *Volumina Legum,* the official collection of laws binding on Poland. The statute was confirmed again in 1507; the last King of Poland, Stanisław-August Poniatowski, confirmed it again in 1765.

"These privileges established the fundamental right of the Jews in Poland down to the end of the existence of the Polish state in 1795. They gave the Jews freedom to hold religious services in public, and assured them such security that the murder of a Jew was punished by confiscation of property, whereas the murder of a noble was punished only by a fine. Further, the privileges granted them the right to conduct business as usurers. Finally, the privileges placed the Jews under the jurisdiction of the *wojewodas*—the administrative provincial governors of the State."

"The general Privilege left considerable autonomy to the Jewish communities, in Hebrew called Canals. The sphere of activity of these communities included pri-

From the fifteenth century Poland was the refuge of the Hussites. In the sixteenth century all sects and religions are not only represented but teeming—Socinians, Calvinists, Zwinglians, Lutherans, Bohemian Brethren, as well as Greeks, Armenians, and even Mussulmen. Rulhière, in general hardly benevolent toward Poland, writes in the eighteenth century: "This country, which in our day we have seen divided on the pretext of religion, is the first state in Europe that exemplified tolerance. In this state, mosques arose between churches and synagogues."[14]

Jan Zamoyski, Chancellor of the Crown (sixteenth century), a profoundly educated man who had studied in Italy and France, says: "I would give half of my life if those who have abandoned the Roman Catholic Church should voluntarily return to its pale; but I would prefer giving all my life than to suffer anybody to be constrained to do it, for I would rather die than witness such an oppression."[15]

King Sigismund-August, the last of the Jagiellons, the fine flower of that superb race of kings, says in the same era: "I am not king of your consciences. I wish to be monarch equally of the

marily religious matters, then jurisdiction in disputes between Jews, matters of social and benevolent assistance, organizational questions, Jewish taxation, and finally the budget of the communities themselves. The broad sphere of autonomy which the Jewish communities enjoyed led to the creation of supervisory organizations for fiscal and religious purposes, these organizations being known as *ziemstwos*, or provincial councils. At the moment of their emergence, in the sixteenth century, there were four of these *ziemstwos* . . . by the beginning of the eighteenth century there were over a dozen . . . The need arose to create a central apparatus which, acting for all the Jewish communities, would undertake the collection of Jewish taxes in the Republic. In addition, a tribunal which would act as a court of appeal from the *ziemstwo* court, and as a higher court for the first hearing of more important cases. In consequence, in 1591 there arose a representative body of Polish Jews, known as the Congress of the Four Lands, or the Jewish Sejm in the Crown. This representative body, which existed down to 1764, possessed two central institutions, the Sejm and the Tribunal." (See *The Polish Spirit of Freedom* and *The Legal Position of Jews in Poland* in *Polish Studies and Sketches*, Nos. 1 and 3—London, Stratton House, 1942.)

[14] See H. Grappin, *op. cit.*, p. 88.
[15] *Ibid.*, p. 89.

sheep and of the goats. I am afraid of tearing wheat as well as tares."[16]

The role of the dietines was to secure for the nobility the conduct of internal affairs; the tribunals, which sat with the Sejm, were likewise in the hands of the nobiliary *tota communitas.* The law, *nihil novi,* had established the principle that no tax could be levied on the community without its consent. The king's power was equally limited in the field of foreign policy. Finally, the elections of the kings were done *viritim* (man by man)—each one had the right to vote. And the king had to give heed to the decrees of his predecessors, being limited at the same time by customary and by divine law. The relations of the sovereign and his people became conventionary, conditioned, by the *pacta conventa,* and there was also established the right of nonsubmission, by the articles of *non praestanda oboedientia* in case the sovereign should be wanting in the prescriptions of law. In the mind of every little Polish noble of that time were engraved several formulas on the subject of what the Polish sovereign ought to be: he ought to be pious—*primum enim in rebus humanis religio est* (the first thing in human affairs is religion); just—*sine iustitia ne Iovis quidem recte regnare potest* (without justice even Jove cannot rule rightly). We can find even in anonymous texts, in pamphlets of electoral propaganda, that modest provincial politicians wrote (citing Aristotle) very certain opinions on the subject of the difference between a legitimate king and a tyrant.

[16] See Paul Super, *Events and Personalities in Polish History,* Pub. by the Baltic Institute, London, 1936, p. 11.

The Polish Ambassador, Jerzy Ossoliński, had every right to say the following words in defense of imprisoned Catholics to King James I of England: "I should never dare ask your Majesty for the release of traitors. If they are such, then they are deserving not of imprisonment, but of the severest of punishments. Yet, if all their guilt is that they are against the oath of fealty because their faith forbids them, I regard them as good Catholics, and not as traitors. It seems to me that no steps should be taken against their conscience, therein following the example of other Catholic Lords, namely my Lord and King, who has within his state people of the same religion as in Britain, but does not therefore violate their conscience."

The tyrant will not submit himself to any law, whereas the king has his royal power and dignity measured and limited by law: "We must choose a king *qui patriae mores amet et patriae leges et instituta et patriae etiam cultum atque vestitum amet et servet.*" But the essential thing is always to govern *iuste et legitime.*[17]

This legitimism and liberalism are truly marvelous. The historian is right in saying that Poland missed her century. "She committed a splendid and lamentable anachronism. In a Europe of hatred and greed, where people were butchered everywhere for thrones or for verses of the Gospel, she had the enormous naïveté to pretend to nothing else but liberty and peace. She turned her eyes away from the Hapsburgs, Guises, Ivans the Terrible and Philips II, to rest them on the ancient republics, the tribune of the Forum and the odes of Horace."[18]

I shall have occasion to speak of the astonishing Latinization of Poland and of the role that classic antiquities played there; here I should like, however, to signalize the fact that the fascination exerted by Rome—republican Rome—is explained by the affinity that existed between the spirit of independence and legalism of the Poles of the sixteenth century and the Latin authors. There existed in Poland at this time just as it had in Rome, love of the civic life, the same national pride, the same attachment to public solemnity and to the public word.

All our political writers of these times constantly cite Sallust, Cicero, Livy, Seneca, likewise Aristotle—much more than Plato, which is very characteristic, for the "statist" leanings of Plato displeased them; their inspiration is essentially republican, they compare Poland to Sparta and Athens, never to the Rome of the Caesars; "they praise, following Cicero and Seneca, republican virtues, courage, simplicity of manners, discipline, justice, con-

---

[17] See *Pisma Polityczne Pierwszego Bezkrólewia*, ed. Jan Czubek, Kraków, 1906.
[18] See H. Grappin, *op. cit.*, p. 85.

sidering much less important the problem of executive power and that of the vigor of juridical laws."[19]

This again is very characteristic; Polish juridical culture was much less advanced in the fifteenth and sixteenth centuries than the political culture. We see in the Poland of this time a weak tradition of Roman law, but beside this subsists a distinct juridical conservatism. The *szlachta* wants no changes, it defends the ancient laws, established by national usage; there was a distinct appearance of juridical nationalism. The one good side to this phenomenon is that there likewise appeared that trait with which we are already familiar—Polish sense of law and order.

Another source of inspiration, as Estreicher demonstrates, was the Bible, the *Old Testament*, and that, because of antipathy to royal power. The Bible is quoted as often as in modern times in America.

There is no wish to follow the example of the neighbors— foreign countries: Venice, Spain, the Empire; all these regimes, if they are mentioned, are quoted and described only to alarm, to show all the abuses of the *absolutum dominium* against which Poland has always defended herself with ferocious energy.

These theories of the "Golden Polish Freedom" and the practice of this freedom are related to movements of Reform abroad, where Catholics in Protestant countries, as well as dissenters, for fear of Catholic monarchs, demand the limitation of monarchical power; they even proclaim rebellion and dethronement. Numerous common ideas attach our theoreticians to French Huguenot monarchomanes; in the first place, the same opinion that the king receives his power from the people and is tied by the laws, that he is therefore only the eye of the law, its ear and its word, and not its creator. However, the French exerted no direct influence on Poland; on the contrary, it is they who praise Poland's ex-

[19] See St. Estreicher, *op. cit.*, p. 92.

ample. I ought also to point out the Polish royalists—a group of theorists that appeared later and had no success; on one hand they advanced concepts of the *absolutum dominium,* in order to limit the liberties of the nobility; on the other hand, they hoped that Catholic sovereigns using greater potency of power could better defend the interests of the Church against the Reformation.

Finally, the Socinians, antitrinitarians, and the "Polish Brethren" import from Italy, Switzerland, the Netherlands, Austria, and Bohemia a whole system of radical ideas, concepts of evangelical humanitarianism and social asceticism; they propagate ideas of absolute social and political equality and the ideal of poverty of the primitive Christians. These ideas had their success, but rather among the bourgeois than among the gentry.

In any case, as I have said, public life in Poland in the sixteenth century had reached a very high level and had become particularly rich.

It is true that the gentry had subjugated not only the king but also the peasants and had not accorded the bourgeoisie the privileges and liberties by which it was itself profiting, but here we must take two things into account: that these privileges and liberties belonged to a very great mass of the population, that proportionately, therefore, a very great number of Polish citizens enjoyed the complete rights of an absolutely free citizen and that, besides, nowhere in Europe at this time were the peasants admitted to participation in the conduct of affairs of state; that, finally, this freedom embracing so great a part of the governing population of the country had formed a high moral culture, which inculcated in this class an ambition to create particularly advantageous conditions of life for all foreigners who came to seek asylum in Poland, and that, guided by these principles of legitimism, respect for law, this nobility never made any attempt on the personal liberty of its peasants nor on that of the bourgeois.

In fact, this respect for law and the cult of good manners in public life is characteristic of sixteenth-century Poland.

The development of this culture, the widening of these privileges, the consequent enfranchisement of the peasants, and laws guaranteeing to the bourgeoisie participation in the management of state, come later, just before the last partition of Poland—after the period of the seventeenth century and the first half of the eighteenth century during which the gentry attained the summit of its ideas of liberty. Gradually, this class, numerous as it was, ended by itself degenerating politically, it embraced the way of social egoism and abuse; it deformed the principles of liberty. These latter finished by degenerating into anarchy and led to the terrible concept that the basis of Poland was disorder; it gradually weakened and disarmed the country—not only from the political but from the economic and military point of view; because it would not pay taxes, perform its military services, and, more and more accustomed to an easy existence the base of which was the work of the peasant—the corvée—it lost all capacity for work and economic initiative itself without having, on the other hand, allowed the bourgeoisie to develop freely and consolidate its own economic resources. For that very reason the cities followed the sloping road of decay. This tendency finally created a state of affairs such that the power it had torn away from the king was in the hands, once again, of the magnates whose political role the *szlachta* had succeeded in reducing so sensibly in the fifteenth and sixteenth centuries. These Polish plutocrats of the seventeenth and eighteenth centuries became little sovereigns of little kingdoms constituted of their immense properties; the nobiliary populace became in their hands a tool of internal struggle, it was led either against the king or else by one set of great lords against another set. Gradually, then, the *szlachta* not only weakened the entire country but unwittingly weakened itself.

The noble inspired by republican Rome saw there only freedom, but he did not wish to see there discipline and the "harsh law"—*"pereat mundus, fiat iustitia—salus reipublicae suprema lex esto."* He thought of only one thing: how to defend himself against the king; and, on the other hand, the example of antiquity, which was wholly based on slavery, justified in his eyes the slavery of the peasant. It was quite difficult to turn him away from this position of individualism and egoism. The efforts of our great kings, such as Zygmunt-August and Stefan Batory, to reduce this excessive liberty were in vain. When once Batory, a king who had on many occasions let it be understood that he did not desire to be *"rex fictus nec pictus,"* apostrophized impatiently and angrily one Kazimierski, a petty noble: "Silence, clown," the latter replied: "I am no clown, but he who elects kings and overthrows tyrants." As early as the sixteenth century, therefore, symptoms of danger could be perceived.

All in all, however, Poland in the sixteenth century seems to us a country whose public morals can be criticized, to tell the truth, from only one point of view: Poland had erected a political system that gave the citizens every guarantee of great material and especially spiritual prosperity—excepting guarantees of security in respect to her neighbors. The nobility had formed an ideal of life, and a life which enervated it and, as I have already said, disarmed the country; and on the other hand, independently of the outer dangers menacing Poland, it could be maintained only if every Polish citizen were an exemplary citizen. The situation in the sixteenth century was neither bad nor unfortunate—quite the contrary—but that situation changed.

Nevertheless, the sixteenth century—that wonderful century in

Poland—remains as historic testimony to certain traits that characterize the nation even today, despite all the terrible catastrophes
which the unhappy country has had to undergo. There is no way
to understand modern Poland thoroughly unless we penetrate
into the study of this historical and political background.

"One is struck," the French historian Grappin tells us, "in
reading these religious or lay publicists of the time, at seeing how
they ordinarily consider the functions of a citizen a sort of sacred
and redoubtable rite. If the Poles clung to their rights, they also
feared their duties and took them for a sacrament. It is superficial
to see in that the effect of classical reminiscence, patchwork on
the ancients. Such sentiments were the manifestation of the deepest
and purest Slavic instincts, of a certain notion of freedom foreign
to the peoples of the west. Whatever the prestige of republican
Rome may have been, it is extremely rare to meet among the
writers of the age an apology for or a simple justification of
slavery. And if the *szlachta* became uncontested mistress of power,
if it more and more restricted the rights of the bourgeois and
the peasants, it made no law hostile to their personal liberty."[20]

We have there, it must be admitted, a beautiful realization—
for the epoch—of the ideal of justice, liberty, and peace which
this Polish nobility had elaborated and constituted. It had, it
possessed this ideal—that is clear after what I have just said;[21]

---

[20] *Op. cit.*, p. 86.

[21] Even the average, anonymous people had ideas illustrating that peculiar Polish
liberalism and legitimism. It was a climate in which even the thoughts of an average
Polish squire became amazingly elevated and idealistic. Let me quote an example.
After the death of the last Jagiellonian, King Zygmunt-August, there were several
parties among the nobles organized for the expected election of the new King. There
were several candidates for the Polish throne, among them Ivan the Terrible of
Moscow. He had partisans: those who thought that a strong monarchical power
would be of some utility for Poland. He had also adversaries. Polemics took place.
One of the partisans of Ivan the Terrible wrote: "After the description of our laws
and of our liberties it is impossible to believe that the King *sua naturali tyrannide
aut rebellione* would be able to punish *sine suo periculo* anybody—in his property
or in his life, because such are our laws and liberties. But even if such *leges et
libertates* did not exist, the generous *magnanimitas* of the Polish nation ought to

but it will become even more so when we become acquainted
with some Polish authors of the time who forged and developed
those ideas, and, what is indeed much more significant and striking, had already, in the sixteenth century, undertaken a profound
and penetrating criticism of certain vicious and alarming sides
of that political system.

I shall begin my rapid review of a few of these Polish political
writers by relating one of the prettiest episodes at the start of
the fifteenth century. After the defeat of the Teutonic Knights by
Poland and Lithuania on the field of Gruenwald in 1410, the conflict with the Order was not yet ended, and King Władysław
Jagiełło was finally obliged to bring his cause before the Council
of Constance. This task was not easy, because very powerful
propaganda was being directed against Poland by the Knights,
strongly supported by the Emperor. This propaganda represented
the victory of Poland at Gruenwald as a defeat of civilization by
barbarism, of the Church by heresy and paganism. They asked
more and more money from the Pope and the West for their
struggle against Poland and Lithuania. They tried to falsify facts
and spread the most fantastic fables about Poland and her King;
counting on ignorance of Poland in Western Europe, they represented Poland as an absolutely uncivilized country, and King
Jagiełło as a cobbler's son. King Jagiełło sent to the Council an
extraordinary embassy, with Bishop Nicholas Trąba at its head.
And the Bishop was accompanied by Paulus Vladimiri (Włodkowicius), Rector of the Jagiellonian University. Our Rector demonstrated this "dubious" Polish civilization. He took part in discussion with the greatest European scholars of the time, and
presented several treatises, among which *Tractatus De Potestate*

mitigate *etiam ferocissimam naturam principis,* because with our Lord the Sovereign
we always have something *commune.*" See *Pisma Polityczne,* etc., ed. J. Czubek,
Kraków, 1906, p. 379.

Papae et Imperatoris respectu infidelium is the most interesting. The form of argumentation, the quotations (the Bible, Church Fathers, Canonists, Doctors, Dante's *De Monarchia*, Aristotle) are purely medieval, but the content, the ideas, the thoughts, the spirit of this treatise are certainly original and very significant. And how timely today! It was written in the form of questions. Here are some of them:

"*First:* Do the Christian princes have the right, without thereby committing a sin, to expel from their countries the Jews and Saracens and to take away their wealth? Is it right for the Pope to order or to suggest this to the Princes?

Second: If the infidels possess countries or states separated from the Christians, if they rule them and live in peace, is it decent in such a case for Christians to make an aggression against them and to take away their lands?

Third: Has the Pope the right, on the basis of the ancient laws of the Roman Empire, to take away from the infidels the possessions which they took away from the Roman Empire?

Fourth: Has the Roman Church the right to keep what was once by violence and arms taken by the Roman Emperors?

Fifth: Is it right to take the wealth of heretics and nonconformists? Is it right and decent to make converts to Christianity by force of arms and by oppression?"[22]

A little later, in 1439, the Council of Basle gave highest praise and recognition to a treatise prepared by the professors of the same Jagiellonian University, in which they defended the thesis of the superiority of the Council against the Pope.

Let us pass, however, to the sixteenth century. Among all the brilliant authors of the time, first place belongs to Frycz-Modrzewski, who so courageously and so wisely attacked all the abuses, sins, vices, injustices committed by the nobles and by the

[22] See St. Tarnowski, *Pisarze Polityczni XVI Wieku*, Kraków, 1886, Vol. I, pp. 9-10.

clergy, and who so generously, being himself a noble, defended the suffering people, the peasants, the poor citizens deprived of all the rights and privileges which were assured only to the nobles.

Here I may be asked, "What is this? You told us that Poland created an ideal system of political and social life in the sixteenth century—and now you are quoting a writer of the same sixteenth century who attacks the vices and injustices committed in the frame of that system?" We must understand here two essential and important points. First: the system elaborated by the *szlachta* was good enough as far as political problems were concerned, but the question of juridical relations between citizens was still awaiting a better solution; the courts were not energetic enough, and the immunity of the noble was too strong. As a result, murders among the *szlachta* occurred often—not so often as, for instance, in Germany, but for Frycz' conscience often enough. On the other hand, Frycz was a man of great moral exigency; he looked further than the present, he was warning his nation against dangers menacing her.

Some of his texts are deeply touching. Here is a really Tolstoyan text of sixteenth-century Poland:

" 'The blood of the peasant will never be benevolent and sympathetic to the blood of the noble.' Behind such words and in a country in which such an epidemic exists there is no place for any unity, friendship, any kindness, understanding, any justice. Removing from the rich their high self-consciousness, from the nobility their pride and haughtiness, from the powerful their self-confidence, she will be able to put on the same level the superiors and the great of this world with the inferiors and poor—and then it will be revealed that all estates have the same hearts and the same brains, and the poor will no longer complain about their misery, and the one who is not a nobleman, that he is not noble. And those who are enslaved will no more protest against their en-

slavers. For the achievement of the above a new law ought not
to be imposed by force; it is necessary to create mutual kindness."[23]

Another text: "Laws are like medicines. No expert physician
has regard for the status of the individual. It is sufficient for
him to know the disease. He does not inquire whether his patient
is a peasant or a lord, a noble or a serf. He knows only him who
has to be cured. In the same manner ought laws to apply to
citizens."[24]

Modrzewski goes so far in his feeling of justice that he would
like to eliminate nobles from tribunals which judge the peasants,
because he is afraid of their fatal injustice. He extends the same
respect for freedom to international affairs, and it is true, though
perhaps astonishing, that in the sixteenth century Frycz, in order
to avoid wars, proposed international arbitration for international
conflicts.

Among all Polish political writers of the sixteenth century it
is Frycz-Modrzewski who appears to us the most noble figure, the
most attractive of his time. There was in him a peculiar sweetness
and moral elegance; he was certainly the superior mind of the
time—then better known and recognized abroad than in Poland.
The striking thing in his writings is on the one hand their practical
character; the writer wishes to be the physician of his country,
and on the other, it is his point of departure for a higher theory,
Aristotelian in its essence, of the state as having to be the vigilant
protector of the material and moral prosperity of the whole population. Thence flow all the duties of the state in the sphere of
education, police, hygiene, protection of the poor; thence, the
importance the writer gave to the betterment of mores; thence, the
interest he took in the oppressed and the poor; thence, his care

[23] See St. Tarnowski, *op. cit.*, p. 153.
[24] *Ibid.*, p. 177.

for good courts, for a severe penal code; thence, his propaganda in behalf of a solid and firm organization of the bureaucracy and the administration. In truth, one cannot but be surprised when he reads those marvelous passages on the unemployed and the state's duties toward them, on international arbitration, on the concept of the aggressor;[25] when one reads Frycz' warnings against the menace of social movements which social inequality may provoke, one would not believe himself in the middle of the sixteenth century![26] That needed a refined civilization—a civilization which was neither accidental nor banal.

Here is another figure: Krzysztof Warszewicki—noble, son of a castellan; adversary of "gilded freedom" and defender of royal power, a rare case for Poland. But it is not in connection with these items that I should like to present you this very interesting writer. I should like to speak here about his book on the *Ambassador—De Legato et Legatione.*

He has been criticized by one of our outstanding historians of Polish literature, Stanisław Tarnowski, for not having written an essay on the Polish foreign policy of his time. Tarnowski thinks the reason for this was lack of ability, of creative and independent thought. Therefore, thinks Tarnowski, he gave only a sort of diplomatic guide—a description of that special instrument of every foreign policy which is diplomacy.[27] He was a man of the world, who saw many people and observed interesting events;

[25] The oldest written statute of Poland, dated 1347, namely, the Wiślica Statute, makes a distinction between defensive war, which a knight undertakes at his own cost, and war beyond the country's frontiers, in which the knight was to be recompensed for his participation by the prince or king. This distinction is found again in the Pact of Koszyce of 1374, and afterward emerges again and again in numerous manifestoes of the Polish nobility, which declare that they will willingly hasten with all help to defend their frontiers, but are against any war of invasion and aggression. The famous Erasmus wrote from Rotterdam to the King of Poland, Sigismund I: "The peace of thy kingdom and Christian blood were always incomparably more precious to thine eyes than conquests and subjections of hostile territories, and this has the approbation of the crowds." (*The Polish Spirit of Freedom*, pp. 18-19.)

[26] See Stanisław Kot, *Andrzej Frycz-Modrzewski*, Kraków, 1923.

[27] See Tarnowski, *op. cit.*, Vol. II, p. 190.

therefore his description of his time ought to be very useful. I think that Tarnowski's evaluation is too low; Warszewicki's book is a striking book, full of interest even for today. He begins his exposition by saying that ambassadors are the eyes of the country: "they must look at every side and warn from whence may come the menace, where on the horizon of the Republic dark points appear."

His precepts and judgments are of astonishing perspicacity and often full of pertinence for today. For instance: a foreign ambassador is to be treated in exactly the same way that our ambassadors are treated in the respective country—this so as not to be wanting in proper dignity.

An ambassador going abroad obviously has an "instruction" of directives concerning his mission. But he must be left a wide margin of freedom of action; his own talent must be given confidence, for it is impossible to foresee everything.

What are to be the capacities and aptitudes of an ambassador? In the first place, he must be educated, especially in the field of history . . . He must avoid all infatuation and arrogance . . . It is bad, he says, to present your arguments in a haughty, blustering, insolent, rude way; it is always clumsy. If you wish to see them accepted, such a tone makes your task difficult; if you desire a refusal, even in such a case it is better to give the appearance of calm and benevolence by casting responsibility for the rupture on the foreign court. *Fortiter in re, suaviter in modo.* The spirit of national sufficiency, the desire to show the superiority of the country represented, that is the greatest danger threatening an ambassador . . .

He must be reserved, discreet, never too loquacious, graceful but never obtrusive, in personal relations courteous, easy, captivating, but full of dignity in official relations. But even in private conversations with his best friends, when he speaks of things, people, affairs of the country of his residence, let him criticize nothing, let him not permit himself any sarcasms—not forgetting that he is among foreigners, where every pleasantry, every word can be remarked and hurt him and his country. Let him receive often at his house, let him receive representatives of different opinions and parties, let his house be hospitable, gay, and agreeable, for often at a merry dinner a word may escape a man who would never have pronounced it even under torture. It is well to have a fine house, fine horses, a fine carriage—in short, everything that attracts the curiosity of the populace and everything that creates popularity. The ambassador must be handsome himself—but not doll-like—of noble stature, well-built, elegant—but without excess, never too much splendor lest the court to which he is accredited take umbrage! For great occasions he must, heedless of expense, appear *en grande tenue*, but in the circumstances of ordinary life he must preserve modesty. Never appear in public in clothes too new, for they bother you and make you awkward. Never go in debt in the country of residence. Never be too intimate with the ambassadors of other countries, for their missions are generally opposed to yours and they are prone to try to pump you. It is always the first steps that are important, the first impression that counts—when people do not yet know you well, that is the time to maintain an air of dignity and nobility. Avoid shady places, gaming, frivolous amusements—you should not be stiff and suspicious, but, on the other hand, never fall into sloppiness. With sovereigns, never insist overmuch. "Kings have the same nature as fish; if you push them toward the bank they go away to deep water; when you let them be, they come of themselves to the bank . . ."

Is not all that charming, does it not prove an astonishing fineness of mind, an admirable *savoir-vivre*, a political culture of the first order?

At royal audiences—speak with eloquence, but never too much, listen with patience, and never—never—let the sovereign see that you know the question better than he does—for they would always rather lose a castle or a kingdom than lose the glory of a good knowledge of affairs! Never praise your own sovereign too much; foreign sovereigns don't like that. Never lie, for a lie is easily detected; never advance doubtful matters as sure ones, probable matters as certain ones. Do not importune sovereigns, wait until they call you, be patient, and never be wanting in the established etiquette of the court. Never begin a talk, but reply to questions. Avoid trying to amaze, praising your country too highly . . . That calls to mind the Muscovite ambassadors of the same time . . . When the ambassadors of Ivan the Terrible had been shown the monuments and ancient buildings at Rome, they answered that in Moscow they had much finer buildings and monuments. When at Ratisbon the Kurfuerst of Bavaria invited them to dinner, they answered that they should eat dinner at home, for it was not fitting, said they, for ambassadors of so great a monarch to stroll about anywhere and accept dinners at strangers' houses . . .

There remains to us a third field, that of the duties of an ambassador in respect to his own government. Here again Warszewicki astonishes and amazes. The first task is to inform, justly and precisely. Never represent, in dispatches, facts not accomplished as accomplished facts. Report everything in greatest detail: who did it, how, when; what the inhabitants of the country think of their government; what goes on at court; and everything must be reported with precision but in an amusing way, so as not to bore the king. The ambassador should keep well in mind— and here once again appears this extraordinary political culture —that he must never sow enmity between the two countries, he must recollect that in his quality of ambassador, of interpreter, he is to consider himself a friend of the country of his residence, as a maker of peace and good relations between the two countries, and not of discord and misunderstandings.

When the ambassador takes a trip, he has to observe everything he sees, take notes, write down the number of inhabitants in the cities he visits, take notice of their commerce, industry, army, atmosphere . . . He must be prudent; above all, he should avoid beautiful women, for they are for him the greatest of all dangers. There is a grievous stipulation . . . it must be confessed.

And here, finally, a list of ambassadors that Poland ought to send abroad, choosing them according to the habits and tastes of different countries:

To Turkey they should send brave, vigorous, and generous men, for the Turks love to threaten and they are greedy, so they must be sent someone who can give them a good deal but will not let himself be intimidated. To Moscow, men prudent and sly, for there reigns *graeca fides*, and they lead you by the nose for a long time in order to dupe you later, they haggle for a long time before coming to anything. To Rome should be sent serious men, orthodox Catholics, only not ecclesiastics (what admirable wisdom!), but laymen, for it is more difficult for a priest to oppose the Holy See and ask him something with determination. To Spain—solid and serious men, quite aloof from political or religious novelties; to Italy, civil, polite, attractive men; to France, men of wit, supple and with a well-hung tongue; to England, imposing, majestic men, good to the eye, for the English love that, all the more so as they well know, and feel with sorrow, that these qualities are deficient in them. (*Sic!*) To Germany, constant men, men of their word, for "the Germans have for centuries been renowned for their constancy"[28] . . . (*Sic!*)

It is necessary to quote here another Polish political writer,

[28] See Tarnowski, *op. cit.*, Vol. II, pp. 191-200.

whose fate has been particularly happy, in the sense that he was
well known in Europe in the sixteenth and seventeenth centuries,
in Italy and in England. I have in mind Wawrzyniec Goślicki, a
noble, Senator and Chancellor of Poland, later Bishop of Poznań.
We do not know the date of his birth—we do know only that he
died in 1607. In the year 1568 he published in Venice two volumes in Latin, *De Optimo Senatore*. A new Latin edition was
published in Basel in 1593. Later on it was translated into English
and published in three editions. *The Accomplished Senator* presents the purest example of Polish political philosophy and
science of that time. The author, of course, quotes Plato, Aristotle,
Cicero. He was an educated man. His chief subject is the art of
government. His aims, as in the case of Frycz, are practical . . .
"Plato's *Commonwealth*," he says, "and Cicero's *Orator* are airy
topics, which I shall not presume to meddle with: for my enquiries
are all entirely confined to common life, agreeable to the customs
of mankind, and altogether intended for public use and benefit"
. . . "No government," he says further, "can be happy or miserable without involving its people in the same state and condition." This is his first important assertion. And the second? . . .
"In the private happiness of the subjects consists the general and
public happiness of the commonwealth" . . . The third assertion
deals with the conception of a citizen.

But who, in Goślicki's opinion, is a citizen? . . . "It is very
evident, that in all commonwealths and cities whatsoever, those
men who have a right to give their opinion and vote in all matters relating to the public, and are capable of being made magis-
trates or officers, in the government or city, to which they belong,
have the best claim to the name of citizens . . ." The fourth
assertion contains his concept of the "People." "By the word
People, I do not mean a mixed multitude of rustics, boors and
mechanics, the mob and rabble, the scum and lees of a country;

but a regular body of citizens and subjects, generous by birth, civilized by education, and every way duly qualified to fill the public offices of a state, whenever they shall be legally invited and advanced thereto . . ."

The Senator is the most important factor in the political life of a state, he is to be the intermediary between the government and the governed. In his book Goślicki gives a detailed analysis of all the traits of an "accomplished" Senator. The Senator represents the legislative power, and Goślicki's idea as to the nature of "wholesome laws" is very characteristic: *laws should rather prevent than suppress crime and evil.* "A good legislator will always take care, that his laws should rather appear as precepts and persuasions to good manners and discipline, than in a prescribing and mandatory form. The end and design of all laws is to make the people good and happy, and agreeable to this ought the mind and intention of the legislator always to be. For the punishing of delinquents is rather a case of necessity, than of choice . . ."

Goślicki's theory of monarchy is no less interesting. He is a partisan of a limited monarchy, based on perfect harmony between the king, the senators, *i.e.*, a representative body of the king's councillors, and the people, *i.e.*, responsible citizens. This harmony can be reached when each of the three orders observes the law. There are in his reasoning some suggestions of a revolutionary character. Kings are made not for their own, but their people's sake . . . therefore . . . "Sometimes a people, justly provoked and irritated by the tyranny and usurpations of their kings, take upon themselves the undoubted right of vindicating their own liberties; and by a well-formed conspiracy, or by open arms, shake off the yoke, drive out their lords and masters, and take government entirely into their own hands . . ." ". . . Kingly government is very aptly represented by the power

and authority which a father has over his children, whose office
it is to be careful of, and watchful over them; to provide for
their sustenance and welfare . . . In the very same manner,
all good kings ought to behave toward their subjects . . . Now
as a father, when he becomes eminently wicked and is remark-
ably cruel and inhuman toward his children, does thereby lose
the very name of a father, and is no better than an unnatural
tyrant. So when a king is under no restraint, but of his own
will and lusts, when he tramples all law under foot, is by
his life a scandal, and his government a plague to his people, he
immediately forfeits the name of king, and cannot justly be called
by any other title, but that of tyrant . . ."

These texts are astonishingly simple in their power of intrinsic
legitimism. As such they are immensely eloquent examples of
the style of Polish political philosophy, they represent also a
striking contrast to the Muscovite theories of despotism of the
time. Exactly at the same time Ivan the Terrible was making up
his "Apology of Absolutism" to which Goślicki's book is really
a very Polish answer.[29]

I have left out—there, in that brilliant past, a whole mass of
writers of the first order, whose names I have not even cited. I
should like to present here, however, but three more personages:
Łukasz Górnicki, writer of the sixteenth century, the Jesuit
Skarga, also of the sixteenth century, and Staszyc, belonging to
the eighteenth.

Górnicki was a bourgeois, a clever, supple courtier, favored
by Kings Zygmunt-August and Batory, a man of remarkable culture and education, admirer of antiquity and especially of Italy,
one of our greatest stylists of the sixteenth century, writing—

[29] See about Goślicki in Tarnowski's book—*op. cit.*, Vol. I, pp. 357-374. My quotations are taken from *The Accomplished Senator* by Tytus Filipowicz (Polish Ambassador to the United States)—see Proceedings of the American Society of International Law, April 23-30, 1932, pp. 234-238.

despite his great Latin culture—a splendid Polish, elegant, fine, brilliant. He was firmly persuaded that stupidity and ignorance are the source of all iniquity. He therefore decided to enlighten the Poles by acquainting them with antiquity and Italy, which he considered the finest examples of human civilization.

In 1566 he made a translation—an adaptation (very adroit and fine) of the *Cortegiano* by Balthazar Castiglione, Polonizing it profoundly, so that his *Polish Courtier* can be considered in certain respects a profoundly national work. I shall have occasion to cite next time some ravishing passages from this book, notably the chapter "on the grace of writing and speaking." Today I should like to cite to you only some political opinions of Górnicki which are in his book published in 1588, *Conversation between a Pole and an Italian*. In this book it is the Italian that expresses the ideas of the author; the Pole represents that stupidity which Górnicki wishes to enlighten.

The Italian, replying to the praises of "golden liberty" lavished by the Pole, pronounces a very severe judgment: the election of the kings is perilous, for it opens the door to the influences of the powerful lords who can with the aid of corruption subject the electors to their will; the Polish laws are bad, because they are unjust; they protect the nobility, they wrong the peasants and the bourgeois; the courts are bad because perjury is an instrument of defense; the organization of military defense is bad because the frontiers are provided neither with fortresses nor with military castles. The Pole will accept nothing and understand nothing of all this.

Górnicki's arguments are firm, solid, wise, richly developed; his book is a great book; I have cited here only a few essential ideas. What is striking in his book is that Górnicki advanced, in the sixteenth century, arguments and judgments to which the School of Cracow had little to add. His perspicacity is astonishing;

it gives proof of great political wisdom and great solicitude for the welfare of the Republic. He was not the only one; he represented the ideas of our great kings and of Poles who had already, in this era, a high conception of the nature of a state and who on the other hand kept their eyes open to the internal and external dangers that threatened the Republic. "The judgment of God," wrote Górnicki, "pushes us as the wind pushes the ship on the sea, and who knows—toward port or toward danger? . . . The wise men of antiquity are right in saying: the enemy will never be able to blight either principality, or kingdom, or monarchy; each state rots of itself when the time for it to wither arrives. And the time arrives when a republic or a kingdom commits so many sins that God can no longer suffer them, for there are not only sins that each separate man can commit; there exist likewise sins, much heavier, that can be committed by a Republic."[30]

The same tone and sense run through the preaching of the greatest Polish orator, Piotr Skarga, a Jesuit, apostle of Catholicism, of moral perfection, powerful preacher of the sixteenth and the beginning of the seventeenth centuries—a man called by Poland "the tyrant of human hearts."

Skarga preached, wrote, imposed the iron moral discipline that the hard school of the Jesuits had carved into his heart and mind. The sources were different from those of Modrzewski and Górnicki, but the end was the same; the good and the welfare of the Republic.

Piotr Skarga (1536-1612)—real name Pawęski—belonged to the Polish gentry of the central part of Poland, the so-called Mazowsze. He was a student at the University of Cracow. In 1557 he was in Vienna, where he went to continue his studies. After

[30] See Tarnowski, *op. cit.*, Vol. II, pp. 234-258. See also Ignacy Chrzanowski, *Historja Literatury Niepodległej Polski*, ed. V., pp. 140-154.

that trip he donned the cassock of the priesthood and became preacher to the Catholics in Lwów. In 1569, while in Rome, he entered the Society of Jesus. Upon his return to Poland he went to Wilno, where he became the first president (rector) of the University. In 1584 he became Superior of the Jesuit Fathers in Cracow, and later he served as the King's Sermoner. He discharged this latter duty for twenty-four years. Among his publications are included *Lives of the Saints* (1573), *Sermons for Sundays and Holidays* (1593), *Occasional Parliamentary Sermons* (1597), and many others. His greatest achievements are his parliamentary sermons in which he appeared as Poland's most eminent orator and stylist.

His writings represent—in addition to an enormous talent for expression—a brilliant Polish style and means of suggestive eloquence, a beauty of language and richness of metaphors, a fusion of great emotional tension and mighty power of logical analysis and persuasion. All his sermons are focused around several chief ideas, which he develops in a sort of system. He is the classic representative of a firm religious conception of life, combined with a very strong patriotism. His sermons display a deep devotion to the truth as he understood it.

He is the defender of the idea of the necessity of establishing in the state a rigid political order based on the executive power of the king and the national unification of the country. But even in this defender of a strong monarchical principle—so unpopular among the Poles of the sixteenth century—there appears the characteristic Polish respect for law, to which I have so often referred as the Polish spirit of legalism: "That kind mother (the motherland) has given you a golden freedom, the assurance that you shall never serve tyrants, but only God-fearing lords and kings whom you choose yourselves, whose power, being limited by the laws, does you no injustice; you suffer no oppression from foreign lords or from your own. It is only you who are tyrants over yourselves when you do not execute the laws and you put up barriers against justice by a false freedom or rather license. Look at the citizens[31] of the Turkish and Muscovite states, what oppression and tyranny they suffer! Not such is your motherland: she is a mother to you and not a stepmother!"[32]

The same idea is expressed in the *Sixth Sermon, On Monarchy,* defending a "good" *absolutum dominium* and explaining that completely unlimited power is good only in the hands of the Lord, who never errs, never is wicked, and never is a tyrant.

"Therefore does human reason provide the monarch and the king with counsel and laws, limiting and defining his power, and helping his judgment that he may not err and become a wicked tyrant. We praise not such a monarchy as is found among the Turks, the Tartars, and the Muscovites, which has a lawless domination, but such as is supported by just laws and wise counsel and has its power reduced and defined by righteous codes."[33]

He also courageously attacks the political and social vices of the time. As a firm Catholic he opposed the Reformation as well as the Greek Orthodox Church and tried to consolidate the nation around the Catholic religion.

We may, therefore, find in him some of the traits of Frycz-Modrzewski, Orzechowski, and Górnicki; but, unlike Modrzewski, he was a strongly convinced and even a militant Catholic; unlike Orzechowski, he never trod the way of religious intolerance; and unlike Górnicki's purely secular attitude in government he represented an intensely religious approach to the great national prob-

---

[31] Characteristically enough, he uses the word "citizens" (*obywatele*) when speaking of the subjects of Moscow and Turkey; the word "subject" (*poddany*) appeared only after the Partitions.

[32] From the *Second Sermon, On the Love of the Motherland.* See I. Chrzanowski, *op. cit.,* p. 239.

[33] *Ibid.,* p. 243.

lems. He certainly was, except for Hozjusz, the greatest advocate
of Catholicism in Poland, but not so intolerant as Hozjusz.

When speaking about dangers menacing and errors charac-
terizing the life of the Republic, he passionately attacks, first,
the lack of public spirit, of unity. He deeply believes that the
Catholic religion itself can cultivate the virtues capable of com-
batting these dangers. He also thinks that possession by the king
of strong political power would be a sufficient medicine for this
sickness.

Skarga's figure is engraved in Polish minds by the famous picture of Jan Matejko, for which Matejko drew his inspiration from
the *Eighth Parliamentary Sermon* where Skarga reached perhaps
the acme of his eloquence and of his prophetic warnings.

Indeed, some of his sermons really do achieve a mighty power
of feeling and of art,[34] especially when the preacher is speaking
about the motherland and expressing sentiments of patriotic love.
An instance of this is the *Second Sermon,* one of the most beautiful, in which we may find some passages of striking pertinence—
and not only for Poland, and not only for his day. After depicting
all the advantages derived from the Commonwealth by the Poles,
Ruthenians, Lithuanians, Prussians and the peoples of Livonia
and Żmudź, after portraying all the benefits of peace and wealth
which the Commonwealth gave everybody, he asks: "What more
could she have done for you? Should you not indeed love her
with all your hearts and keep her intact and, if need be, sacrifice
everything for her well-being? In loving her you love yourself,
and you do not lose yourself; having no attachment to her and
no faith in her, you betray yourself. Singly do you each love your
own gains and destroy the Republic's, and you think that you
do well and provide for yourselves . . . When a ship is sinking

[34] However, there are to be found also some defects in this art which sometimes
becomes too crudely "realistic." See L'Abbé A. Berga, *Pierre Skarga (1536-1612),*
Paris, 1916, pp. 360-372.

and the winds are upsetting it, the foolish one looks to his bundles and chests and lies on them and goes not to the help of the ship; and he thinks that he is protecting himself; but he is destroying himself. For when the ship has no help, then it itself must sink with everything aboard. But if he despises all his chests and goods which are on the ship and goes to its assistance with all the others, forgetting everything that is his, then only will he gain all and preserve his own health . . . On this ship you have sons, little children, wives, wealth, treasures, and everything you love; on that ship there are as many souls as this kingdom and the states united with it contain. Let them not sink, but have mercy on your own blood, on the people, and on your brethren; and serve them not so much with your wealth as with yourselves, you who have taken them under your dominion and under your protection . . . O great lords! O earthly divinities! Have magnanimous and open hearts for your brethren and your nations, for all the souls which this kingdom with its states embraces. Do not confine and compress your love within your homes and your own private concerns, do not shut it up in your closets and coffers. Let your love flow from you onto the whole people, from you high mountains like a river that waters the flat fields below."[35]

There is no doubt that these suggestions and pictures did not perish, and we see them two hundred years later in Mickiewicz's *Ode to Youth*, where the poet opposes to the selfish, the enthusiastic and generous.

Sometimes his voice becomes terribly threatening, especially when he is trying to frighten, as for instance in the *Third Sermon, On Domestic Harmony*: "And you will be as a childless widow, you who have ruled other nations, and you will be for ridicule and mockery to your enemies. You will forsake your language, in which alone this kingdom has remained free among the great

[35] See Zdzisław Dębicki, *Pisarze Polscy*, Warszawa-Poznań, 1920, Vol. I, pp. 407-409.

Slavonic peoples, and you will ruin your nation, and the rest of this nation, so old and widely flourishing in the world, you will lose. And you will be turned into a nation which is foreign and hates your very selves, as has happened to others. You will be not only without a master of your own blood and without the choosing of him, but also without a fatherland and without your own kingdom, exiles everywhere miserable, despised, poor, wanderers, you will be trodden upon where once you were respected. Where will you be able to find a second such fatherland in which you will have the same glory, the same affluence, money, treasures, and luxuries, and goods? Will another such mother be born for you and your sons? If you lose this one you can have no thought of another."[36]

He reaches the same level of Biblical pathos in that famous *Eighth Sermon, On the Impunity of Flagrant Sins,* which as I have mentioned inspired Matejko: "Were I Jeremiah I should take shackles on my feet and fetters and chain on my neck, and I should cry out on you sinners as he cried: 'So will the Lords be fettered, and they will be driven like rams to foreign lands.' And I should show the mouldy and rotten dress, shaking it that it might fly asunder in shreds, and I should say to you: 'So also shall be annihilated and turned to shreds and smoke your glory and all your gains and your possessions.' And taking a clay pot, and summoning you all together, I should dash it to the wall before your eyes, saying: 'So will I smash you—saith the Lord— like this pot, the shards of which cannot be again put together nor restored.'

"Were I Ezekiel I should shave my head and my beard; I should divide my hair into three parts. I should burn one part, another I should cut off, and a third I should scatter in the wind, and I should call out to you: 'Some shall die of the famine; and

[36] See I. Chrzanowski, *op. cit.,* pp. 229-250.

others shall fall by the sword; and the third part shall be scattered throughout the world.' And I should not leave my dwelling-place neither by the door, nor by the window, but I would destroy the walls, and as if running away I should call on you: 'So it will happen to you. There are no castles and fortresses to defend you. The foe will smash them all and will ruin you.'

"Be ever afraid of those perils! I have no special revelation from the Lord about you and about your ruin. But I have a message to you from the Lord. And I have this instruction: to show you your evils and to tell the vengeance that will be wrought on them if you do not put away your evils."[37]

No insistence need be made upon how prophetic these words appear to us in the light of the Polish catastrophe of the eighteenth century, of the Polish insurrections, in the light of the calamities through which we all are now passing. There is nothing astonishing in the fact that Skarga inspired not only Jan Matejko but also our Romantic poets, who created a literature of exaltation, revelation, and also of expiation; that this classic preacher, rigid in his Catholicism, but ardent in his patriotism, came to be called the "tyrant of consciences" not only by his contemporaries but also by later generations.[38] The Abbé Berga, writing in 1916, said that Skarga is "too Polish"—I wonder whether he would appear to be so to readers in 1944.

After the decline and decay of Polish political international prestige, and just at the last moment of Polish independence, in 1791, Poland made in the Constitution of the Third of May a new and wonderful effort to restore the greatness and generosity of her political thought, to "modernize" it, to spread the liberties and privileges to the "middle" class, to the bourgeoisie; to abolish the serfdom of the peasants; to reorganize economic life; to create

[37] *Ibid.*
[38] See about Skarga in the works of Brückner, Chrzanowski, Kot and others.

a strong executive power, to fortify the power of the king, to reduce the privileges of the Sejm. This constitution abolished the *Liberum Veto*, provided for a strong military defense and a new organization of education. The Constitution of the Third of May was much more a continuation and a development of Polish traditions, of the thoughts of the Polish reformers of the sixteenth century, then an imitation of the concepts of the French Revolution; it was inspired by the Polish political writers of the eighteenth century, such as King Stanisław Leszczyński; Stanisław Konarski, with his four volumes *On a Method of Effective Government*; Hugo Kołłątaj's *Letters of an Anonym*; and Staszyc's *Admonitions to Poland* and his *Remarks on the Life of Jan Zamoyski*.

In the works of Staszyc, who was one of the chief inspiring spirits of this constitution, in those of his works even formally connected with the sixteenth century (with Jan Zamoyski), we may find opinions very near the ideology of Frycz. But Staszyc insisted not only on the necessity of spreading Polish liberal and democratic traditions to all social classes, but also and perhaps even more on the concept of responsibility. This concept was based on the necessity for the individual to subordinate his aims to those of the community. For Staszyc this community represented a moral unity, but this moral unity was possible of realization only in the State: "Without the State, there is no moral unity for a nation, but the nation does not exist for the State's sake— on the contrary, the State exists for the Nation. The State is not the Master, but the Servant of the Nation."[39]

It is not a new opinion that the Third of May is more a Polish than a French product. And this in spite of the address of King Stanisław-August, sent on May 5, 1791, to the French Assemblée Nationale in Paris, in which he insisted on this relationship.

[39] See I. Chrzanowski, *op. cit.*, pp. 560-575.

Already Mickiewicz had attested the Polish genealogy of our Constitution: "This law did not emerge from the brain of an isolated sage, from the lips of a few administrators, but was drawn from the heart of the great mass: it is not merely written in black on white, but it still lives in the memory, in the desires of the generations, and so it is a living law, rooted in the past, and developing in the future . . . In the May Constitution . . . the national element, the child of past traditions, is nurtured on the new present-day needs of the Nation. Hence, it has been well and justly said that the May Constitution is the political testament of the former Poland . . ."[40]

And now let me come to the end. Among those who tried to save Poland at the end of the eighteenth century from disaster, among those who were the creators and guides of our wonderful renaissance in the second part of the eighteenth century, was also a man, a great man—a man who belongs to two worlds and to two histories—to that of Poland and to that of America, a man about whom Thomas Jefferson said: "He is as pure a son of liberty as I have ever known and of that liberty which is to go to all, and not to the few and each alone." This man is Thaddeus Kościuszko, the fighter for Polish and American independence, the friend and protector of peasants in Poland and of Negroes in America.

The Constitution of May 3, 1791, had declared that "guided by justice, humanity, and Christian duties as well as by our own well-understood interest, we take the peasants, from under whose hands flow the most abundant source of the national wealth, who constitute the most numerous population in the nation, and therefore the country's greatest strength, under the protection of the law." Kościuszko went further: having called all the inhabit-

[40] See *The Polish Spirit of Freedom*, "Polish Studies and Sketches," Vol. I, issued by the Polish Ministry of Information, London, 1942, p. 49.

ants of the country to arms, he proclaimed in the Połaniec Manifesto of May 7, 1794, that "every peasant is free and is allowed to move freely from place to place." And they moved; they moved for the first time in order to join Kościuszko's armies fighting against Russia. They gave the best proof, by this, of their attachment for their country, despite all the lies that our enemies have told about us and about them.

In America, before leaving his second mother-country, Kościuszko wrote a testament on May 5, 1798, by which he authorized his friend Jefferson to employ his whole property in America "in purchasing Negroes from among his own, or any other estate, and giving them liberty in my name, in giving them education in trade or otherwise, and having them instructed for their new conditions, in the duties of morality, which may make them good fathers, good mothers, husbands or wives, in their duties as citizens, teaching them to be defenders of their liberty and country, and whatsoever may make them happy and useful."[41]

And now, when we know not much, but anyway something about Polish political ideals, where have we to look in order to discover the "crimes" and "sins," the "errors" and "mistakes," of the Poles?[42]

[41] See L. Krzyżanowski, *Thaddeus Kościuszko and Abraham Lincoln*, "Nowy Świat," New York, February 14, 1943, p. 21.

[42] The French historian, H. Grappin, says: "Poland has been reproached with not having been able to 'assimilate.' But what does that word mean? Zygmunt assimilated Hussite Bohemia, and the Ivans assimilated Novgorod, and the Turks assimilated the Balkans, and Saint-Bartholomew the French Huguenots, and the bands of the Duc d'Albe the recalcitrants of the Low Countries. Poland, certainly, did not know how to do it. That terribly brave and arms-loving country was not a conquering country. She used her sword only to defend herself and protect others. She made herself mistress of immense Lithuania only by a marriage, and patiently, through the stormy vicissitudes of that union, she waited nearly two centuries for time to do its work and elaborate a common soul. No other nation can rise to accuse Poland. And it is for that, doubtless, that she has not lived. The rude way would have been more fruitful for her. Muscovy and Prussia taught her too late how one fabricates an empire, and how the blows of force astonish the world better than the deeds of justice." (H. Grappin, *op. cit.*, pp. 81-88.)

In fact, instead of "assimilating" the Teutonic Order after we had beaten it,

When I read the book by Mr. Walter Lippmann, *United States'
Foreign Policy,* I found the answer. Mr. Lippmann says: "In fact
we shall find that we have been the victims of a blinding prejudice
—that concern with our frontiers, our armaments, and with al-
liances, is immoral and reactionary." This is said about the
United States of America in the twentieth century; the same may
be said, exactly the same, about the vast, enormous Polish Empire
of the sixteenth century. But America was protected on both sides
by two mighty oceans; Poland was threatened from both sides
by two mighty nations: This is not mere geography.

---

we did not; instead of "assimilating" Prussia, as we frequently could have had
occasion to, we let it grow in strength and vigor. And with Moscow? When Batory's
armies had retaken Połock, cleared up Courland, and entered Muscovy, Ivan the
Terrible, seeing himself lost, had "the magnificent inspiration" to call the Pope to
his succor, promising to become "good apostle and lead his whole empire to the
Church of Rome." The Jesuit, Antony Possevino, intervened, sent by the Pope, and
won the cause. That was the "trickery" of the Peace of Kiwerowa Górka.

Poland kept Courland, which belonged to it, and the territory of Połock, which
had been stolen from it. "The operation was a sorry one," writes Grappin (*op. cit.*,
p. 100): "Poland, holding Muscovy under its thumb, released it naïvely on parole.
Having a precious occasion to get it over with, at least for a long time, she gave it
grace. Capital fault." (*Ibid.*) Always the same means, based on the spirit of peace
and compromise; always, also, pacifism, emanating from generosity and . . . lazi-
ness.

III

Religion and National Life

NATIONALISM, national ideas, emotions, and conceptions—in all times and in all environments, uncultured and cultured—has been fain to use two kinds of arguments: apologia and opprobrium, sublimation of national values and belittling of foreign values; thus came the definitive appearance of chauvinism and xenophobia. At the very base of this dualistic, "antinomic" attitude are ignorance, for uncultured environments, and bad faith, for cultured environments. Ignorance, like bad faith, justifies apologia just as well as it does belittling. It is thus, for instance, that even in the fifteenth century the Czechs advanced "theories" on the origin of the Germans which it would be difficult to cite here. In like manner, the *Word of the Merciful-hearted Christ* (*Slovo Khristolubza*), a monument to Church Slavic bears witness to the fashion in which "the lying books of the Saracens of Mahomet and Bakhmet the Holy" explain the inconvenient birth of Osiris and the reasons why "he was named God," which it is impossible for me to reproduce.

It is pointless also to insist on physical traits of foreigners, such as odor. Apparently it is difficult to hide an odor (perfumes being objects of luxury), but there are, on the other hand, some other physical traits which it is easier to hide, and, of course, moral traits. Thus, the Blacks of the Congo would have it that Europeans wear clothing in order to conceal their bodies, which are supposed by them to be covered with wounds. The inhabitants of Ruanda claim that the white man wears shoes to conceal his donkey-like hoofs.[1] Others maintain that foreigners hide tails under their clothing, that they bleed from the navel, that they have hoofs, and so on.

The popular Polish songs of Galicia represent the Russians as cannibals; likewise, in France in 1815 no child dared leave the house, because the Cossacks were universally known among the French people as eaters of babies.

On the other hand, we know that the inhabitants of Haiti considered their island to have been the beginning of Creation; we know that the Jews considered Jerusalem the center of the world. Like conceptions characterize the Japanese, Chinese, Greeks, English, and I need not mention the Mormons—and numerous other genealogical and historical conceptions of the same order, which we can find everywhere, among the Roman, Germanic, and Slavic nations.

It is pointless at the present hour to harp on the Germans, who have pushed all these theories to the extreme, meeting the Negroes on this felicitous path; the Germans, for instance, claim that Jesus Christ was the son of a German,[2] a Teutonic official in Palestine, and Marcus Garvey for his part teaches that Christ was of Negro origin.

Religion often aids the nation; and the nation aids religion. What is worse is that the Christian religion often permits itself to be exploited not only by patriotism and nationalism, but by

---

[1] J. Fraessle, *Die Negerpsyche*, 29, 33, cited by J. St. Bystroń, *Megalomanja Narodowa*, Warsaw, 1935, p. 65; J. Czekanowski, *Forschungen in Nil-Kongo Zwischengebiet*, I. 127. See also Bystroń, *op. cit.*

[2] See "Heimdall," 1911, pp. 64-65.

imperialism and, in our day, by statism and totalitarianism. I do not intend to avail myself of the examples of modern Germany and contemporary Russia; I prefer to cite their great adversary *avant la lettre*, Tolstoy—his pamphlet, *Christianity and Patriotism*, in which the illustrious Russian writer, speaking of the Franco-Russian Alliance, demonstrates how God could be either French or Russian, as the case might be. Need I recall the pamphlet which before this War made quite a stir in Europe—*Is God French?*

Yes, we well know that the good Lord knows all the languages in the world; that, still being polyglot, he has preferences and for the English speaks English, for the Germans—*unser Deutscher Gott*—speaks German, for the Russians, Russian. The Polish peasant has no doubt either that in Paradise the customary and privileged tongue is Polish.

If our peasant were educated and cultivated, if he had read the Church Fathers and Dante, or studied at Harvard at the time of President Dunster, he would have known that God speaks Hebrew. In any case, as to Poland, she began her conversations with God, and continues them, in Latin. This is a capital, very important fact, especially given Poland's geographical situation and Slavic origin. This fact determined her history, it assigned to Poland her historic mission, it bound it to the Catholic Universe, to Western Europe, detaching it in large part, in major part, from the Slavic family and from the East of Europe.

This fact came into being in 966 when the first historically known prince belonging to the royal Polish dynasty of the Piasts —of peasant origin, according to legend, Mieszko I, espoused Dąbrówka, daughter of Prince Boleslav of Bohemia, and at the same time embraced Christianity, as did his entire nation. I should like to accentuate here two very important circumstances: first, Mieszko received baptism from a western source; on the

other hand, he succeeded in escaping the Germans in this circumstance, and escaping their spirit of conquest—the Germans being
wont to conceal their encroaching appetities with religion and to
destroy Slavic tribes in the name of the Faith. Having embraced
Christianity, Mieszko defended himself against them by its very
means, and on the other hand, having done so through the medium
of Bohemia, he pushed still further the work of political and cultural emancipation; he disembarrassed himself of German wardship. We may note, too, that his daughter, Świętosława, was the
wife of King Sweyn of Denmark, conqueror of England, and
mother of the famous King Canute. For four centuries the dynasty
of the Piasts labored tirelessly at the work of developing Poland's
cultural and political relations with the West. The Jagiellons
continued this great task with, certainly, no less success.

It is not incumbent on me to insist here on the importance of
the Christianization of Poland. The creative forces of Christianity
were, one might say, limitless; they delivered man from the
clutches of destiny, of the Fate of pagan antiquity, and from the
imprisonment in which he was held by nature. The effects I
should like to present here, however, are not those of an universal, general, philosophical order. I have in mind something
else. In the tenth century, at the very moment of the conversion
of the Slavic peoples (some were converted before then), Europe
was, as we know, in a profoundly troubled state. The essential
thing for us at this moment, however, is to take into account one
capital fact, so well interpreted by Mr. Sturzo in his fine book,
Church and State: namely, that by the ninth century the West had
already realized a unitary conception as a development on two
fronts: one against Byzantium, although the open break of the
churches was to occur later, in 1054, and the other against the
Saracens. "It is thus that little by little, without the most representative men's being even conscious of it, arose what was later

to be named Christendom, no longer the Western Roman Empire, nor even what we call the Franco-Roman Empire become Roman-German Empire or, more simply, Holy Roman Empire, but the unitary and resolvent Christendom of the entire Christian West."[3]

I should like to stress one other fact, also a capital one, which, too, is directly related to what I have just brought out: the creative forces of history were transported at this moment from Byzantium to Rome, and it was Rome that became the center of spiritual organization of Europe's historic life. The creative, dynamic energies of history were there; they had left Byzantium forever, and although the latter, on the eve of succumbing, again mobilized all the spiritual resources to "cast one last glitter"[4] over the world, the hearth of civilization was finally formed and established at Rome. Therefore Poland did not have to repine at having had the great, the immense historical privilege of being allied to Rome, not to Byzantium. The breath of the Roman West has animated numerous activities in European society, and consecutively, little by little, in Poland too.

From the beginning we see that in Poland it was the Church which assumed responsibility for education and science; it was the laymen who governed the country. The struggle for the separation of the two powers—*that of the keys* and *that of the sword*—assured to the spiritual power an autonomy and authority which enabled it to play a very great part in the moral development of society. This western organizational *diarchy* affirmed the prestige of the Church and saved it from the subjugation that lay on the Eastern Church—in Russia, for example. This diarchy weakened the political power of the state in Poland, but it certainly developed the social and spiritual forces of the nation and its national conscience. The dynamic, active element of Western

[3] Luigi Sturzo, *L'Eglise et L'Etat*, Paris, 1937, p. 68.
[4] See Ch. Diehl, *Byzance*, Paris, 1919.

Christianity manifested itself equally in the organization of the
religious orders whose goal was to labor in the "earthly city" for
the "heavenly city." These Catholic monks, in Poland as elsewhere, were the apostles of spiritual energy—the best Christians
did not desert the world—they did not abandon the lay world to
itself, or even merely to the often inoperative protection of the
clergy—as in Russia, for example. In Russia the monasteries
were based and organized on a different principle: personal
salvation, tending toward asceticism; social didacticism came
only as satellite and not as immediate goal, as was the case in
the West.[5] In Poland, then, the best Christians did not abandon
the world; quite the contrary, they stayed in it and endeavored
to make it better.

We ought not, however, to exaggerate the spiritual role of the
first monks who came to Poland from outside. They were foreigners, and for that reason it was not easy for them to get into
intimate communication with the population. But their contribution in the material world was very great from the beginning;
they brought us the art of building in stone and brick, they developed our agriculture and horticulture. The monasteries, sub-
sidized by the lords, became more and more numerous. At the
end of the tenth century, under Bolesław the Great, there were
several of them (both for men and for women), in the eleventh
century Poland had a great number, and in the thirteenth it
teemed with them. Among them all the Benedictines were the most
active; Poland owes to them its most beautiful churches, its paintings, its stained glass, its belfries and its crypts. Next came the
Cistercians from Burgundy, from Germany, from Citeux, from
Clara Vallis, from Altenpforte, and, with their severe doctrine of
death and asceticism, with their propaganda of good deeds, they
began to model the Polish soul and also to cultivate Poland's

[5] See W. Lednicki, *Russia and Her Culture*, "New Europe," New York, 1941.

forests and fields. Then—the Carmelites, the Hospitaliers of St. Esprit de Saxia, and all the others who in the thirteenth century founded hospices; finally, the Dominicans, who had already established themselves in Poland by the thirteenth century, not in the woods and the fields like the Cistercians, and not to save the individual soul, but to save the people by the Word—in which they were seconded by the Franciscans. And note that the first Dominicans and Franciscans in Poland were Poles.

At this moment, also, was established the cult of the Polish Saints, Saint Wojciech, Saint Stanisław and others who replaced foreign saints. The Polish Church was emancipated more and more from foreign influences. Religious nationalism was, therefore, already established.[6]

With the church was constituted the organization of education in the country, the nuclei of which were for a long time the cathedral, parochial, and monastic schools which were divided in two sections—the *trivia*, where grammar, dialectics, and rhetoric were taught, and the *quadrivia*, with instruction in singing (music), arithmetic, geometry, and astronomy. The benefits of these medieval schools, everywhere accompanied by the switch which was the primary source of education, profited the burghers, peasants, and clergy. The Jagiellonian University, founded in 1364, became already in the fifteenth century a center of the humanistic movement in Poland. We see at that time Grzegorz of Sanok (d. 1477), who gave lectures on the *Bucolics* of Virgil and on other similar subjects. We see there also Grzymała developing activity of the same sort; and at the end of the fifteenth century a foreign scholar Conrad Celtes settled in Cracow, where he became an eloquent advocate of Humanism. At the same time Poland saw the appearance of a new type of school—a purely humanistic school (e.g., the Collegium Lubranscianum, 1519). By

[6] See A. Brückner, *op. cit.*, Vols. I and II.

the middle of the sixteenth century Poland already had *gymnasia* —high schools, some of five classes (years) and some of ten—as in Germany. The humanistic *collegium trilingue* was established. These new schools were under two kinds of leadership—Protestant and Jesuit. The schools of the first group were populated by the bourgeoisie—the schools of the second by the nobility. But in general—the humanistic school—contrasting with the medieval —becomes more and more aristocratic.

I should like to stress, finally, that in the sixteenth century two new universities were founded: in 1579 the Academy of Wilno and in 1594 the Academy of Zamość. All these schools became more and more devoted to the interests of laymen and to public affairs.

But in the Middle Ages the Church had taken into its hands the intellectual and moral education of the country. It is particularly in this latter field that its role was very great; in a very energetic fashion, it molded morals, customs, the life of the family; it set marriages and conjugal customs to rights, little by little destroying and liquidating the moral and social disorder that subsisted as heritage of the pagan era.

With this is bound the role played by another factor, that of Latin. It is true that the establishment of linguistic dualism arrested—in Poland as everywhere in Europe—the development of literature of national expression; but, on the other hand, Latin became a conduit leading Poland to the universe, bringing European science to Poland, so that Poland became a member of the European community.

Poland was Latinized very swiftly and very profoundly. Schoolmasters imposed on their pupils notions borrowed from Italy and France. Thus, by about 1200 we already have the famous chronicler, Wincenty Kadłubek, author of the first Polish

Chronicle.[7] Kadłubek wrote an *histoire romancée,* so to speak, and his documentation was dubious, his Latin of an elegance adapted to the tastes of his time; but it is precisely his style that can bear witness to the cultural level already attained in the twelfth century by the Polish elite.

"The bravest of kings," he says, "being desirous of bequeathing to posterity the merits of our ancestors, has cast upon me, who write with a pen puny as any reed, he has laid on my dwarfish shoulders this enormous weight, guided probably by the conviction that the glitter of gold and the splendor of precious stones do not pale in the inexpert hands of the artisan—as stars be in no wise dimmed even when they are pointed out by the terribly black fingers of the Ethiops."[8]

Polish civilization had a very dignified and very sure rhythm of development, but it was interrupted by the terrible catastrophe of the invasions of the Tartars; these invasions, though they were stopped, penetrated into the very center of Poland, even to Cracow, which was put to the torch, and Lignica, which was the site of our first great historic battle, waged in 1241 for the defense not only of Poland but of the entire West. It was after the disasters of these invasions that Poland commenced the work of her restoration, assisted by German colonists; it was then that the *ius teutonicum* was introduced into Poland as a basis for civil organization; it was then that Polish life in general took a great leap upward: we see cities begin to grow, architecture develop, commerce and industry enriched, and Poland establishing more and more frequent and intimate contacts with the outside world —Italy, Germany, the Low Countries, and especially France.

[7] Stanisław Kot, *Five Centuries of Polish Learning,* Oxford, Basil Blackwell, p. 2. "He seems," says Professor Kot, "to have known Gervaise of Tilbury and to have given the Englishman information about Poland for his work *Otia Imperialia.*"

[8] See I. Chrzanowski, *op. cit.,* pp. 3-7.

The last king of the dynasty of the Piasts, Casimir the Great, a sovereign of immense merits in regard to his country, founded the University of Cracow, as I have mentioned, in 1364—that is, sixteen years after Prague. By this time there was no essential difference between Poland and the rest of Europe; in the principles of the organization of its public life—the Royal Court, the nobility, the cities, the clergy, the monasteries, justice, education.

The University of Cracow, one of the oldest in Europe, takes up its truly great tasks a little later, however, after its reorganization in 1400 under the auspices of Władysław Jagiełło, Grand Duke of Lithuania. In this he followed the tradition of the attachment to this university, cherished by his wife, Queen Jadwiga, whom he had espoused in 1386, accomplishing then and there the union of Poland and Lithuania. This union was accompanied by a great event: the baptism of Lithuania, which until that moment (1386) had kept her pagan faith, defending herself against the oppression of the Teutonic Knights. The union had been the fruit of political conceptions of the Polish lords; it was, therefore, the fruit of Polish wisdom. A little later, in 1400, the University of Cracow, from that time forth called the Jagiellonian University, began a new existence. King Władysław was himself a barbarian and an illiterate—but he had a cultivated Polish entourage, and we have preserved some royal documents of that era which illustrate the cultural level reached by the country at this moment.

This is what the neophyte and illiterate barbarian, Jagiełło, said at the new erection of the University of Cracow: "We will direct our attention principally to this, that the inhabitants and subjects of our Lithuanian territories, above all those who live in superannuated error and lead our companions in the shadows, shall be converted to the light, that they may become the children of the light with the aid and collaboration of those whose mind is adorned with wisdom and science; that is, with the aid of people expert in the principles and secrets of writing, whose counsels fortify the royal throne and whose virtuous acts enhance the health and strength of the Republic . . . We see that Paris, having convoked and assembled learned and expert scholars, adds an aureole to France and imposes respect, just like Bologna and Padua, which reinforce and embellish Italy, Prague which brightens Bohemia, and Oxford which fertilizes and instructs all Germany *(sic!)*. Thanks to divine Grace, we have come to govern over numerous lands, and we have received the Crown of the Kingdom of Poland, in order to make the illumination of scholars radiate through the realm and with the help of science, to remove shadows and faults, and to make our Realm the equal of the others."[9]

In 1418 Jagiełło wrote to Pope Martin V apropos of the University:

"I love it like a daughter and I am faithful to it as to a mother; its sufferings are my sufferings and I resent its adversities like my own misfortunes, and even more; I regard every lack of respect toward it as a crime of *lèse-majesté.*"[10]

The dynasty kept lavishing favors on the University—especially the women, who all became protectresses of the Academy of Cracow: Hedwig, Elizabeth, Barbara; Sońka, *benefactrix singularissima;* Ann—sister of Zygmunt-August, wife of Stefan Batory, was its *benefactrix liberalissima et clementissima.* Its role in the country was very great; it is enough to say that during the fifteenth century the University had 18,338 students.

On the other hand, its work as a center of science soon became very important. This was accomplished under the inspiration of Italy, Paris, and Prague, and the number of early books of that time preserved by Poland is eloquent though indirect proof of

[9] Polska Akademja Umiejętności, *Kultura Staropolska*, Kraków, 1932, p. 269.
[10] *Ibid.*

it; fifteen thousand incunabula, showing that the Poles did not spend their time doing nothing. What interested them in particular was the doctrine of Nominalism. Another proof of this academic activity is furnished by the ten immense volumes of the History of Poland by Jan Długosz (fifteenth century), written in Latin and representing the best source for knowledge of medieval Poland.

Medicine as a study was not brilliant, but theology, astronomy, and, above all, mathematics (the latter two were unique in central Europe), created the glory of the University: this activity in the fifteenth century and the beginning of the sixteenth prepared the way for Copernicus—enough said.

The Academy became known outside of Poland; already in the years 1501-1510, 1,714 of 3,215 students were foreigners.[11]

Literary life was also better and better organized—but, until the last part of the sixteenth century, or, to be exact, until the year 1543, belles-lettres were the prisoners of Latin.

It is necessary to stress that there was no other country at that time in Europe—with the exception of Hungary—which was so deeply, so completely Latinized as Poland was. Latin, once established, fascinated the Poles. As Nevill Forbes (University of Oxford) justly says: "If they wished to create anything which they hoped would have permanent value, anything, in fact, except that which they considered ephemeral and trivial—personal satires, facetious tales, epigrams and novelettes—they wrote in Latin, while works of grave import such as histories, political and philosophical disquisitions, even memoirs, they continued to compose in that language . . ."[12] And all this in spite of the fact that Poles possessed already in the Middle Ages "extraordinary

[11] See Kot, *op. cit.* (*Five centuries*, etc.), p. 5.
[12] *Polish Literature*, a lecture by Nevill Forbes, M.A., Ph.D., Oxford University Press, p. 9.

national vitality, which was symbolized then," says Forbes, "as it is today, in the language . . . this admirable medium of expression . . ."[13]

Everything was in Latin at that time—all instructions, acts, accounts, diplomatic correspondence of the King's Chancellery were written in Latin. In the Church, Latin was supreme. The judge, the prosecutor, used Latin. The schools also were under Latin rule. The poets wrote in Latin. Even private letters, letters addressed to women, were written in Latin; Latin was a proof of culture, civilization, good education, and good manners.

The Poles knew other languages too. The result was that a really great level of culture had been reached; so that the French historian, de Thou, who met some Polish nobles when they came to Paris in 1573 to offer the Polish crown to Henri de Valois, expressed his amazement: "Ce qu'on remarqua le plus, ce fut leur facilité de s'énoncer en latin, en français, en allemand et en italien; ces quatre langues leur étaient aussi familières que la langue de leur pays . . . Les Polonais parlaient notre langue avec tant de pureté qu'on les eût plutot pris pour des hommes élevés sur les bords de la Seine et de la Loire que pour des habitants des contrées qu'arrosent la Vistule et le Dnieper, ce qui fit grande honte à nos courtisans qui ne savaient rien."[14]

This is splendid testimony; and surely, the knowledge of Latin, spread throughout the whole Polish-Ruthenian-Lithuanian Commonwealth, as well as the knowledge of European languages, acquired through many trips and voyages of Poles to Italy,

---

[13] *Ibid.*

[14] H. Grappin, *Histoire de la Pologne*, Ed. Larousse, Paris, 1922, p. 92.

("What was most noticeable was their facility of expression in Latin, French, German and Italian; these four languages were as familiar to them as the language of their own country . . . The Poles spoke our language with such purity that they would have been considered men brought up on the shores of the Seine and of the Loire, rather than as inhabitants of countries irrigated by the Vistula and the Dnieper, which ashamed our courtiers, who did not know anything.")

Germany, France, England, and the Low Countries, enriched our civilization immensely and engraved universalistic ideals in Polish minds.

But for literature it was not very advantageous. In this respect Polish literature was handicapped. No doubt, we did have traditional folk-epics, folk-tales, ceremonial songs, which in other countries "form an inexhaustible mine of material for ethnographers and philologists." No doubt, we had all those "productions of popular imagination, anonymous creations handed on from generation to generation, elaborated and embellished by each in turn"—but perhaps "because they were not cherished . . . they fell an easier prey to the jealous and prudish censoriousness of the (church) hierarchy"—they vanished and disappeared.[15] "In the national language, not as in Latin—there had been no continuity of development, no tradition," as Brückner says, speaking about Polish national literature. "The Polish literature of the first half of the fifteenth century is an accidental collection of all sorts of translations; it did not at that time have any national character . . ."[16]

It is an amazing fact, but at the time when the French, the Italians, the Germans, and even the Czechs were already printing books in their national languages, in Poland there were Latin books only. Even as late as 1577 the great Polish historian Kromer wrote (he wrote in Latin, of course) that "everybody writes officially as well as privately in Latin, because our language is neither as rich, nor as easy to read and write, as other languages." In 1540 Decius says, "All Poles know Latin, but they do not write anything in their national language."[17]

In the sixteenth century, however, the situation was already a little different: in 1535 Marcin Bielski, a historian, translated

---

[15] See Forbes, *op. cit.*, p. 10.
[16] See *Dzieje Kultury Polskiej*, Vol. II.
[17] See Brückner, *op. cit.*

the *Lives of Philosophers* from Czech into Polish. In 1514 Ungler printed the first book in Polish, *The Garden of Souls;* the translator was Biernat of Lublin, who gave Poland his excellent *Aesop* and who may be considered the pioneer of the *Polish book.*

But the first writer who gave his country an *original* Polish book, written in Polish, was Rey, and this book appeared in 1543. *(Brief Talk between Three Persons: a lord, a Bailiff, and a Curate.)* It is a modest work, but enormously important for the history of Polish civilization. It is the first and even the only Polish satire which does not moralize in a dull, obtuse, heavy way. The author speaks sincerely, sharply, he gives a vivid and bright picture of Polish life, of its vices, errors, and sins. All these traits will appear later in his masterpiece—the *Mirror of the Honest Man.*

All this is expressed in excellent, picturesque, racy Polish—unspoiled, not obscured by Latin, as Rey did not know Latin and did not consider Latin the only decent language for the conveyance of serious information. He was a Pole born in the very depth of Polish Ruthenia, a Pole during his whole life deeply attached to Cracow and to the province of Cracow. He was a noble and an autodidact, who found himself among abecedarians, doctors, priests, and clerics; he knew the popular songs, proverbs, Polish and Ruthenian; he was a good storyteller, ignorant but realistic and full of human curiosity for anything human and true. He began to write dialogues in which he depicted life as he saw it; from those dialogues arose his *Brief Talk* of 1543, which opened a new era in Polish literature.

Some ten or twenty years later, immediately after his work of 1543 appeared some very beautiful Polish texts in poetry and prose, which put Polish national literature on a level equal to the best European writing of that time. It is enough to mention here Kochanowski, Sęp-Szarzyński, Orzechowski, and Skarga, men who created a marvelous, rich, polished, elegant, penetrating language. When we read it now, we can scarcely believe that this language is almost four hundred years old.

Rey was a Protestant, and this is one of the most important elements in the case. Because the Reformation—in spite of a very strange assertion made by one of our famous historians, Professor Kutrzeba, who once advanced the opinion that the Reformation brought nothing to Polish civilization—played an enormous role in the development of Polish thought, in the development of Polish social consciousness and finally in the field of the evolution of the Polish language. Those who fought against Rome and the Church in Poland wrote Polish in order to be understood by the democratic masses of the nation. "The Reformation," says Brückner, "was a spring thunderstorm breaking the ice of the winter." From it flowed the torrents of the Polish word and the Polish language; in some ten years, from 1550 to 1560, everything was changed: in literature Latin had been finally overcome by Polish forever.

In the same year of 1543 two great Polish writers, Andrzej Frycz-Modrzewski and Stanisław Orzechowski, began to write. The first wrote in Latin, the second in Latin and Polish; the first was a Reformer, defending Protestants, representing universalist ideals and true Christianity in his writings as well as in his deeds and life; the second, a nationalist and an orthodox Catholic, intolerant and intractable, author of a theocratic system, defending the predominance of the Church and of the Pope, but at the same time cynical and brutal, unfaithful, disloyal . . . living a life full of disorder, of scandals; but writing wonderful Polish, among the best in our history.

The first was one of the most idealistic, generous, wise and democratic of Polish brains and hearts—one of the greatest Polish patriots; and as often happens, just because of these fea-

tures, he was severely attacked by his contemporaries, the nobles
of his time, who blindly and jealously defended their privileges
and abuses.

The second—flattering the human mob, his country, of which
he is a panegyrist; full of cunning demagogy, a most repulsive,
anarchic personality, but highly endowed with a brilliant literary
talent, with a fantastic power of eloquence and expressiveness—
Orzechowski represents the classic type of Polish brilliance and
at the same time the degree to which arrogance and insolence,
intolerance and cynicism may reach.

Here we come to a problem over which I should like to linger
a bit. It is precisely that of the Polish language. Formed and
developed as a branch of the Slavic tree, it preserved several
purely Slavic phenomena in the field of phonetics and morphol-
ogy. It underwent a period of great influence and penetration by
another Slavic language, Czech. Through the secular co-existence
of Poles and Ukrainians, it absorbed some few Ukrainianisms
into its vocabulary. And it assimilated also some Turkish, Hungarian, and Rumanian elements. But besides these few Slavic
and Oriental infiltrations, the Polish language took over an
enormous quantity of German, Italian, and especially Latin
words, terms, expressions. The Latin element particularly became
a very important factor in the development of the Polish language: Latin suffixes, Latin constructions, Latin proverbs and
classical locutions immigrated into Polish and became there
powerful and important citizens. Latin, for Polish, played a role
not far inferior in importance to its role as a source of learned
words, for instance in the development of English, as well as of
the Romance languages. It gave that Slavic language a distinctly
Western European aspect; this language was elaborated by the
nobility in the sixteenth century, that is, by the cultivated class
of Poland, which at that time had intimate cultural and social

relations with Bohemia, France, Italy, the Low Countries, England, and Germany, and the majority of writers and poets belonged to that class of society. As a result, Polish is, of all Slavic languages, a product of an aristocratic intellectual élite, the most polished and elegant, and was early adapted to aesthetic purposes and uses. At the same time, it is one of the most difficult and capricious languages among the Slavic family.[18]

These great and rapid cultural conquests were the results of the currents of the Renaissance and the Reformation, as I have just now said. If the Reformation woke the moral and religious conscience as well as the individual and national conscience, the Renaissance brought the love of antiquity, the cult of erudition, the love of the arts and poetry, the cult of the human personality. At a very early date the Poles had begun their tours of study in Italy, France, and the Low Countries, even in England and in Germany, travels which knitted them in personal, intimate contact with the great centers of European civilization at that time. The study of the humanities, the study of Latin, of the poets of antiquity, polished their minds and their thought, their tastes, their intellectual habits; so that, when suddenly, under the influence of the Reformation and on the example of Rey, they began to write Polish, they did a really marvelous piece of work. They also conducted propaganda in behalf of the Polish language. So says Górnicki in attacking the Polish petits maîtres of the time: "Every Pole, if he take but one small step abroad already wishes to speak no other language but that of the country where he has lived for a little; if it is Italy, he will say to you at every word, *signor;* if it is France, it will be *par ma foi;* if it is Spain, *nos otros cavaglieros;* and sometimes another such, who need never have been in Bohemia and for whom it will be enough merely to have crossed the Silesian border, will wish to speak

[18] See A. Brückner, *Dzieje języka Polskiego,* "Nauka i Sztuka," Lwów.

nothing but Czech—and God knows what sort of Czech it will be! And if you tell him to speak his own tongue, he will say to you that he has forgotten it, or that this maternal tongue seems gross to him, to demonstrate the which, he will drag out one word of old Polish, which he will find in the *Bogurodzica* and he will compare it with some polite Czech word in order to cry up the beauty of a foreign tongue and the grossness of his own . . ."[19]

It is quite true; this rapid development of national Polish literature was a surprising phenomenon. Let us take one writer, Kochanowski, whom Professor Noyes has so gracefully translated; he studied at Padua and at Paris, he read the poets of antiquity but also Petrarch, Ariosto, and perhaps Dante; he read Ronsard and Joachim du Bellay; indeed, it was at Paris that he wrote in Polish his famous *Hymn to God*, which became a first swallow, flying from Paris to Poland to herald the summer of *Polish poetry*.

Kochanowski, it has been well said, is a born poet. Not very profound, without any especially rich imagination, he was a faithful disciple of the Greek and Latin poets, whom he knew wondrously well, and his sincere, pure, elevated, and very human poetry touched on all the disappointments and all the joys of the human heart. He wrote comic poetry, illustrating the life of the Polish court and at the same time representing a sort of intimate journal of the poet; he wrote satires; he touched on political events and religion—just like Ronsard; he wrote a beautiful tragedy; he had polemics with Desportes—in Latin—he sang his own unhappiness, the death of his adored daughter Orszulka. The laments are a poetic document of the grief of the human heart, poignantly eloquent, thanks above all to their simplicity. France always repeats the verse of Lamartine,

[19] See I. Chrzanowski, *op. cit.*, pp. 145-146. *Bogurodzica*—Polish religious song— hymn of the thirteenth century.

"Un seul être vous manque et tout est dépeuplé," and ever
unforgettable for France is the touching avowal, like a pure tear,
made by Marguerite de Navarre,

"Un tout seul à qui seul j' étais une me fut ôté"; and Kochanowski moves our hearts with the same strength, though his pain
is not the pain of the lover:

> You left a great void in my house,
> Cherished Ursula, with your vanishing;
> We are many, and yet it is as if there were no one;
> One lone small soul bereaved us of so much!

He is distinguished by perfect taste; a high idea of, and
esteem for, poetry; very great elegance of expression; vast humanist culture; and a varied richness of language.

And note well that he was not the only one at that moment!
Take the ravishing Sęp-Szarzyński, a sort of Polish Leopardi of
the sixteenth century, master of the sonnet, which he filled with
his fierce pessimism and profound eroticism, presaging the
"philosophies" of the *Crimean Sonnets* of Mickiewicz, the great
glory of Polish poetry in the nineteenth century! He too is a
pupil of foreign universities and disciple of Petrarch. Take the
bourgeois Klonowicz, writing, like Kochanowski, in Latin and
in Polish, his attention directed above all to the lot of the peasant,
bewailing it and teaching that the true privilege of noble origin
is first of all to serve virtue. In this he is equal to Frycz, to Rey—
who also had not forgotten the peasant. This "philanthropic"
tradition, this humanitarian attitude, will be taken up again
later by our last great humanist and poet of this era, the bourgeois
Szymonowicz, who belongs to the seventeenth century but represents the same literary school.

To these names let us add that of Sarbiewski, author of Latin
odes which were at that time known abroad as in Poland; our
historiographers of that epoch, Kromer and Bielski; the great

preacher Skarga, whom I have cited already on several occasions; and then we shall have a certain idea of the richness of the flowering of belles-lettres in Poland in the sixteenth century and in the seventeenth—for this development was by no means arrested in the sixteenth century.

Kadłubek already knew Aristotle's *Poetics*. On the other hand, utilitarian Roman didacticism was broadly spread through our letters. Nevertheless, our poets of the sixteenth century had not forgotten to establish a very high conception of pure poetry and of the poet "bard of the Gods." "I sing to the Muses as well as to myself," said Kochanowski in his celebrated sonnet, opposing to the common riches of life the high price of poetic song—although the latter competes only with "the song of grasshoppers" . . .

However, the striking thing—with just such poets as Kochanowski and Szarzyński—is the precision, the manly sobriety, the powerful modesty of their expression, which seeks no exterior effects but, merely with the help of a sometimes intentionally difficult syntax (Sęp-Szarzyński), compels thought and seizes you by a sudden rapture at the moment when you have perceived the goal of the poetic effort.

I have also mentioned several times the effect of the Reformation, and the fact that Poland had become a refuge, an asylum for every species of dissidents who propagated the Reformation. You have seen what these currents did for Polish letters. But Poland at this time was not merely a country of asylum, passively observing religious discord; she took an active part in that movement, and that movement spread among us with great rapidity. The conditions in which the movement was developed in Poland were peculiar, and it is those conditions that determined the distinct character taken on by this movement among us.

As our greatest historian of Polish letters and civilization, Professor Brückner, attests, it is certain that the first factor was

foreign influence. I have already said that the Polish nobility had
become accustomed during the fifteenth and sixteenth centuries to
travel abroad to study. Without exaggerating the facts, we may
say that Italy, the Low Countries, France, and Germany were
swarming with Poles. Poland had never been separate from the
outside world; quite the contrary, she abated no efforts to become
better and better acquainted with Europe. On the other hand, we
had among us a large number of Italians, especially in the era of
Zygmunt I, whose wife was Italian—Bona Sforza. The Italian
influence betrayed itself everywhere: in letters, in the language,
in architecture, in clothes, in customs, in cookery . . . I have
already mentioned that our cities were peopled by Germans; let
us add to that the Dutch; Jews, coming from every country of
Europe; Armenians; Greek émigrés after the fall of Constantinople; Tartars; Czechs; and then we shall have the exact image
of the life of this state, swarming with representatives of every
European country. Victims of religious persecution found in
Poland a country guiltless of the slightest leaning toward
xenophobia . . .

By the time the currents of the Reformation reached Poland,
the soil was already prepared for them as a result of local conditions. To be cited first of all is the antagonism that separated the
nobility and the clergy. This antagonism was not based simply on
causes of an economic order. The nobility was struggling against
the privileged situation of the clergy in regard to taxes, it is true,
and against the export of Polish money to Rome. But aside from
these economic causes there were others of a more serious nature.
The Catholic clergy had at this era attained in Poland a high
degree of secularization, and an evident moral decadence. The
life of the priests, their morals, life in the monasteries, above
all in the female monasteries, left much to be desired. The higher

clergy was corrupt and sybaritic; enjoying great revenues, it was addicted either to political life or to the pleasures of voluptuousness. The lower clergy was ignorant and ill-behaved. Therefore the situation in Poland was not very much different from the rest of Europe.

Secularization embraced not only the clergy but everybody— and that, under the influence of the doctrines of the Renaissance, under the influence of rationalism and the cult of pagan antiquity. The first adepts of the Reformation were recruited among the German Poles—in Prussia, in Poznań, in Cracow. Trade with Frankfort, Nuremberg, and Breslau had opened the way for this propaganda. In the Polish provinces of Prussia and Poznań Lutheranism spread and has been preserved to our own day. Little Poland (Galicia) adopted Calvinism, as did Lithuania, after 1550. After 1558 appeared Italian sects, rationalists and Arians, Socinians, coming from Switzerland and Bohemia with their social doctrines, etc. This great mass of doctrines, contemplating not only the reform of the life of the Catholic clergy but submitting to criticism the very essence of dogmas, often suggesting subversive concepts in the domain of political and social life, attacking the established order and the state—this mass of opinions, of currents fighting one another, weakened the Reformation. Its partisans were too differentiated and too divided among themselves. An effort of unification was undertaken: the "Peace of Sandomierz," 1570—an accord between Lutheran, Calvinist, and "Czech" pastors and ministers—created a sort of common strategy for the defense of the principles of the Reformation.[20]

The Reformers ended by attaining a great result—a guarantee of tolerance, accorded them by the King and the Diet. These laws are the glory of Poland, which succeeded in assigning complete

[20] See A. Brückner, *op. cit.*, Vol. II.

equality of laws and privileges to all the sects represented in Poland, and complete liberty of conscience.[21]

However, the triumphs of the Reformation, clamorous, noisy, giving the impression of great scope—especially as numerous families of magnates protected these movements and adhered to the Reformation in the beginnings—were rather superficial and transitory as a purely religious, ecclesiastical movement. The Protestants did not succeed in enlisting in their ranks the high Catholic clergy; they continued to be divided; they had no eminent leader; their dogmatic discord compromised them. Finally, there were desertions. On the death of those lords who had adhered to the Reformation, such illustrious families as the Radziwiłłs, the Łaskis, the Myszkowskis, the Boners, returned to the bosom of the Church. The result was that when Jesuit propaganda began to be developed, when the court of the king—of Batory and above all under Zygmunt III Vasa, a fanatical Catholic— became more and more set in its militant Catholicism, the Reformation found itself confined to a small part of the nobility: only a sixth part of the nobility had embraced the new faith. As for the people, it did not budge. The new faith, then, was from

[21] "In 1573, after the death of Sigismund Augustus, the so-called Confederation of Warsaw (*Pax inter dissidentes de religione*) reaffirmed in a solemn pledge the principle of equality of rights without any regard to religious confession. By this document the Polish Protestants of all shades were granted religious freedom. It is a proof of unusual tolerance, unknown then in Western Europe, that this Confederation was voted unanimously, the bench of bishops alone abstaining from voting. Of the ninety-eight deputies to the Diet who signed the Act of Confederation, forty-one belonged to the Catholic party. The Senate gave an even more eloquent expression of tolerance, because, of the twenty-eight Senators who signed this historical act, only three were Protestants.

In the same year, at the election of the new king, Henri de Valois of France, who in his own country was reputed to be an active opponent of the Huguenots, the Protestants succeeded in forcing him to take an oath that he would abjure any attempt which might lead to the persecution of the dissidents. This, however, was the last offensive of Polish Protestantism, which at this time was slowly but surely declining." (*The Protestant Church in Poland*, "Polish Studies and Sketches," No. 4, London, 1943, p. 15.)

its inception a faith of the "lords"—of the nobles, of the "intelligentsia."

Protestantism was broadly spread in Poland, in Lithuania, in Ruthenia; it touched the great Polish houses, but its action was not deep. The situation is presented in the same aspect in the cities—Poznań, Cracow, Wilno; the masses did not rally to the Reformation. The clients of the new religion, then, were the *szlachta* and the patriciate, and their communions in Poland and Lithuania never exceeded 600 in number. "During the seventeenth and eighteenth centuries Protestantism declined in Poland and the majority of Poles returned to Catholicism."[22]

But, as Brückner says so justly, the Reformation rendered immense cultural services to Poland. It assured the Republic a great glory abroad; the Low Countries, France, England, Italy, Spain, Germany, were ravaged by religious wars—and only Poland remained at peace herself and assured peace to all the dissidents of the world, to her own and to aliens.[23]

It was then that illustrious statesmen and European scholars rendered Poland eloquent homage, sending letters of admiration to Poland's sovereigns and great lords. It was then that Europe became acquainted with two great Polish adversaries: Łaski, a great lord, a humanist, a statesman, famous in England and the Low Countries, a protector of Protestants; and his opponent, Hoziusz, the champion of Catholicism. It was then that, especially under the influence of Hoziusz and the Jesuits, Polish Catholicism awoke, took cognizance of itself and its duties, and reformed itself.

[22] See *The Protestant Church in Poland*, "Polish Studies and Sketches," No. 4, London, 1943, p. 21. "In 1937 the Protestants of all denominations in the entire area of Poland numbered some 830,000." (*Ibid.*, p. 34.)
See also A. Brückner *Różnowiercy Polscy*, Warszawa, 1905.
[23] *Op. cit.*, Vol. II.

Polish polemics penetrated abroad; they were translated; Poland became known abroad. In Poland itself, the Reformation re-awakened conscience, it animated letters, it rendered immense services to the language, it provoked rich religious literature, it deepened religious interest, thought, sentiments. It rendered just as great services to Catholicism; it imposed on it a more noble, more dignified, and more exalted style of thought. It ennobled and deepened the spiritual life of the country; it changed and bettered the morals of the Catholic clergy.

But the Reformation had, as well, its bad effects: it inaugurated an inauspicious method which later became habitual, a method which consisted of making common cause with foreigners and producing foreign intervention—a method which in the eighteenth century brought Poland to her ruin.

This method was inaugurated on the occasion of a very serious event that took place in the same era. That was the affair of the Orthodox Church. The Eastern Church had many adepts in our Ruthenian territories, but since the fourteenth century it had fallen into complete decay. In 1589 Moscow had established a patriarchate dependent on the Czar. This was a threat to the independence of our Ruthenian Church. At the same moment conflicts loomed between the Metropolitan of Kiev and the Patriarch of Constantinople. A movement of renovation, guided by Possevino and our great Skarga, took place. Finally the Metropolitan of Kiev, Rohoża, convoked a Synod at Brześć, where the union of Florence with Rome was renewed. The Act of Union was concluded in Rome in 1596. The dissidents revolted against this act, which reinforced the Catholic Church, and waged propaganda against it in Ruthenian circles, provoking movements against the union. Once on this road, they were enlisted on the side of the Muscovite Church, and shortly the Czars began their activity, looking toward the expansion of their influence over our Ruthenian countries.[24]

On the other hand, it must be remembered that the Eastern orthodox church which existed in Lithuania and Ruthenia used to be autonomous. After the union of Florence the orthodox church in Poland received from King Władysław Warneńczyk in 1443 a privilege which assured it rights equal to those of the Catholic Church.

Armenians also belonged to the Eastern Orthodox Church. In 1439 the Armenian or Gregorian Church joined the Roman Church. But this union was not a durable one either—it was renewed in the seventeenth century. Since 1666 Lwów has been the residence of three metropolitans—Latin, Greek, and Armenian.

All these conquests of the *szlachta* in the political and social field, in the field of the sciences and the arts, of belles-lettres, and, finally, in the religious field created a new national ,atmosphere in the Poland of that day. Poland then no longer considered herself a younger sister, an illegitimate child in the great family of the European peoples. Quite the contrary, she felt strongly that in many respects she was at the very least equal to them.

In the fourteenth and fifteenth centuries, when Poland was just about to forge that life and civilization which became so brilliant and elegant, she had again to suffer from a complex of inferiority. The national sentiment was freely manifested with the help of, so to speak, outward gestures. The Pole of the fifteenth century had to defend himself against degrading opinions with regard to Poland, spread abroad above all by the Germans, who persecuted us with propaganda filled with such epithets as *durus Sarmata, crudus Sarmata, cruda ingenia, Sarmaticae linguae barbara verba.* People had always insisted that the Polish nation was *bibacissimum genus hominum,* that our material civilization was

---

[24] See Grappin, *op. cit.,* pp. 102-103; M. Bobrzyński, *op. cit.,* Vol. II.

poor, that our dwellings were not to be compared with those of Western Europe.[25]

It was then that one Ostroróg, in his speech to Pope Paul II in 1467 in Rome, lauds his sovereign and his Republic, displaying all the splendors of his erudition to defend the thesis that the only defeats Julius Caesar had ever known were those he suffered on Polish territory! The women of the Polish royal family wear Polish dresses, different coiffures; the men follow the same customs; and the son of Jan Ostroróg, Stanisław, arriving at Rome in 1513, *totus aureus gemmatusque more barbarico fuit*—to dumbfound, to sparkle, to manifest the power, the richness, the civilization, of his country.[26]

It is true that the taste for ostentation, luxury, rich garments, parade, and that infatuation and vanity which Warszewicki and so many others tried to destroy, have forever remained with the Poles. They are innate traits, but they were developed under oriental influences, the contacts of the Poles with Moscow and the Turks. The Polish historians of the fifteenth and sixteenth centuries, as well as foreign observers, speak about it unceasingly. However, at this era Poland's material and domestic life had greatly changed, and under foreign influence too.

We know that the dwellings of nobles as well as bourgeois were more richly furnished, with utensils of silver and gold, that pictures began to appear on the walls; candelabra, clocks, wainscoting, frescoes, rich Turkish, Persian, and Polish carpets, Polish Gobelins, arras from Flanders, our famous Polish tapestry and the cummerbunds of Słuck embellished that life. Manners became more and more studied, drinking became more and more restrained, the tournaments became more and more a game of skill and equitation, language more and more elegant and select. So

---

[25] See Kot, *Polska Złotego wieku wobec Kultury Zachodniej (Kultura Staropolska)* pp. 645-646.

[26] *Ibid.*, p. 644.

that Decius could remark in 1512: "Having then and there abandoned their long tight-fitting clothes and their long curled hair, they began to manifest temperance in their drinking and feasting. Upon the example of the king, drunkenness was condemned; sobriety began to be enormously appreciated; and thus an immense change has been swiftly produced in the manner of existence and morals of the Sarmatians. From this beginning, other virtues were strengthened and developed, and that is why many nations are taken with respect for the conduct of the Poles."

In fact, the Poles began to earn that respect: "The humanist of Ferrara, belonging to the retinue of Hippolite d'Este, Celio Calcagnini, made an enthusiastic visit to Cracow and its vicinity," Professor Kot tells us; he admired the buildings, the aqueducts, the libraries, fish-cultures; he admired Polish Latin poetry.[27]

The Swiss historian Joachim Vadianus writes, after his visit to Poland (I continue to quote Kot), "that this nation, though it be of Scythian origin, is glorious and very different by its culture from the simple ancient Sarmatians."[28]

The great Erasmus writes to Decius in 1523, "I congratulate this nation which used to have a bad reputation for its barbarity and which now, in sciences, jurisprudence, morals, and religion, and in all that separates us from barbarism, is so flourishing that it can rival the first and most glorious of nations."[29]

At that moment—while Górnicki was writing his *Cortegiano*, making propaganda for trips abroad, while Orzechowski was doing the same job—this propaganda was, to tell the truth, useless. The Poles were already somewhat saturated by the outer world; their life had become so polished that one de Thou, as we have seen, was full of admiration for their education and their

[27] *Op. cit.*, p. 682.
[28] *Ibid.*
[29] *Ibid.*

way of life. Note that, on the other hand, it was not only the
nobility that profited by these benefits of European civilization;
in the cities, the bourgeoisie, under the influence of German
émigrés, who were quickly Polonized, adopted many German
habits, customs, and morals. This is a very important point. All
these factors—Catholicism; Humanism; the Reformation; trips
to Italy, France, and other countries; the presence of foreigners
in Poland; literary activity; the University of Cracow; the acad-
emies of Wilno and Zamość; the translations from foreign books
—all these detached Poland from the east of Europe, from the
Slavs belonging to the eastern group.

It all bound Poland to the west and made her a European
nation in the strict sense of the word.

The plastic arts[30] and music bear the same testimony. If in the
beginning Poland had, in the eleventh and twelfth centuries,
reared Roman-Byzantine churches, great Polish architecture later
expressed itself above all in the Gothic style, then the Renaissance,
and finally the Italian and Austrian baroque.

The Polish Gothic style, represented by the magnificent
churches of Cracow and Toruń—not to mention others—offers a
specimen of Western architecture, although the Poles, due to the
material in which they built, introduced characteristics unknown
elsewhere. Polish churches are more sober, more majestic, more
simple on the outside, than French or English churches, which
display to the eye the crochety interplay of lacework and scaffolding in stone added to those on the outside, in the guise of
ornament. The Polish churches present to the glance great surfaces
on which it rests; they do not play games with the laws of
gravitation, they are not the paradox of the adaptation of stone
to ends contrary to its nature, it is not their feats of mechanics

[30] See R. Soltynski, *Glimpses of Polish Architecture*, Standard Art Book Co.,
Ltd., London.

that are dazzling. No, they are serene and grave, imposing, dignified, grandiose and finished, limited, accomplished, firm, tranquilly silent. Inside, they are "furnished" churches—opulent, vivid, impressive by the ostentation of culture, adorned with rugs, arras, sculpture, tombs, cut-glass chandeliers, painting, with their stained-glass windows and their grandiose doors . . .[31] Such are the Church of St. Mary, the Cathedral, the Church of St. Catherine at Cracow, such the superb churches of Toruń.

And the Italian Chateau of the Wawel in Cracow! With its galleries in arcades, light as a song! And the superb Baroque of Lwów and Wilno, the classicism of Warsaw, the Italian and French palaces, the "empires" in the country, the old quarters of Warsaw, the magnificent Great Square of Cracow, that of Warsaw, that of Kazimierz—all that is western, while remaining profoundly Polish.

Also Polish is the architecture in wood—the Uniate and Orthodox churches; but these, very beautiful and very picturesque, are oriental specimens (Ruthenian, Armenian, Byzantine).

In the fourteenth century a fine school of painting had already made its appearance in Cracow, and in the fifteenth it reached a high level of development, and Polish sculpture regards as its master the famous Wit Stwosz, certainly one of the great sculptors of the time.[32] These two arts developed; painting sees its triumphs particularly toward the end of the eighteenth century and in the nineteenth; sculpture populates all the churches of Poland with tombs and bas-reliefs, sometimes of very great appeal—the churches of Cracow and Wilno offer good testimony of it. In the nineteenth and twentieth centuries we have Jan Matejko—the Sienkiewicz of Polish painting, creator of famous historical paintings but especially powerful in portraiture, a little later appear

[31] See St. Tomkowicz, *Sztuka Plastyczna* in *Polska w Kulturze Powszechnej,* Kraków, 1918, Vol. II, pp. 3-10.
[32] See H. Gotlib, *Polish Painting*, Minerva Publishing Company, London, 1942.

the marvelous *paysages* and *scenes de genre* of Chełmoński, preceded by Alexander Orłowski, Piotr Michałowski, Juljusz Kossak. Finally I am citing only our greatest modern painters—Juljan Fałat, Jacek Malczewski, Józef Mehoffer, Wyczółkowski and Wyspiański, to whom I would like to add Henryk Rodakowski, Stanisław Lenc, Teodor Axentowicz, the Stykas, and Olga Boznańska as our best portrait painters, and Stanisław Noakowski with his brilliant "architectural visions." Also our sculptors—Dunikowski, Wittig, Kuna, August Zamoyski, S. Ostrowski and M. Lednicka.

I cannot enter here into the details of the development of music in Poland. It will suffice to say, however, that by the fifteenth century Cracow entered upon a period of rich musical evolution, thanks to the orchestras of the court, especially those of the sixteenth century; thanks also to the Church (the Jesuits did much for that); to Polish virtuosos—such as Jacob the Pole, "the most excellent lute-player of his century" (the words are those of Sauval, author of the *History and Researches of the Antiquities of the City of Paris*, 1724, Vol. I, p. 322), and to our first great composer Gomółka (sixteenth century).

Finally our dances contributed richly to Poland's music. In the seventeenth century the *polonaise* was crystallized so neatly that Jean le Laboureur says—speaking of this dance in his *Journal* (published in 1647) of his voyage to Poland, where he had gone in the suite of Marie de Gonsague, wife of Władysław IV of Poland—"I have never seen anything graver, sweeter, more respectful." This *polonaise*, called in Italy *alla polacca*, is introduced into German music in the eighteenth century by Johann Sebastian Bach (for the piano as well as in orchestral works), to live in Europe in the works of Mozart, Schubert, Wagner, Liszt—and I need not cite our Chopin.[33] The role of the *mazurka* is paral-

[33] See Zdzisław Jachimecki, *Muzyka* in *Polska w Kulturze*, etc., Vol. II, pp. 47-69.

lel. By the fifteenth and sixteenth centuries, the famous German composer Henry Finck pays homage to the Polish musical culture of his time.[34]

The development of Polish music in the nineteenth century was by no means poor; such composers as St. Moniuszko, H. Wieniawski, Różycki, Karłowicz, I. Paderewski, and K. Szymanowski, and the great number of Polish performing musicians, give the best proof of it. (Barcewicz, Paweł Kochański, Bronisław Huberman, Józef Śliwiński, I. Paderewski, Józef Hoffman, Artur Rubinstein, E. Młynarski, and A. Rodziński.)

I would like to stress also the fact of a comparatively early development of the theatrical art in Poland.

In the beginning the theatrical performances were attached to some special occasions. Such, for instance, was the case in the sixteenth century of the famous classical play by Kochanowski, *The Dismissal of the Grecian Envoys,* which was written on the occasion of the marriage of the Chancellor Zamoyski to Krystyna Radiziwiłł. Later on, in the seventeenth century, there existed a permanent Italian theater at the court of King Władysław IV. Besides, many private theaters were established at the courts of the magnates. Finally, in the eighteenth century there appeared in Warsaw two theaters, one in the Łazienki Palace and the other a public one. The performances included operas, ballets, comedies and tragedies. In the nineteenth century this art played a great part in Polish cultural life. Excellent companies were organized in Lwów, Cracow, Warsaw and Poznań.

Polish dramatic literature is very varied and wide. It produced great romantic dramas, satirical and realistic comedies, symbolic and historical plays. In the very last years Warsaw became an especially active center of theatrical life which embraced both the serious theater and the light genre of operettas, vaudevilles and

[34] *Ibid.*

cabarets. Warsaw had many talented actors and stage directors. To this should be added the school theater, in the development of which, in the seventeenth and eighteenth centuries, the Jesuits played a particularly important role.

Then the folk theater should be mentioned with its puppet shows which have survived up to our time. This theater represents the oldest tradition, going back to the medieval miracle plays.[35]

Finally, the development of the tradition established in Poland by Copernicus on one side, and on the other by the Polish humanists, should not be overlooked. And the rich development of Polish science at the end of the eighteenth and the beginning of the nineteenth century, and up to our own times (brothers Śniadeckis in natural sciences, Marcin Odlanicki-Poczobutt in astronomy, Lelewel in geography, Naruszewicz in history, Hoene-Wroński in mathematics and philosophy, Staszyc in social, political and educational endeavors—to quote only a few names), prepared the way for the great achievements of Polish scholarship in modern times. I need not stress again the thorough investigation in the field of Polish and foreign literature (Piotr Chmielowski, Ignacy Chrzanowski, Józef Tretiak, Stanisław Tarnowski, Marian Zdziechowski, Roman Dyboski, Juliusz Kleiner); in ancient, medieval and modern history (Józef Szujski, Michał Bobrzyński, Tadeusz Korzon, Władysław Smoleński, Szymon Askenazy, Wacław Sobieski, Władysław Konopczyński); in the history and philosophy of law (Leon Petrażycki, Oswald Balzer, Stanisław Wróblewski); in classical philology (Kazimierz Morawski, Tadeusz Zieliński, Tadeusz Sinko, Leon Sternbach).

The famous school of linguistics boasted such names as Jan Baudouin de Courtenay, Jan Michał Rozwadowski and Kazimierz Nitsch. The history of culture is represented by Aleksander

<hr />

[35] See Ludwik Bernacki, *Teatr, Dramat i Muzyka za Stanisława Augusta,* Lwów, 1925, Vols. I-II; also Jan Lorentowicz *Teatr Polski w Warszawie,* Warszawa, Inst. Wyd. "Biblioteka Polska," 1938.

Brückner, Kazimierz Chłędowski and Stanisław Kot. The Warsaw school of mathematical logic includes Wacław Sierpiński, Stanisław Leśniewski, Jan Łukasiewicz. In sciences and medicine— Wróblewski and Olszewski, Smoluchowski and Pieńkowski, Leon Marchlewski, Skłodowska-Curie are among the most notable. The above names are more symbolic and representative than exhaustive.[36]

These contributions of Polish science and learning are all the more striking in view of the fact that Polish scholarship was handicapped by lack of adequate laboratory facilities under foreign rule after the partitions.

Poland, then, had, as respects its general civilization (parallel to its political civilization), reached in the sixteenth century a level that put it on a plane of equality with Western Europe. That was its culminating point. After the sixteenth century appeared some very significant phenomena.

The dynamic, creative currents of this civilization were halted. Poland evolves nothing new; she continues to preserve what she had created up to the seventeenth century. The nobility, more and more softened by the easy life it had succeeded in guaranteeing itself, left the cities and went away to the country, where it led an existence more and more sybaritic, more and more detached from public causes, less and less intellectual and cultured. It succeeded in hindering the bourgeois from acquiring landed property (the Diet of Piotrków, 1496); it reserved for itself all the high ecclesiastical dignities, attached the peasants to the glebe (only one in each family had the right to engage in studies or industry, "lest the land come to lack arms"); it established prohibitive laws against the exportation of public manufactured products and favored the exportation of raw materials; it gave

[36] For more detailed information see Stanisław Kot, *Five Centuries of Polish Learning*, Oxford, Basil Blackwell, 1941.

free access into Poland to the products of foreign industry; it put itself at the humiliating disposal of the magnates rather than work in commerce or industry, and that because of a caste-contempt for the bourgeoisie and the professions.

The Polish nobility little by little lost interest in public life, in the outer world, in letters, in arts, and abandoned itself to the rustic pleasures of the country. At this period Poland appeared to be a country where the fields were worked by the peasant mass; the cities swarmed with Jews—whose presence and activity provoked Starczewski[37] to the angry comparison of them to "parasites on the sick body of the Republic"; and above it all is the *szlachta*—tumultuous, noisy, haughty and servile, patriotic but active only in movements of distress; bigoted and at the same time tolerant; passionate yet indifferent; patriarchal in all its customs, in its traditions, venerating the family, respecting the elders; adoring public assemblies, ceremonies, diets, dietines, confederations, as pleasant reunions; always opposed to war, but brave and valiant when it is necessary. This *szlachta* "Sarmatizes" itself more and more, contrary to the great "international" and "universalist" enterprises of the sixteenth century; it leaves the cities, "disintellectualizing" them and impoverishing them as it finally disintellectualizes and impoverishes itself.

"The Polish knighthood, after the sixteenth century, becomes an agricultural class dreaming of nothing beyond peace, 'sweet peace.' Reading the *Mirror of the Honest Man* by Rey, the masterpiece of the time, we see that the ideal of the nobility in that time was to cultivate moderately, to lead a calm life in the country, to enjoy the ease and sweetness of the hearth and not to bother with public affairs unless it should cost nothing in 'freedom of life' . . ."[38]

[37] *Op. cit.*, p. 94.
[38] Starczewski, *op. cit.*, p. 112. See also J. S. Bystroń, *Dzieje obyczajów w dawnej Polsce, Wiek XVI-XVIII*, Warszawa, 1932, Vol. I, pp. 157-162.

The seventeenth, and still more the eighteenth, century definitely stabilized this order of things. This life itself, by the by, became less and less attractive. All the great designs of the fourteenth and fifteenth centuries were realized—the great achievements of the sixteenth, accomplished; one wanted no more war, no great foreign policy—one wanted to live in peace and with the minimum of effort. In these circumstances, characters were softened, and the former tolerance, the former civic virtues, the old political and cultural ambitions, were transformed into indifference, quietism, egoism, resulting at last in the Polish obscurantism of the Saxon era.

There is only literature, which by a sort of paradoxical obstinacy keeps up its development throughout almost the whole century; but that also undergoes a period of stagnation during the Saxon era, to revive at the end of the eighteenth century and flower anew in the nineteenth, during the time of the Partitions.[39]

The morals of the seventeenth century go to seed; the country, the Republic, inexorably follows a decline that leads her to the catastrophe.

And it is precisely in the seventeenth century that Poland becomes a source of cultural radiation toward Russia—through Lithuania and the Ukraine. It is at this moment that Polish books, the Polish theater, ballet, music, schools, language, clothing, customs, political ideas, arts, artisans, painters, typographers, manuals of rhetoric, psalters, even the *Psalter* of Kochanowski, all the Jests, *Melusines, Magellones, Mirrors,* Polish *Till Eulenspiegels,* the erotic lyric, heraldry, statutes, religious polemic—all that penetrates into Russia, first by way of Polish Ruthenia and Lithuania and later directly, prepares the great reforms of Peter the Great, and continues to exercise its influence just as

[39] See Julian Krzyżanowski, *Od Średniowiecza do Baroku,* Warszawa, 1938, Tow. Wyd. "Rój."

much later—under Elizabeth, and Catherine II, and even Alexander I.

These infiltrations, cultural and political, literary and artistic, had begun earlier, but it was in the seventeenth century that they became particularly potent—just at the moment of the gradual and systematic weakening of Poland!

And later! What an immense quantity, in very truth, of Poles, of cultural forces, of scholars, artistic and intellectual, what a quantity of Polish moral and spiritual energy has not Russia absorbed during the whole nineteenth century—through the intervention of statesmen like Prince Czartoryski; of men of letters; of musicians; of poets who left their immense influence there, like Mickiewicz; the painter Orłowski, the pianist Szymanowska; scholars like Sękowski, later Spasowicz, Petrażycki, Zieliński; engineers, lawyers and great orators (Tadeusz Wróblewski and Aleksander Lednicki), physicians; and all the insurgents of 1830 and 1863—deported to Siberia and to the Caucasus, and all the émigrés, Russified and not Russified—innumerable masses of Poles who all represented Polish culture and most of them the salt of the nation. And I do not speak of our collections of art, our libraries, our museums confiscated and swallowed up by Russia.

And, to tell the truth, it was not a good bargain. Poland never received her deserts. For Russia had nothing to give us, except what she gave to the entire world. That is very considerable, and it is not for me to contest the universal value of Russia's cultural contribution; but let us not forget one thing, that this contribution dates only from the end of the nineteenh century. Second, for Poland this contribution was accompanied by such a destruction of Polish culture that it was quite difficult for Poland—ready as she was—to recognize the beauty of the great Russian literary work and the splendors of Russian music, and everything else that the Russian creative genius produced, without remembering Russia's genius for destruction . . .

Here we have arrived at one of the most essential problems of Polish national culture and its historical development—at a tragic problem. Poland had for long centuries been bound by her historic life and her spiritual efforts to western civilization. Her geographical situation—given her proximity to the eastern side—had assigned her historic mission, which was to push this civilization into regions it had not reached. Poland very quickly understood her role, and she had inaugurated it brilliantly—with the aid of the sword and the aid of culture. The sword was the defensive; culture was the offensive.

In 1241 she had stopped the Mongolian invasion at the Battle of Lignica; in 1444 the brave King Władysław Warneńczyk perished for the policy of the Holy See at Varna in its war against the Turkish invasion; in 1683 King John Sobieski saved Vienna and Austria from this same invasion, accomplishing an act of national unselfishness which, at the same time, showed devotion to the cause of Europe.

Such was the defensive. And the offensive? The union with Lithuania and its Christianization. The establishment of the Universities in the confines of the Polish East—that of Wilno in 1579 and that of Lwów in 1661, of the Academy of Zamość in 1594, schools and colleges in Ruthenia and the Academy of Peter Mohila which was an emanation of Polish civilization, the Lyceum of Krzemieniec in 1803. Finally—this penetration of Polish culture into Russia, of which I have already spoken.

But it is just here that we come to the historical catharsis, to the tragic convergence of causes and effects.

Russia defended herself against this penetration, and the latter was accomplished in spite of her. The Russians' aversion to the

West and to Poland was nourished by excessively powerful religious prejudices. What was worse, this penetration was accomplished in spite of Poland herself! The Europeanization of Muscovy appeared to Poland as a great danger for her; she was afraid to arm Muscovy with weapons that the latter did not yet possess and that could render the Russian threat still greater; and Poland, instead of becoming vis-à-vis Russia an interpreter and an apostle of European civilization, took the attitude of a rampart of that civilization. She interpreted the title of *antemurale Christianitatis,* assigned her by virtue of her combats against the Mongols and the Turks, as that of rampart against Muscovy. (And, to be just, one must admit that Poland's attitude was in great part justified by Russia's ferocious anti-Westernism.) On the other hand, under the influence of Rome she let herself be enlisted in a religious policy whose goal was the union of the churches—a design that Muscovy exploited in order to dupe Rome, a design that was illusory and unreal, having, at any rate, nothing in common with true Polish interests.

There was only one single moment when the destinies of these two countries could have taken a happier development and inaugurated a truly grandiose era for Poland as well as for Russia: that was the moment when the son of Zygmunt Vasa, Władysław, was elected Czar of Muscovy. That was one of the brightest of Poland's political successes, but it was the fruit of the thought and efforts of one single man, one of our greatest statesmen, the Hetman Stanisław Żółkiewski. The Polish prince was to "respect" the Orthodox religion and after the death of his father was to succeed him on the Polish throne, all the while keeping the throne of Moscow.[40] This magnificent project was not realized; mistrustful Russian obstinacy on the one hand and the fanatic Catholicism

---

[40] Moscow demanded that he embrace Orthodoxy; Żółkiewski silently agreed.

and personal ambitions of King Zygmunt on the other rendered Żółkiewski's efforts vain.

Since that moment history turned against Poland and her mission. What King Zygmunt-August had dreamed of was never accomplished. The passion for freedom, animating Poland, did not triumph; what conquered was the passion for power, animating Russia. We had either to crush Moscow or to come to terms with Moscow; we did neither.

Russia was Europeanized independently and against Poland. On the other hand, Poland was never sustained by the West. The West pressed Poland on her western frontiers, despite the victory of 1410 at Gruenwald, which had saved the eastern Slavs from Germanic oppression; Germany gnawed at Poland. When the Partitions came, Europe made no protest. During the insurrections, Poland waited in vain for succor from the West. So she did not succeed in accomplishing her mission; everything was against her, Russia as well as the West, and in such conditions her own strength was insufficient to accomplish this immense task. But the idea of this mission, the profound attachment to European civilization, continued to move her soul deeply; this soul, in its very essence, is Latin, Western, devoted to Europe much more than Europe is toward her; this soul is romantically missionary— our great Romantics of the nineteenth century continued to model it after the same fashion, and it is they, indeed, who, drawing from the deep sources of national history, once again reinforced the European and missionary style of Polish thought.

Poland has been a great crossroads of history. The East, as the Russian philosopher Solovyev says, had worked out an order of ideas in which man was subordinated to supernatural power. The West created the ideal of the independence of man. In the East the state had enslaved the peoples, while Greece had elaborated the ideal of the freedom of the peoples.

The supernatural element and the predominance of the state have given rise to the development of the ideal of resignation. Greece and Rome, with their Republics, developed the factor of spiritual energy and popular activity. These traditions, it seems to me, meet again; they reappear in the powerful development of the human personality, with all its spiritual and moral energies in modern Europe, on the one hand and in the grandiose development of the Russian machine of state, crushing the individual and the human personality on the other. Of course, in western Europe we have the horrible example of the Nazi state in Germany, but this may be regarded as an aberration from the normal western ideals. Similarly, in Russia, throughout the nineteenth century the great Russian writers preached the western ideals of human rights, and of the dignity of the human personality, but that, too, was an exception to the general current of Russian history, which manifested itself in a political system where the individual was completely crushed. Russian abstract thought, in revolt against the social and political system in which the Russian man had to live, created the ideal of a perfect God, who was to compensate for the distress of subjugated man. The West, on the contrary, sought to create the ideal of the perfect man patterned after the ideal of a perfect God.

Poland found herself between these extremes of historic forces forming the evolution of European civilization. To reconcile them she had proclaimed the Christianization of the State. That was her great historical idea, developed particularly in the nineteenth century in the torments and tortures of the era of the Partitions. She failed to impose this idea on the world. Later, under the conditions of her renewed independent existence she also proved unable to remain true to this idea in her own political life.

What will be the destiny of Europe—who can know? Until now it has been the force of the state that has prevailed. However, perhaps there will come the epoch, predicted among us by Mickiewicz and in Russia by Solovyev, the epoch when the "perfect God" will reveal Himself to "perfect man"—to man, powerless to become "perfect" without the help of a God who is "perfect"—and all-powerful.

IV

Squires and Peasants

WE ARE well informed about the life of the Polish landed nobility, because it has been preserved in many social traditions of modern Poland; because the mirror of the novel, comedy, poetry, and memoirs has continued to reflect it; and because our historians have searched its fragments in letters, in the documents of the courts, in trials and in wills, and they have reconstructed it to the least detail; because our painting has delightfully reproduced true scenes of genre; because, finally, the historians of art, architecture, and the applied arts above all have gathered precious indirect information on that same life, because that life, before the last war and even before this one, had its representatives in many "nooks and crannies" of Poland which were well-known to us all, and thanks to which we could savor the slightly gamy taste of the morals and ideas of the good old days of yesteryear.

For documentation on this subject we have hundreds and hundreds of texts; it goes without saying that I cannot hope to present here even a small part of them. Perhaps it will be enough to say that every century possesses at least several representative works. For the sixteenth century, it is the *Mirror* of Rey; for the seventeenth it is the incomparable *Memoirs* of Pasek and the "Trilogy" of Sienkiewicz; for the eighteenth—the *Memoirs* of Mr. Duklan-Ochocki and Kitowicz, the satires and novels of Krasicki, the fables of Trembecki; the novels of Henryk Rzewuski, written later, the memoirs and comedies of Ursyn-Niemcewicz and the "Trilogy" of Reymont; for the nineteenth it is *Pan Tadeusz* by Mickiewicz, the comedies of Fredro, the novels of Kaczkowski, the sketches of Chodźko, the novels and works of Kraszewski and the *Ashes* of Żeromski; and, finally, for the second half of the nineteenth century and the beginning of the twentieth—the novels of Orzeszkowa, Prus, Sienkiewicz, Weyssenhoff, Żeromski, Berent, Marja Dąbrowska . . . And it must be said that all these are first-rate. Let us add the exciting studies of Łoziński, of Bystroń, of Wasylewski, Berent and Brückner's *History of Polish Culture*, and we shall have ample documentation.

The seventeenth century was a century of transition. The nobility had definitely attached itself to the life of the country, savoring in this sort of voluntary seclusion all the pleasures that this existence could assure them. The end of the seventeenth century and the beginning of the eighteenth are the era of "Sarmatism"; the Polish noble cultivates not only the land but also all his national, and particularly domestic, habits and virtues. But his education becomes scant, cursory, and badly organized; the one thing he still knows well is Latin. Take Pasek's *Memoirs* and you will see that in his Polish there are more Latin words than capital letters—every sentence contains a great number of them. He knows Aristotle and Plato, and the Latin poets, whom he cites with the greatest of ease. There is, also, eloquence. When it is necessary, he becomes a truly inspired orator.

What are his habits and occupations while he is at home? He is not always there, what with wars and military service. Then there is—business. What business? Sale of products, crops, wood,

going down the waves of the Vistula to Danzig to give him mediocre revenue but enrich Danzig and the German and Jewish agents
with whom he does business.

Then there are suits with his neighbors. The neighbor is the
worst enemy, worse than the Tartars, the Swedes, and the Germans; the latter come only from time to time, while the neighbor
is always there. So there are constant brawls, suits, and quarrels.
And since courts work and act slowly, justice is done finally by
the accuser himself.

So Mr. Pasek, in return for some damage his neighbor had
done to his fields, collars his adversary's "functionaries" and
obliges one of them to eat, as punishment, half a hare—raw.
Slaughter, full-scale wars are waged for all sorts of conflicts,
offenses, misunderstandings, and suits. Sieges, ambuscades, duels,
battles with guns and cannon . . .

Mr. Pasek, descended from a poor but worthy family, had embraced a military career; his reasonable and respectable parents
had preferred arms for him to service at the court of some great
lord. The latter road was the more usual. A young noble repaired
to one of the magnates and perfected his education and polished
his manners there, learned savoir-vivre and savoir-faire. But there
was also another thing that he very often found in these courts:
humiliation. He had, generally, to follow the road of servility.
The petty *szlachta* played the role of humble clients of the magnates, and this role offered no guarantees of a good moral education. That is why the Paseks had preferred arms. It was in the
eighteenth century especially that this system became maleficent:
the *szlachcic*—if we take the novels of Rzewuski, apologist for
this civilization—unpleasantly combines the "point of honor"
with the most abject servility.

That was not the case for women—given the fact that they took
no part in public life and that their role was restrained. But as con-

cerned education, the way of a girl was similar;[1] many were the
things at a fine court for women to do. It was there that she could
find a husband, and with the help of his patron, that husband
found employment in the administration of the country. Girls did
not go to school; nuns or old women were charged with their
instruction, which consisted of very few things—reading, writing, knitting, singing, dancing: in the great houses they were
already starting to study French. Given the very low level of
masculine education at that time, the women took to it easily.
That is why toward the end of the eighteenth century we already
had so large a number of female authors, and authors of great
quality too.

But the woman of the seventeenth century did not yet have any
apparently great role in life. She was confined to the family only.
And this family was an enormous power. Everything depended
on the prestige of the father, on his will, everything was a function of the children's respect for their parents and their obedience
to their will—absolute obedience. This life was developed in the
frame of the nobiliary confraternity—it was a confraternity in
the strict sense of the word: everybody was related to everybody
else. There were men who knew by heart thousands of genealogies
and relationships and cousinships. This type of born genealogist
maintained himself almost to our own days—an uncle of mine
had ever present in his memory all the relationships of blood and
by marriage in those vast regions of the Eastern confines of
Poland. Marriages were made by the parents—marriages of
reason with an economic and social basis. The girl had no more
right to object than the young man did.

And these marriages were virtuous—we know almost no sentimental or romantic stories. It is striking that down to the end of
the eighteenth century Poland had not one example of great illicit

[1] Comp. K. Hartleb i M. Gawlik, *Kultura Polski*, Warszawa-Kraków, 1925.

passions. With us—no Francesca da Rimini and Paolo Malatesta, no Héloïse and Abelard, no Tristan and Isolde; for Poland had not known feudalism, the cult of Woman, the Troubadours, the pages, who consoled the wives of the Crusaders, the Troubadours and the Minnesingers. There was no Marie de France, no Marianne di Aleoforado, Dante and Beatrice, Petrarch and Laura, Romeo and Juliet, Manon Lescaut . . . No one in Poland says, like that delicious German woman whose words have been preserved in the manuscripts of 1170 by the monk of Tegernsee: *"Ich bin dîn—dû bist mîn—des solt dû gewis sîn—dû bist beslozzen—in mînem Herzen—verlorn ist das Sluezzelîn—dû muost och immer darinne sîn."* (I am thine, thou art mine; of this be thou sure—thou art locked in my heart—the key is lost—thou shalt for ever there remain.)

True, there is Kochanowski, singing of love; Szarzyński, saying, "Not to love is hard, but to love is a wretched consolation." Someone else writes odes *ad diamantam puellam*—but all that is but the literature of poetic speculation, abstract and cold. "Among all the European peoples," it has been said, "brought up on the conquests of western civilization, we alone cannot identify ourselves with amorous traditions . . ."[2]

To be sure, we have had in our history the loves of Wanda and Rytogar, of Walcerz the Doughty and Heligunde, but those are legends and fictions, and the amours of Queen Hedwig and Wilhelm, of King Zygmunt-August and Barbara Radziwiłł, and a few others, form a rare exception with us at that period. Until the very end of the eighteenth century, social life developed along other lines—those of an austere, severe, well-ordered family life, one which knew only the family, the "poetry of marriage and the

[2] See B. Merwin, *Polskie Listy Miłosne od XV do XIX wieku*, Lwów-Poznań, 1922, p. xix.

domestic hearth," it admitted only legitimism—once again, that Polish legitimism!

Now that tree bore no forbidden fruit; on that soil the fruit of love was not developed . . . Our archives know no amorous correspondence, no dramas, no hearts struggling for a unique happiness that demanded great sacrifices. It was necessary to wait until the Dukes of Lauzun should come to be madly smitten with our Polish women and discover them to us ourselves; to wait for a Benjamin Constant, a Sénancour and a Kruedener, a Goethe and a Byron, a Musset, a Mickiewicz, finally to hear the truly poignant word of veritable passion and to teach us to love and to make us, as we are today, great and faithful friends of Woman . . . For three centuries Poles spoke without one second's let and wrote thousands of letters—but never on love. For one reading the poets of the nineteenth century and the love letters of that century, it is difficult to believe that they have so brief a national tradition. Trials; public affairs; supplications; political and religious polemics; compliments addressed to kings, great lords; friendship; attachment to the spouse, to the legitimate companion; devotion to children—those are the themes of this "literature"—but never Woman, never passion.

Mr. Pasek, during the Swedish wars, found himself in Denmark. There he met a young Danish girl, Eleonore in Croes Dyvarne, who fell madly in love with him and wished to marry him. She addressed to him a long letter in Latin, confessing her love. "That letter," he said, "was not very much like a feminine concept, and I myself should not have believed it if I had not already known her *scientiam* in advance, and if I had not often heard her *extemporaneos discursus* . . ."

But that is not the question. Mr. Pasek avows that this letter "put chains on his heart." He is smitten. He replies to her, "term for term." He struggles with his *affectum* "as with a bear," he says prettily; then, with his comrades, "We drank—as is the Polish way"; "during this refreshment, every time love came to mind, the drink became colored with tears"; but the Abbé Piekarski explains to him "that if he lets himself be taken by this *dulcedo* and her good fortune *et usus cohabitandi*, he will never see Poland again, for the *persuasiones continuae* will come, and he will have to remain abroad, become a devil of a Lutheran, and his parents will not even see him when he arrives in Heaven, where there is anyway a *regnum amplissimum* of far greater opulence than the fortune of Monsieur Dyvarne." After these arguments Mr. Pasek, "having kissed the feet of the Lord Jesus" on his holy medal, "felt an immediate desire to return to Poland . . ." So they went happily to the frontier, he says, "and, after shedding some tears, casting a look whither they awaited him for the winter," he went away.[3] Recollect that even Pantagruel deliberated with more persistence whether or not he ought to marry.

His "bear," then, does not after all seem to have been very strong; common sense and the spirit of discipline—self-control —had conquered *affectum*.

Back in Poland, Mr. Pasek at thirty meditated as follows: "To take in marriage a widow with children means to take cares along with her; the first husband will have made debts, he will leave after his difficulties, children, *litigia;* and you yourself—you will waste away on other people's account, you will lose your health; what you have been able to get together for yourself you will spend in the courts, and instead of thanks you will win ingratitude. I advance this *pro memento:* he who would do such a thing—let him come to take counsel of me." And behold, on Thursday, September 8, 1667, Mr. Pasek, still aged thirty,

---

[3] *Pamiętniki Jana Chryzostoma Paska,* opracował Jan Czubek, Wyd. Z. N. im. Ossolińskich, 1923, pp. 51-57.

meets a widow of forty-six, mother of five children; the same day he proposed, and on the eleventh of September they are united. It is true, she was so pretty that Mr. Pasek confessed: "*Supponebam*—she was thirty . . ."[4]

Pasek's memoirs show us that his life in Poland was very active, representing the usual existence of the *szlachcic* in the seventeenth century—diets and dietines, as public affairs; for "social" affairs—what were called "friendly services"—agreements, "condescensions"—deeds in confirmation of this or that, the placing of girls in convents, compromises, acts of marriage and burial. Then, too, the general convocation of the nobility took place twice, in 1669 and 1672; besides that, trials—several suits a year; export of wheat for Danzig . . . As we see, life was full. Add to that the many "social" parties; burials, baptisms, marriages, Yuletide dinners, Easters; trips . . . In these conditions, who was it who managed the house, who supervised work on the peasants' holdings, who prepared the wheat for Danzig and procured the money for all these trials and trips and public services? The virtuous and worthy Mrs. Pasek; she it was who did all that, always staying home, never leaving her domicile—with one single exception, when she went with her husband to Cracow to make out the deed of the life-annuity that she had settled on her husband. And Mr. Pasek was happy and content; he would have been even more so, he admits with a certain melancholy—thinking of the energetic Mrs. Pasek and her "rule that anything that has to be done has to be done right away"—"if only the good Lord had given me one son by her . . ."

As for Pasek himself, he is the classic type of the Polish *szlachcic* of the seventeenth century with all his faults and his few merits. Religion—superficial, bigoted, full of superstitions: he is certain that the good Lord assists the *szlachcic* on every oc-

[4] *Ibid.*, pp. 307-308.

casion. He fasts, goes to confession, makes pilgrimages to Częstochowa (image of the Miraculous Virgin—revered by all Poland
—in the Convent of Częstochowa). But he mixes all that with
actions that are sometimes pretty ugly. He vexes his peasants;
he has duels; he raids other people's houses; he is chauvinistic
and nationalistic—for him, the Swedes are "pigs," Muscovites "a
people of lizards," Germans "Lutherans and therefore dogs."
Above all he detests the French, because of the Polish Queen,
Marie Louise. His patriotism is provincial; his devotion to his
country, interested; he does nothing without demanding good
pay for it.[5] However I do not think that he represents an exception when compared with average non-Poles of any time. Anyway
how far superior to him must his wife have been! This Polish
woman in the seventeenth century—and later—had an important
and greatly responsible role in life, but a role without glitter;
she was still always the respected matron, the "legitimate one,"
the woman whose virtues were domestic; she was a stay-at-home,
who accomplished her duties as spouse, mother, and mistress of
the house in exemplary fashion but discreetly, modestly, silently.
Thus, as in bourgeois Germany, the four K's reigned: *Kirche,
Kinder, Kleider, und Küche.* Often she was married against the
dictates of her heart, but she accepted her fate with resignation,
as our peasant women do even in our own day. Rare were di-
vorces, but many the serene, virtuous, peacefully happy hearths.

By the seventeenth century, however, there were already cases
of mésalliance—proof that Woman was beginning to conquer
the imagination of Man: such as Princess Anne Lubomirska,
bourgeois, cause of a duel and of the death of Tarło. All the same,
it is only the era of the *Saxe Galante* that will assign a more
showy role to Woman—an impertinent and equivocal role; at
that moment the Pole will begin to be distinguished from the

[5] See I. Chrzanowski, *op. cit.*, pp. 364-378.

Czech, the Russian, the German, becoming more and more the "ladies' man," more and more the "Frenchman of the North." It is in the eighteenth century that comments appear in the reviews read by the nobility:

"There are some of them who scarcely wolf down two slices of toast before they go to see their two mistresses; he readily fasts every Wednesday, but every Wednesday with a different woman; he eats no meat on Fridays, but he goes and has his love-affairs with the spinning-woman behind the stove; he fasts on Saturdays, but it doesn't prevent him from seeing the girls."[6]

So we see that it was a busy week, and that Woman—Woman of every condition—gained more and more ground, and the Polish man became a Don Juan. The Polish language itself signalizes these changes, this evolution undergone by Woman. At first, she is called respectfully *białogłowa*, fair-haired, because of her coiffure—an appellation which was, so to speak, anonymous, official, ceremonious; then she is the *niewiasta*—a designation always respectful and cold; finally, she becomes the *kobieta*—formerly a common appellation which now became plain, bald "woman," a form that is intimate, affectionate, familiar, and friendly. All this is aside from the fact that a rich amorous vocabulary was of course established.

This linguistic evolution symbolizes a road that had been taken by the Polish woman as well as the Polish man.

However, let us return once more to the *Memoirs* of Pasek. There is one page on Schleswig which is very instructive, as much so on the subject of seventeenth-century Poland as on that of Denmark. "The people there are charming; the women *(białogłowy!)* polished and very fair, they are prettily dressed, but they wear sabots (wooden shoes)—the woman of the city as well as of the country. When they walk on the city sidewalks, they

[6] See A. Brückner, *op. cit.*, Vol. III, p. 68.

make such a din and hubbub that there is no way to hear what they say to you; but the women of higher rank have shoes like the ones customarily worn by women in Poland. In love (affection) they are not so reserved as Polish women; although at first they manifest extraordinary modesty, after only one meeting and a conversation of a few words they become exaggeratedly and furiously amorous, without being able to hide it; they are ready to forget their fathers and mothers, their dowries, and follow the one they love to the end of the world. Their beds are recessed into the walls, like closets, and they use a great many bedroom trimmings. They sleep quite naked, as their mothers brought them into the world, and feel no shame undressing and dressing in one another's presence, and they even take no heed of the guest—they remove all 'embellishments' by candle-light and, when all is said and done, they even take off their shift. They hang all that on a nail and—stark naked—closing the doors, they enter these closets to sleep. When we told them that it was really unsightly for them to act in that way, and that with us even a wife would do nothing of the sort in the presence of her husband, they said that 'for us there is nothing shameful in so doing and there is no reason to be ashamed of the limbs of the body, God having created them!' As concerns this nudity in sleep, they said to us that 'the shift and the other clothes suffer quite enough in the daytime—why not give them a bit of rest at night'; 'and besides, why should I,' she said, 'take with me into my bed all the insects and fleas that I have in my shift and permit them to eat me and spoil my sleep' " . . .[7] This page is proof that Polish habits of that time were very different.

Family life in Poland in the seventeenth century, as I have said, was measured, sober, based on obedience and discipline, severe—

[7] Pasek, *op. cit.*, p. 12.

but not monotonous.[8] The gentleman found his greatest pleasure
and distraction in the chase—the national occupation, which will
even in the twentieth century make Princess Bibesco jest at the
"best guns in Europe," riding to hounds, hunting with dogs
alone, hunting with guns. Look at the delightful paintings of
Juljusz Kossak, Andriolli and Fałat and you will see there the
unspeakable sweetness of the Polish sky in the autumn, and the
charm of Polish snow landscapes, the inexpressible beauty of
the Arab horses raised in Poland by the *szlachta* down to our
own day, the quantity of dogs, and especially of game—that
staple of the Polish cuisine . . .

Then we must mention the holidays: that of Christmas with
Christmas trees, with Punch and Judy, masquerades, the Jesuit
"mystery-plays," the theaters, all the innumerable ceremonies
of religion; the holidays of Easter with their artificial fires, with
cannonades, with immense "hallowed" tables—the *święcone:*
cold dishes of all sorts—roasts, game, smoked meat, pies, tarts,
cakes, cheeses, etc., prepared all Easter week so as not to make
the kitchen staff work during the holidays; Corpus Christi, with
its processions and long religious ceremonies; the *Kuligs*—
nocturnal escapades in sleighs; amusements attached to the
carnival; the *ridottos* of Warsaw—public, masked balls,
where the nobility mingled with the bourgeoisie; the "little
games," games of chess, checkers, the innumerable card games
—*piquet, tresette, marchand, mariage, tryszak*—games of chance
came later, in the eighteenth century.

Drinking—Hungarian wines, mead, Malvoisie, Alicante, beer
of different kinds, *wódka, gorzałka,* rye, prunella, cherry, aqua-
vitae—anisette, English porter, French wines, Malaga, Ma-
deira, and so on, drunk from morn till evening. The art of drinking

[8] See Bystroń, *op. cit.,* Hartleb, *op. cit.*

became a Polish art, especially in the eighteenth century. We have not to forget, however, other examples in this field—Scotland, Sweden, Russia . . . In those days there were *amateurs* who could absorb whole kegs, drink all night, and continue in that manner week after week. Libations were not generally pacific; stories, quarrels, duels, scandals became the inevitable concomitants of these drinking-bouts, and often blood was mixed with the wine, since the *szlachcic* always had his *karabela*— his saber—and even his pistols, at his belt, and a very strict notion of personal honor in his head.

No *szlachcic* who could be called more or less worthy or honorable ever left his house without being followed by a large pack of flunkeys; so every Sunday, when people went to church, there was a reunion of little "courts" on the journey, of little "courts" —armed. "War" began on any occasion. Sometimes it was of very long duration, for in Poland, too, the *vendetta* played a great role. There were battles, real battles. Thus, in 1630, for example, in the affair of Wydżga and the Łodzińskis, the house of the latter was defended with twelve culverin-cannon, twenty-four mortar, fifty German muskets, thirty-five Polish muskets, twenty from Wilno, six from Toruń, eight janissaries'-guns, twenty-two "gouldines," and so forth.[9]

One can easily imagine what forces of defense and of aggression were at the disposal of the magnates! They had regiments, militia—in short, whole armies. Thanks to the impotence of the courts, certain gentlemen had become veritable brigands, quite in the style of the American gangsters. They permitted themselves the most violent abuses, unbelievable banditry and piracy—such as in the case, for example, of the famous "Devil—Stadnicki."[10]

Polish cuisine was rich in the seventeenth century; it became

[9] See W. Łoziński, *Prawem i Lewem*, Lwów, 1931, Vol. I.
[10] *Ibid.*, Vol. II.

still more so in the eighteenth. All sorts of meats, roasted and boiled, baked, with sauces; game—hares, pullets, young partridges, grouse, peacocks, venison, wild boar, bear; poultry; cranes; the cold Polish soups; curdled milk; fruits, preserves, walnuts, hazelnuts; pastries—made of rancid butter to give them more taste. In the eighteenth century we get accustomed to French bouillons (King Stanisław Poniatowski began his day every morning with a cup of broth that his chef had prepared for him through the whole night by continually adding new ingredients to it). Then came fricassees, ragouts, pâtés de foie gras in the French style, sauces, stuffing, oysters, frogs, ices, tarts, pies . . . all that, prepared by French chefs or by Polish chefs who had studied a good apprenticeship in France and in Poland. Coffee appeared by the seventeenth century; it was taken after dinner, and the men and women conversed over coffee. It was a real social revolution![11] At any rate, hunting, drinking, and cooking formed an immense vocabulary, a rich lexicon in the Polish language—to such a point that one of our best poets in modern days, Juljan Tuwim,[12] has published a *Drunkard's Dictionary*, very rich and very varied. Another poet, Ejsmond, and a writer, Weyssenhoff, have introduced hunting into letters, for which they have a great precursor in Mickiewicz. The many manuals of Polish cooking still await their poet—although *Pan Tadeusz*, by Mickiewicz, has already given a fine specimen in this connection.

But the presentation, the framework, the decorum, the etiquette of all these feasts and hunting parties and banquets in the seventeenth century were modest enough. Only in the center of the table did crystals and porcelain and silver plate appear. The ordinary *szlachcic* had in his belt, beside his saber and his pistols, a knife,

---

[11] Brückner, *op. cit.*, Vol. III, p. 76. See also W. Łoziński, *Polnisches Leben in Vergangenen Zeiten*, München bei Georg Müller.
[12] See Juljan Tuwim, *Polski Słownik Pijacki i Antlogja Bachiczna*, Warszawa, 1935, Tow. Wyd. "Rój."

fork, and spoon—so he helped himself anywhere. The plates, although changed for the different courses, were washed in water that was kept in the dining room and was not changed during the whole dinner; the manners and precepts of hygiene were simple.

There was, however, one very important element in this life—the domestics: lackeys, valets, heyducks (Hungarian foot soldiers), grooms, bootjacks, coachmen, jockeys, runners, hunters, hussars, equerries, chefs, cooks, scullions, dishwashers, maîtres d'hôtel, maids, servants, waiting women, chambermaids, charwomen, hostlers, pages, stitchers, butlers, footmen . . . it is impossible to enumerate that catalogue.

But it was hunting, above all, that imposed this immense livery, and many fortunes were spent in honor of Saint Hubert. The magnates organized parodies of hunts, even, to make it more complicated—with glass game, with mannikins astride wild boars . . .[13]

It was the court of Zygmunt III which had already, in the seventeenth century, exemplified pomp and luxury. The *szlachta* used to tell it around that at the ceremonies of his marriage the king wore one costume that had cost a million *złotys* and another of six hundred thousand. The silver and "other appurtenances" of his luxury amazed the *szlachta*, and—what was worse—became the object of imitation. It was the magnates who began it; then the *szlachta* did their best on their own account. It is difficult to imagine what a number of all kinds of precious materials, carpets, woven goods, hangings, rugs, carpeting from Daghestan, Smyrna, Aubusson; Gobelins; quilts in brocade, silk, damask, and so on, were owned by the châteaus of the great lords and the houses of more or less wealthy noblemen in Poland at that time.

And the precious stones! The furs! One of the cloaks of a cer-

[13] See A. Brückner, *op. cit.*, Vol. III.

tain Bobola—who was no great shakes in the aristocracy—had buttons that were priced at a hundred and thirty ducats apiece. His house contained one hundred pieces of silver plate, twenty-one chains of gold, basins, goblets, and carafes in gold and in silver, brilliants, emeralds. Suffice it to say that at one single fair at Jarosław—a little city in Eastern Galicia in the seventeenth century—David de Lima, merchant from Amsterdam, sold six hundred thousand *złotys* worth of jewels! Take the trappings on horses, the accoutrements of riders, the saddles—the saddle belonging to Charles Fredro had one hundred thirty-three rubies and twelve emeralds, not counting the innumerable pearls and encrusted gold![14] In France, Italy, England, the nobility used to spend even more money for luxury.

Unfortunately, all these riches were preserved, in great part, only on paper, in inventories, wills, records of trials, literary descriptions . . . The wars, the Tartar invasions which continued up to the seventeenth century, and then the ravages made by Russia, Austria, and Prussia took up the greater part of that rich national patrimony.

Money was spent beyond all moderation. In a single year, 1602-03, the *szlachta* of Sanok drank sixteen hundred and sixty-six tuns of Hungarian wine, not counting the Malvoisie, Alicante, and Rumanian wine that it had made sure to take in that same year.

Fortunes were powerful and revenues immense. I have mentioned the Danzig transactions of Mr. Pasek—those were certainly modest. But—Peter Potocki, for example, in the beginning of the seventeenth century sells to Kraus, a merchant from Danzig, twenty-one hundred oxen at a clip! A certain Sulatycki, a gentleman of Łuck, sends to the Łuck Market four thousand rams, two thousand sheep, three thousand oxen, and six hundred heifers![15]

[14] W. Łoziński, *op. cit.*, Vol. I, p. 124.
[15] *Ibid.*, p. 137.

In the eighteenth century, fortunes became fantastically tremendous. One Charles Radziwiłł possessed scores of cities and
six hundred villages; Felix Potocki, one hundred and thirty thousand peasants and six hundred thousand acres of land. His revenues were about three million *złotys* a year. The Lubomirskis,
Branickis, and Czartoryskis by no means lagged behind him. For
these immense fortunes the magnates had to thank the kings and
the considerable rise in the price of land, the fact that they paid
no taxes, the exploitation of the salt-mines, the forests . . .

The kings of the Saxon dynasty and, later, Stanisław-August
Poniatowski continued the tradition of immense luxury. The
magnates followed this example. The budget of Puławy, a property of the Czartoryskis, amounted in 1793 to one million, four
hundred eighteen thousand, six hundred and ninety-six *złotys;*
four hundred sixty thousand, eight hundred and twenty nine
represented the interest that had to be paid, and five hundred
five thousand, six hundred and sixty-six—the salaries of the
officials! I do not propose to enumerate here the crowd of
managers, valets, cooks, musicians, and the tremendous *Frau-
zimmer* that the Prince kept. A "world of people," we might say,
ate every day at Puławy, and it really meant a whole world! The
cost of the kitchen alone amounted to one hundred fifty-one
thousand, eight hundred and eighty-seven a year; the stable,
to fifty-five thousand. The Prince had eight saddle horses for
himself alone . . .[16]

Radziwiłł spent still more. He had a militia of twenty-three
hundred men; at the stable, more than one hundred men—
twenty-six coachmen! More than twenty ballerinas, forty-four
musicians, more than thirty valets of every kind, fourteen cooks.
The banquet Radziwiłł gave in 1788 to receive the Lords of the
Crown cost two million *złotys.*

[16] Brückner, *op. cit.,* Vol. III, pp. 174-175.

Vanity no longer had any limits: in 1751, at the burial of Joseph Potocki, Crown Constable and Castellan of Cracow, the participants included ten bishops, sixty canons, one thousand two hundred and seventy-five Catholic priests, four hundred and thirty Uniates and Greeks. And one hundred and twenty pieces of cannon were shot off, using up four thousand seven hundred stones of powder in six days.[17]

Luxury on a grand scale was fully established; expenses became mad, for the sake of life's uninterrupted pomp. Balls, receptions, ballets, theaters, carriages, clothes, cookery—everything became organized now in the French manner. French was incrusted on the "Polish-Latin" of the preceding epoch. Wigs, clothes, manners had all become Parisian. A Polish dude now sleeps wearing gloves, under six covers, his hair and neck covered with powder; he wears a three-cornered hat, he has a hundred jackets and as many outfits, he is familiar with six hundred coiffures, his costume is a rainbow of color, he is covered with lace, his buttons are a complete zoological garden—for under the glass of the buttons are butterflies, caterpillars, lizards, frogs . . . He wears gewgaws, eyeglasses . . .[18]

This is the time of the appearance of the perfumed and elegant cleric. "Nothing could be more amusing," Bernouilli relates, speaking of the Polish Sejm of that era, "than to see the bishops. For the most part, they are young, elegant aristocrats, coquettish, their violet robes competing in richness and charm, they wear magnificent lace and head-dresses, bordering on the comical . . ."[19]

And now also came the appearance of *Woman.* Life is dominated no longer by the Sejm and the dietines, but by the boudoirs. The stay-at-home Polish woman of the sixteenth and seventeenth

[17] See *Ibid.,* p. 67.
[18] See Stanisław Wasylewski, *Na dworze króla Stasia,* Poznań, p. 28.
[19] *Ibid.,* p. 29.

century gets around everywhere now. It is she who governs life. She has love affairs, adventures . . . Houses of rendezvous and assignation are set up . . . This new woman is ridiculously bedecked; her dresses cover a scaffolding of iron wire and whalebone, her coiffure is a mess, her face a painting, her bosom a jeweler's window. The French femme galante becomes her model; King Stanisław becomes the "Grand Master" of all these ceremonies—he "who loves all women," as Bernardin de St. Pierre said. The art of conversation, above all the trick of "saying nothing, agreeably and ingeniously"—develops; erotic poetry, sentimental, frivolous and light, obtrudes itself more and more; hunting with packs of greyhounds, mad "country-days," déjeuners champêtres, trips on boats covered with flowers and garlands, Strephons and Phyllises, gardens with trees cut à la Française, porcelains, miniatures; palaces with unheard-of parquetry, the most beautiful in Europe; songs, elegies, pastorals, idylls; bathrooms with porcelain from Saxony; trips to Paris; purchases in Paris of town mansions and sometimes of entire blocks—two wings of the Palais Royal, for example;—that is what life is made of . . . Luxury, prodigality, levity, heedlessness—giddy, distracted, mad . . . Radziwiłł buys fifteen hundred bottles of champagne for the Christmas holidays—three hundred of Rhenish wine, two hundred of Burgundy, and eight hundred pounds of coffee ... Countess Kossakowska, perceiving an orange-seller in the street and having no money with her, takes off her necklace of pearls and buys the oranges, paying at the rate of one pearl to one orange.[20]

The "Journal of Commerce" of 1787 (No. 104) announced that in 1785 Poland had imported thirty-six thousand tuns of Hungarian wine alone! "Our tables," relates one sermonizer of the times, "are like geographical maps on which must be found

[20] Wasylewski, *op. cit.*

every specialty of every country in the world."[21] And again it must be stressed that this picture does not represent anything unique for those times: let me recall the France of Louis XV and England in the same eighteenth century.

Social arrogance and the vulgarity of amusements and attitudes had become impossible. One Uniatycki makes his prayers in church under an insulating glass-bell to protect himself against the unpleasant breath of the "faithful." One Dulski had a harem of maidservants at his personal disposal, and he was not the only one; one *Wojewoda*, Brzostowski, being in Dresden, hired an apartment opposite his own, would stretch string across the street to amuse himself with the sight of the passers-by as they tripped backward, or else at night would ring at doors and douse the heads of those Germans who opened them, with tar. One Komornicki used to travel in a carriage drawn by goats and subsist exclusively on their milk. One Dyliński proposed to castrate all the Jews; one Wolski built a frigate, manned it, raised a Spanish flag, and declared war on Algeria. Attacked and beaten, he fled to a Papal port, was disarmed and, on the intervention of the Queen, set at liberty . . . The rigmarole would be too long to continue.[22]

The noble begins to sell his lands—often for nothing, because he needs money too badly; now he goes into business—with his lands, he pawns them, he contracts debts, the Jew becomes everybody's money lender . . . Corruption spreads; the ambassadors of Prussia and of Catherine buy the votes of the deputies in the Sejm for mediocre prices; women arrange their husbands' fortunes by lying with foreign agents; King Stanisław, during the thirty years of his reign, spends two hundred millions for all his pleasures and women. The game of Faro takes whole, enor-

---

[21] See A. Świętochowski, *Historja chłopów polskich w zarysie*, Lwów-Poznań, Vol. I, 1925, p. 298.

[22] Świętochowski, *op. cit.*, pp. 298, 299, etc.

mous fortunes in a night . . . The Ambassadors of Russia and Prussia humiliate the King, the deputies, the senators, offend them in public, create juicy, scandalous situations—scandals that a Dostoevski could not have imagined . . . Poets write the praises of Catherine II; magnates as well as statesmen sell themselves to foreigners . . . People sing, dance, amuse themselves, play cards, make love—and all that takes place at the very moment when Russia and Prussia, systematically, gradually, successively prepare the Partitions . . . the dismemberment of the Republic . . .[23]

One might say—a nightmare, a terrible and fantastic dream, beyond all probability, a feast in time of the plague. It is impossible to believe that such was the truth when one reads the memoirs of the time, the history of that epoch, the observations and narrations of foreigners, the historical novels of our novelists. And yet it *was* true. The life of the Polish squires had indeed reached its apogee, but what an apogee! This life represented a mélange of barbarism and civilization, of Sarmatian habits and French taste; the magnificent coaches, drawn by blooded horses whose manes were painted in red and whose harness glistened with silver and gold, crossed through streets filled with filth and garbage; the palaces—those magnificent palaces of Warsaw, of Białystok (residence of the Branickis), of Wilno and of Grodno—rose beside miserable huts; the hunting parties, costing hundreds of thousands each, were paid for by money borrowed from the Jews—or, indeed, taken from the Ambassadors of Russia and Prussia; the elegies and the sentimental idylls, ex-

[23] Once more I wish to remind my readers that similar examples of corruption in high places and widespread denunciation could be cited in abundance from the eighteenth century history of other European nations, such as the "Causes Célèbres" in France, the corruption at various times in Sweden, and at the time of the two first Georges in England, the court of the Russian Empresses, etc. See Albert Sorel, *L'Europe et la Révolution*, Vol. I; Lecky, *England in the Eighteenth Century*, Vol. I; Ralph Waldo Emerson, *English Traits;* Władysław Konopczyński, *Poland and Sweden;* the works of K. Waliszewski, Bilbasov and others on Russia.

cellent novels, satires, poems of marvellous taste appeared side by side with a literature that was outmoded, vulgar, destined in time for the people, actually read by those whose ancestors had been accustomed to read the poets and sages of antiquity . . .

One would say, then, a world in a state of chaos and complete perdition, consecrated and given up to catastrophe, to a catastrophe not only political but economic, social, moral, cultural; definite, irrevocable, absolute. And yet, this world did not perish. The Republic collapsed—but the nation rose again, woke again, set to work, to penitence, to the hard labor of him who has lost all save honor, and is determined to make his fortune anew. How did this miracle come to pass? I have already explained it on several occasions. It was this same *szlachta*, assisted, it is true, by the representatives of other social classes, that accomplished this miracle of the moral resurrection of the country, of its *own* rebirth in the first place.

For, in spite of everything, in spite of the corruption and decay of that epoch, the society always contained forces of moral resistance and a reserve of spiritual energy which could not be exhausted . . . It is precisely the fact of the depth of the abyss into which the country had let itself be swallowed, that furnishes an eloquent—and how eloquent—proof of the fantastic vigor of the nation which was able to get out of it, to recuperate, to set to work, to survive morally, and not merely to survive but to attain, in the nineteenth century, a magnificent level of spiritual development. But who, then, at the very moment of the catastrophe, represented these inexhaustible forces of the nation?

Men like Staszyc, who said, "A great nation can fall, only a degraded one can disappear," were there, and they kept vigil. Hugo Kołłątaj, an illustrious writer of the time, says, "The Poles will not let themselves be digested by the foreigner if their memory remains faithful to liberty, if they broaden their minds, if they continue to enlighten one another, and if they renounce frivolities and twaddle to hold themselves ready for any event. They will not save themselves either with vain chatter or with the hope that someone will come to take their hand. It is a question of having a stable enthusiasm, of being able to count on one's self, of seizing the occasion, of biding circumstances wisely, and of not executing resolutions until after long deliberation." There you have a whole program! Then, too, the satires, fables and novels of Naruszewicz, Krasicki . . .

On the other hand, King Stanisław-August had not only dallied with love affairs and feasts; he had instructed the nation, he had given it the taste for arts and letters that the Saxon era had destroyed. He had erected the most beautiful Polish buildings. There were magnates, who were not all scoundrels. There were Potockis, Zamoyskis, Załuskis, Czartoryskis, Czackis, whose patriotic merits were great models. Let us not forget the fine endowments, the libraries, museums, collections, donations of all sorts, constituted in Poland by the magnates; let us not forget their castles and palaces, which were works of art and centers of culture. There were men like Kościuszko and his insurrection organized with the help of many aristocrats, of the priest Bohusz, the banker Kapostas, the shoemaker—yes, the shoemaker Kiliński and the general Działyński. And we have not to forget either the important role of the freemasons in the regeneration of the country.[24]

Then, the *szlachta*—that part which lived in the provinces, far from places of perdition like Warsaw—continued to cultivate those delightful domestic virtues that characterize it to this day. It is family discipline, respect for one's parents, for age, for authority . . . submission to the laws of life and religion, truly

[24] See Władysław Smoleński, *Przewrót umysłowy w Polsce wieku XVIII*, Warszawa, 1923.

Christian resignation, often finding expression in a charming simplicity and moral dignity.

These traits appeared especially when they were face to face with death. Here is the charming story of the death and the last will of a seventeenth-century gentleman of Halicz, named Raszko. He was on his deathbed; he asked his friend Łychowski, who was there: "Master Jacob, do you believe that I am going to die?" He answered, "You are going to die, Sir." "When?" Mr. Łychowski answered him once more, "Today." "Really?" "To be sure." Whereupon, the dying man: "Take paper and the inkstand." He dictates his will in a clear and peaceful way; then, asking for the pen said, "I don't know whether I am in a state to sign . . ." "But he signed just as he used to sign when he was in good health, which greatly astonished us," as the witness of this scene terminates his story.[25]

Another—testaments often open beautiful pages in the story of the life of the squires: Bernat Suchorabski asks to be buried hard by his house, to have a very modest funeral, to have generous alms distributed among the poor . . . He speaks in his testament with touching tenderness of his daughters and of his wife—he advises the latter to marry again, immediately after the marriage of her oldest daughter, choosing a "handsome, honorable, and home-body husband." Finally, one other, Zborowski, gives a large sum to found a hospital in Lwów for "old soldiers" who, "having no *modum vivendi*, live in poverty, wretchedness, and vagrancy" . . .[26]

So these people had a conception of life and of their own duties which rendered them resistant to the temptations of moral disorder that had spread through the country with such terrible

[25] See W. Łoziński, *op. cit.*, Vol. I, pp. 152-153.
[26] *Ibid.*, 153.

rapidity—like the invasion of an epidemic, blasting and paralyzing the whole of life. There were some who escaped, who escaped unhappiness thanks to a "prophylaxis" of the past, those "preventive measures" established by the code of family life.

Look, too, at the world that appears in *Pan Tadeusz;* it is a world of 1812, and so a world that has survived the catastrophe of the Partitions. Look at what a spirit of order, hierarchy, and common sense reigns there! Everyone has his place, his rank, his functions, and his role. And all that in spite of and in artistic contrast to the anarchic theme of the poem. Here, no usurpation, no posing—all is loyalty, sincerity, solidity. Authority and obedience—two principles that the life of the Republic lacked—are the cornerstones of family life, they are the fundamental laws, the basic principles of this system.

Here the son, like the daughter, kisses not only his mother's but his father's hand. The son, when he grows up, kisses his father on the shoulder, he makes this gesture to every older man. We still do it now; these customs are powerfully alive, they have not disappeared. Girls kiss the hands of all older women, relatives or not. The priest always has his place of honor. When the bishop arrives, he is received with a gesture that is symbolic of genuflection. This world, in *Pan Tadeusz,* is neatly "hierarchical"—but with that, it is welcoming and benevolent, it is humane, it is good and charitable—for the peasant, for the Jew. And we have there a very important point. The *szlachta* had long waited to vote liberal laws with respect to the peasants. But its natural good-fellowship and clemency always prevented any crying abuses, ferocious conduct toward peasants—as happened so often in other countries, especially in Germany and Russia. Our annals know no stories like those of the famous Russian *Saltychikha.* The stick and the knout never had the role that they have had elsewhere. The peasant suffered misery, but he suffered it particularly in the small estates; in the large estates, often, he lived under a regime that was not essentially hard.

This world of *Pan Tadeusz* is a patriotic world. It is quite true, for it is just this provincial nobility, this petty nobility—often touching the life of the peasant, so humble and modest was it— it is indeed this nobility that enrolls under Napoleon in the legions of Dąbrowski and Prince Joseph Poniatowski, as it had arisen in the era of the Confederation of Bar or under the flags of Kościuszko; it is this class, again, that wages the insurrection of 1830 and that of 1863; it is the nobility that, deported in chains, goes to people the desert steppes and mines of Siberia and the Caucasus, accomplishing there not only the inhuman work of the prisoner but also a civilizing task, often intellectual labor . . . It is there that Wonlarlarski in 1723 translates Thomas à Kempis into Polish; it is there that the confederates of Bar and the insurrectionists of 1830 write memoirs, like Chojecki in 1789 and, somewhat later, Brig. Kopeć; it is there that they go to inaugurate new cultivations of the land, a new horticulture, scattered as they were in the snows of Siberia. It is there that the Princes Lubomirski are born, and the Princes Sanguszko and the Princes Czetwertyński live after the insurrection; it is there that, at the end of the nineteenth and the beginning of the twentieth centuries, Sieroszewski, one of our greatest writers, writes his Siberian narratives and novels, translated into every language.

The life of this *szlachta* in *Pan Tadeusz* is simple, modest, and sober; property pays for itself; it is a *self-sufficient* existence. There—no luxury or extraordinary phantasies; there are only some few aristocrats who manifest them, but even they do not fall into excess and exaggeration. It is nature, the seasons, and the toil of the countryside—and hunting!—that determine everyone's existence. But that is how it is in time of peace. When history intervenes, when the signal for the historic hour is heard, this people of squires rises and is ready for sacrifice and heroism. And that is the striking thing: gallant Saxony and the nightmare of the Partitions have not destroyed those two essential virtues, patriotism and courage, the disposition to sacrifice and the faculty of heroic resolution. The lesson of Napoleon—harsh and deceptive as it was—is not to be forgotten. The Emperor said, "The Poles must not rest on foreign aid. They must arm themselves. All the fine words that others will tell them will come to nothing . . . A nation crushed by its neighbors can rise again only with weapons in hand." Certainly—"without Polish legions we should have neither the Duchy of Warsaw, nor the Kingdom of Poland after the Congress of Vienna," affirms Starczewski with justice.[27]

The advice was not forgotten by the squires. In 1830, Mochnacki, a great man of action and political writer, writes: "After the dismemberment of his country, liberty or oppression, gentleness or brutality of government, all leads the Pole to the same result, to the bloody struggle to reconquer the political existence which he has lost but which he has never ceased to be worthy of. Such is our immutable destiny. When the foreigner's government is gentle, the Poles rise up because they can; when it is severe, they rise up because they must. Nothing will accommodate them to the ruin of their fatherland, and moderation no more than cruelty. This necessity for some to be tyrants and for others to be rebels, this fatality which, since the Partition of Poland, weighs on the country as on its oppressors—that is what gives dignity to all our national movements, and to our history a character belonging only to it."[28]

Here we come to a particularly striking conception—these words make us understand, especially if we read them with the

[27] *Op. cit.*, p. 118.
[28] Cited by Starczewski, *op. cit.*, pp. 118-119.

image of Poland at the moment of the Partitions before our eyes, how the nation was able to take advantage—moral advantage—of the terrible catastrophe of the eighteenth century. By advancing this paradoxical contention I mean that the catastrophe awoke Polish consciences, and opened the door to everything in the spirit of the nation that was best, honest, energetic, independent. The foul scum, the riffraff, was absorbed by the oppressing regimes; the soul of the nation was saved. And the squires more and more "spiritualized" themselves; the constructive, sane, honorable elements came to the fore.

It was at this time, too, that Woman became in the world of the gentry, a moral factor whose prestige continued to increase. It is true that the world of *Pan Tadeusz* is essentially masculine; one would say there that one is in a men's country club in England. Besides, it is not without reason that one of our most brilliant historians of literature at Cracow, Professor Windakiewicz, published in the *Slavonic Review* of London a study entitled "The Anglomania of Mickiewicz!" At any rate, women, attractive and charming though they be, play a role of a second order in this par excellence *male* epopee. But later, above all after the insurrections, you see the Polish woman taking so great a place in life, morally so important a place, that she appears wearing this halo even in painting. You see her, for example, in Grottger's cycle of pictures connected with the insurrection of 1863. Woman there is outlined as a Madonna, charitable and merciful but heroic, full of dignity and moral authority before which Man must needs bow.

That authority, that great dignity—that moral carriage, that allure of the superior, sovereign creature, created a legend; they created the prestige enjoyed by the Polish woman abroad; even Poland's oppressors could not help admiring her. Our custom of kissing a woman's hands, a custom established by the nobility and adopted by the bourgeoisie as well as the peasants—yes, the peasants—spread to every European society. But in Europe only Society follows the custom; in Poland everyone does. Polish letters, like painting, give the same image of Woman.

It is an aristocratic stylization, if you please, but it is life that made it. Take the novels of Orzeszkowa; you will say to me that she is a woman and so is partial; well, take the novels of Prus, Prus the positivist, the champion of "organic work," inviting the country squires, as Sienkiewicz will do later, to industry and commerce, wishing to make bourgeois out of them . . . This Prus gave us a present, a delightful gift, in the person of his unforgettable Madzia one of the characters in the novel, *The Emancipated*. This Madzia represents—what? What has been called "the genius of the heart," the fairy of sentiment, that great and so often misunderstood architect of life, that patient and silent worker for universal harmony, that mysterious artisan who appeases conflicts, who makes everyone in life be still and get along together . . . As the tears of Kitty Scherbatzkaya that she can no longer retain and that bring her back to her sister Dolly become what Tolstoy had so justly called the "grease" of the "machine of the relations between the two sisters"—so Madzia represents the same business of "lubrication" in the human relations in the world where she is.

We see this same moral prestige of women in the novels of Sienkiewicz, reproducing the same class of society—such as, for example, *The Połaniecki Family*, where the authority of Marynia Pławicka-Połaniecka is similar to a sacred image protecting the house. She is silent, she takes no very active part in the life of her energetic, willful, violent, ambitious, egoistic, and passionate husband . . . But she is there, she is present—she is vigilant, like a soul mysteriously and secretly present, like that delightful Madonna of Pushkin's ravishing poetry—she is there with the unspeakable beauty and purity of her moral being. The husband, guilty of certain sins, leans over her to embrace her feet, covered by the quilt, when he comes to sit on his bed after her childbirth; he bends with sobs in his throat before the silent beauty of his wife's soul.

Żeromski follows the same road, for there is no other road for them, it must be the road of truth that they wish to follow: Woman has become *all* for the Polish man, she is his guide, his friend, his wife, his mistress, but above all his mother. The prestige that women had won in the nobility was likewise established in the other classes of the nation—in the bourgeoisie and among the peasants. The peasant was submitted to this authority to such a degree that the old widower Boryna, one of the principal characters in Reymont's *The Peasants*, lying on his bed and meditating a second marriage, all at once and with stupefaction catches himself in the act of suddenly and aloud asking his wife, years dead, her opinion on the marriage he wants to enter into!

In Poland, as elsewhere, the peasant did not have an easy life. It is evident, however, that the fact that Poland did not know the system of feudalism made the lot of the Polish peasant at all times less cruel than that of the peasants of other countries in Europe. The reforms introduced by Poland on the eve of its ruin did not have the time necessary to ameliorate the conditions of the peasant's life. The latter then underwent the lot of the peasants of the co-partitioning countries. The fact is, however, that a great number of peasants, after the first partition of Poland, had taken flight from the territories annexed to Russia by Catherine II, and had come to Poland; we have there a proof that their lot in Poland was better than under the Russian regime. Then, in the second half of the nineteenth century, the co-partitioning regimes did all they could to create conflicts between the Polish

landed nobility and the peasants; they favored the peasants with
the aim of weakening the nobility, cultivating social discord, and
breaking up the national unity of the country. In spite of the great
means at the disposal of these governments, that goal was not attained; the Polish peasant was neither Germanized nor Russified,
he remained faithful to his country, and during this last war he
has shown, and he is showing, that his attachment to his fatherland is not an invention of Polish propaganda.

The peasant has always had his eloquent defenders in Poland.
I have already cited to you Rey and Modrzewski in the sixteenth
century, as well as writers and poets of the seventeenth, even entirely devoted to the defense of their cause, who had pronounced
a very severe judgment on the lot that the nobility had assigned
to them.

It was particularly in the nineteenth century, however, that a
powerful current of sympathy and interest was established in
our literature and in the social sciences. We even arrived at a
kind of "peasant-mania," springing from various roots. There
was the interest of the Romantics for folklore, for the picturesque
peasant; there was the interest of the anthropologists in race;
there were socialist and populist doctrines; there was the tradition of Lelewel in our historiography, which continued developing in a more and more democratic direction; and, finally, there
was a whole line of writers and poets who, guided by sentiments
of humanitarianism and philanthropy and reinforced by the influence of George Sand, later that of Harriet Beecher Stowe,
and still later that of Tolstoy and Turgenev, devoted themselves
to that cause.

It must not be forgotten that in the eighteenth century even
Rousseau, in the advice he gave Poland, was opposed to emancipation without preliminary education . . . Nor must it be forgotten, either, that the co-partitioning governments had done all

they could (except for Austria, and she only in the later period) to maintain the Polish peasant in the night of complete ignorance.

That does not by any means change the fact that, until the end of the nineteenth century, the majority of the landed nobility was certainly opposed to the abolition of serfdom. As I have said, the Polish nobility, intemperate, violent in the expression of its sentiments, could often fall into excess, but it was never coldly cruel toward the peasant, as was the French or German nobility. Anyhow, the general sentiment was that the peasant belonged to an inferior class, an inferior race, destined to serfdom by divine and by human laws. In the eighteenth century people avoided even having domestics of peasant origin—every domestic had to have a family tree!

On the other hand let us bear in mind that the "Castle" was always, in spite of everything, a center of civilization and help for the peasant. It was there that he resorted before going to see the physician; it was there that he was given the most necessary attention in case of accident; it was there that he was assisted in time of misfortune such as the death of his cow or his horse, in case of fire . . . It was there, above all, that the peasant received clothes, gifts for his children. It was there that his children clandestinely studied in secret schools, under the regimes of the oppressors.

Besides, as early as the eighteenth century men like Kołłątaj, Staszyc, Kościuszko, reasoned in a fashion very different from the opinions of the "obscurants" of that century. As I said, in the last half of the nineteenth century especially, opinions changed radically, and a strong team of writers took up this cause, never again to yield it up. It would be difficult to cite all the names. First of all, come two women, one a poet, the other a novelist, both of them famous, illustrious, surrounded by great respect and admiration. The poet was Marja Konopnicka, whose moving poetry has modeled the soul of many generations in the last sixty years, and who wept for the present—in this sense, she was the Nekrasov of Poland. Eliza Orzeszkowa apotheosized the peasant. Under her pen, as under Tolstoy's, the peasant became a master of conscience, an example of moral heroism; the hero of her novel *Cham—the Brute* accomplishes deeds of resignation, charity, goodness, that are evangelic. It is a husband, who pardons his wife not only betrayal but even an attempt on his life.

This woman, on the other hand, represents a most unfortunate social "product"—that layer of the petty middle class, whose declassed offspring cling to the class of the nobility and are demoralized, assimilating nothing of this class but its vices and faults, vanity and a wholly superficial polish that covers a bottom of moral rottenness. Such is this horrible Amelcia, a kind of criminal Madame Bovary of the village. Her husband is no Mr. Bovary; he is an inexhaustible source of goodness and chivalrous generosity, and it was not a coat of arms, but nature, that made him a veritable knight. "There are some souls," writes Orzeskowa, "who are like wells—when the flower of love falls in it, no wave will ever be able to cast it out." In another work she promulgates —long before *The Wedding* of Wyspiański—the idea of conjugal union between squires and peasants.

Some decades later, one Weyssenhoff takes up the same subject and relates the romantic story of the loves of a young "lord" and a ravishing Lithuanian peasant girl—woven, incidentally, against a delightful background of landscapes and hunting scenes. This story influences many young Poles in the era before the War of 1914 to embrace dreams, if not bonds, of this kind.

Then come the powerful, pathetic, stormy, revolutionary, violent, indignant and choleric, charitable and pitiful poems of Kasprowicz, himself a peasant but highly cultivated, Professor of Comparative Literature at the University of Lwów, translator of ancient authors, of Shakespeare and Shelley.

Next, the poems and novels of Tetmajer, on the mountaineers of the Tatras; the novels of Orkan, attached to the same region; and, finally, *The Peasants* of Reymont, the great peasant epic— the four volumes, *Autumn, Winter, Spring,* and *Summer,* recalling the *Terre* of Zola, but richer, broader, grander than Zola's—a novel that won Reymont the Nobel Prize.

This immense fresco represents the entire life of the peasant, under the sky and on the glebe of the four seasons, in the forest, in the fields, in the garden, in the stable and in the barn and in his house. His family life, his dramas, his affairs, his work, his distractions, his loves, his passions . . . It is the life of the country—with the priest, the Jew, the court, the church, the tavern, with dances and songs, marriages, births, deaths, and adulteries, cows and horses, with everything the peasant eats, drinks, thinks, feels, believes, says, or does not say. All his customs, all his beliefs, all his illusions, and all his hopes, his goodnesses and his cruelties, his generosities and his ferocious appetites, his poetry and his down-to-earth spirit, his folly and his good sense—everything is there. Everything is there to such an extent that when the Germans attacked Russia in 1914 and invaded Polish territories, the German soldier had Reymont's four volumes in German in his sack as a manual for the "Overseas Administration" of Poland. They considered that novel the best introduction to the life of the Polish peasant.

In fact, you can find there, in that Polish village, the rich and even opulent peasant who eats well—not only cabbage and curds and potatoes, but bacon, meat, sausages, chickens, turkeys and geese for holidays; who possesses several cows and horses, pigs, enjoys good crops, living in a suitable, well-kept, well-furnished house. You see also the gloomy misery of so many others.

What is especially striking in this book is that the author, who was of very modest social origin himself and had been able to observe the peasant's life very near at hand and very attentively, shows us to what extent the peasants are sufficient unto themselves and possess full consciousness of that self-sufficiency. They have a peculiar social ethic and do not in any way preoccupy themselves with that of others.

Their life is regulated by the seasons. They follow the furrow of the plow, but sometimes passion leads them astray; that is the story of Antek and Jagna, of their terrible and heavy love. In this story they appear like the powerful figures of a Michelangelo . . . Their passion makes them silent, it immobilizes them in an elemental tension of the body, which dreams and cannot make a single movement—so great is their desire. It is possible, however, that that is the effect of the author's creative imagination, making up, in a certain measure, for the reality of the erotic life of the Polish peasant, which is generally full of modesty and very reserved in this field of human existence.

In independent Poland the role and situation of the peasant changed greatly. It is enough to say that Poland created about thirty thousand primary schools, which enormously reduced the number of illiterate peasants. The most powerful and numerous political party during that period was the peasant party. Agrarian reform did not definitely settle the agrarian problem, but at any rate six million acres were distributed. The peasant continued to climb the social ladder—especially in Galicia, where a large number of lawyers, physicians, and university professors were sons of peasants, whose parents lived in the village. The leader of the peasant party, Witos, was on several occasions President of the Council. It was no longer necessary for literature to defend the rights of the peasant; it consecrated itself to the study of his life, to the story of that life—such are the classic monographs on the peasant of our distinguished sociologist, who is here now, the Professor of the University of Poznań—Florian Znaniecki; such, full of rancor toward the past, are the two volumes by Świętochowski on the peasants; the same purpose inspires the two immense volumes, *Memories of the Peasants,* published by the Institute of Sociology of Warsaw, which give us the image of the peasant's life painted by himself.

Poland changes its social and demographic character; the most numerous class in the nation, that which, according to legend, gave her her first kings, after long centuries of mute existence in the shadow and in oblivion, now returns to power . . . And yet, the general aspect of life does not much change, for during the centuries of very close and intimate existence with the numerous Polish gentry, after many and frequent ennoblements in the past, as a result of education and of the political role that the peasant has already begun to play now, he is stamped with the customs, usages, and manners of the gentry.

This is a fact: the modern Polish peasant is a very well-brought-up man, often better than his neighbors still living in the castle, he is distinguished and physically handsome. He is aristocratic. While disappearing, the nobility has not left it without heritage. There is nothing for it; Poland *is* an aristocratic country; but it is not, as Lamartine said, "an aristocracy without people," it is an aristocratic nation without an aristocracy.[29]

[29] See the Polish Peasant in the following recent publication *From Serfdom to Self Government,* etc., translated from the Polish by W. J. Rose, Minerva Publishing Co., London, 1941.

V

The National Poet: Adam Mickiewicz

IN MY OPINION we have nothing greater or finer in Poland than this man, this poet. His life and work, completely united to each other, represent a phenomenon that is singularly human, deeply national, and at the same time essentially universal in its higher, symbolic sense.

The biography of Mickiewicz is stirring, above all because his life, taken altogether, represents a constant evolution of the moral personality; an evolution whose dynamism is hidden in the constant and ferocious travail of a conscience which never stops forming and modeling that being, constituted of powerful passions and immense means of expression. There is in him the same titanic inner struggle that appeared in Tolstoy—the same desire for happiness and bliss, the same love of life, and on the other hand the same moral and religious control, which leads him to acts that definitely detach him from Art and oblige him to sacrifice everything, even poetry, for "the sacred cause." But—while for Tolstoy this "sacred cause" is personal salvation, for Mickiewicz it is the nation.

There is something Gogolian in this great drama—*toutes proportions gardées*, but Gogol's personality was infinitely inferior to that of Mickiewicz as well as to that of Tolstoy. There is ambition, as in Tolstoy and in Gogol, ambition to become the master, the "tyrant of conscience"—a moral Napoleon of the nation, its hero, its spiritual leader. There is innate, immanent authority which makes this man dominate and command, speak as leader— to everyone, to princes, to poets, to popes, to the mobs . . . And always, from the beginning; *he* alone, *he* believes, *he* has the notion of power—inner, secret, tranquil, and mute—like dynamite—until the moment when forces that cannot be seen but can be sensed will come into play, and play an irresistible and, if need be, a terrible role. His whole entourage felt this at the very moment when he appeared before it, for there are men, as Wilde said, who have a regal air—although he was, particularly in his youth, modest and gentle . . . gentle, yes, but agile as a leopard. Free, absolutely, essentially free; always aware of his means and his strength, and everywhere audacious, hurling his claims and his inspirational laws at men, at the nation, at . . . God. At the same time, resigned, and ready for penitence—which was never a symptom of weakness in him . . . Capable—like a leopard—of making a great leap, a bound, without needing to exercise his muscles beforehand, unacquainted with the tension of exercise experienced by the weak who would become strong. Nothing in him of the impotent and terrible hero of Dostoevski's *Notes from the Underground*. Women felt and admired in him this latent, secret strength, and they yielded to him—all save her who was his first and only love; but such was to be her role in the poet's life—without her, Mickiewicz would not have taught Poland how one can and how one ought to love.

A born improviser, he was a sort of magician, who, even when improvising in foreign languages (in French), even before foreigners (Russians), brought his hearer to a kind of delirium, of frenetic raptures. And that occurred not only with women but

with men, poets—great poets, skeptical and wise, like Pushkin
and his Pleiades in Moscow.

As a poet, he completely changed the Polish poetry of his
century; he truly *animated* it, he gave it a soul, a soul so great
that till now, even, it overflows this poetry; this poetry is smaller
than its soul. Beside him all the others are dwarfs. The language
he spoke and wrote was full of provincialisms, regionalisms,
dialectisms—that beautiful language of the Polish Lithuanian
regions—expressive, uniting sweetness with energy, simplicity
with the picturesque; and there again he manifested his freedom
of action, the nonchalance of a superior being, his carelessness.
He knew all the great men and great personalities of his time, and
each time, after each encounter, he captivated them and made
them friends of Poland—Goethe, Alfred de Vigny, Delacroix,
Montalembert, Lamennais, George Sand, James Fenimore
Cooper, Michelet . . . Pushkin was the sole exception. "Among all
the Poles, none interests me but Mickiewicz," he had said. This
ferocious enemy of Poland did not change his attitude toward
Poland under the influence of Mickiewicz, but neither did his
admiration for Mickiewicz change under the influence of his
hatred of Poland.

Frenchmen, Italians, Germans, Americans, Russians—especially the Russians—all revered and loved him. At no time has
any Pole ever played a role similar to his in Russia, where
Mickiewicz left an ineffaceable trace of his sojourn; it is a tradition a century old and it is still vivid. This really touching attachment persists, and it withstands all the mishaps of politics.

This man did not take part in the insurrection of 1830-31,
although he could have been in the ranks. He suffered from that
fact, and he expiated that desertion all his life; but it did not
hinder him from imposing on the nation the poetic image of his
own martyrdom for the Polish cause, which was certainly not

comparable to the martyrdom of the nation, and from making out of it a gospel, a compendium, of the martyrdom of Poland. Here again is revealed that soul's bold and captivating force, which was really—and it still is today, it will always be—peculiarly penetrating.

There is another trait in this poet that I should like to note: his poetry is the poetry of truth, intrinsic truth. In spite of his supremely romantic élan, in spite of his adoration for Byron, Mickiewicz was a great realist, one of the greatest. Beside Byron he adored Goethe. He himself, as it happens, has said—and very neatly—what he thought on the subject of truth in poetry. It was his good friend Odyniec who preserved in his *Travel Letters* the admissions Mickiewicz made in this regard: " 'Verses and poems are two different things,—as different as the sky and the earth. Books have given me one conviction, that all the great poets there have ever been in the world, from Homer to Goethe, have drawn from the same source.' 'and what is that source? Folk poetry?' I asked. 'Folk poetry is not a source, but like a girl from the village it fetches up with its hand and drinks directly *in* the source, before conduits bring the water to the cities, fill the fountains with it and supply it for tea.' 'Well then, what *is* the source?' 'Reality and truth. To the people's eyes this source is the rock; but it is precisely from the rock on the Greek Parnassus that the Castalian spring gushed out. Imagination is like Hebe, drawing from this source and filling the cups—or, indeed, like that girl from Karlsbad who distributes *Sprudel* in glasses . . .' "[1]

Mickiewicz was born on the twenty-fourth of December, 1798, three years after the first partition of Poland. He came into the world at Nowogródek, a little provincial town situated in that Lithuania which since the fourteenth century had been united to

[1] See *Sto lat Myśli Polskiej (Wiek XIX)*, Warszawa, 1907, Vol. III, pp. 325-326.

the "Crown." That part of the Polish Republic had been taken by Russia. As Catherine II had not yet had time to abolish everything that the old Polish regime consisted of, local autonomy, courts, and schools in Lithuanian Poland still kept their Polish character.[2] Mickiewicz was born in a modest family of Polish country squires; his father was a lawyer and owned a house at Nowogródek where the poet spent all his childhood, in a milieu with which you are already familiar, in the milieu which appeared partially in *Pan Tadeusz*. At any rate, the life of this provincial *szlachta,* removed from the highways of events, had not changed since the Partitions; you were still, so to speak, living in Poland, in a Poland that was politically dead but which Russia had not yet even tentatively tried to assimilate and absorb from the national and cultural point of view. I ought to take especial notice, however, of one great historical event which became carved in the memory of the poet, at that time a boy of fourteen: the Campaign of 1812. He saw the Grande Armée and Polish troops at Nowogródek! Likewise, he saw its terrible, tragic retreat. Therefore, in the lapse of several months he had— like all Poland—lived through the hopes of resurrection attached to that campaign and also through the sinister eclipse of those hopes.

After studying in the secondary school at Nowogródek, he went to the University of Wilno, which had been founded, as you know, by Stefan Batory in 1579 and which had just been reorganized under the auspices of Prince Adam Czartoryski, at that time its curator, appointed by Emperor Alexander I.

That was, it must be said, the most brilliant period in the history of the University; it had reached a very high scientific

[2] Especially after the death of Catherine II, in the beginning of the reign of Paul I, who demonstrated a sort of Polonophilia, the conditions of life became, for a while, a little better in this part of Poland. See Henryk Mościcki, *Dzieje Porozbiorowe Litwy i Rusi,* Wilno, 1910.

level, and it was greatly esteemed even abroad. Astronomers like Jan Śniadecki, and before him Odlanicki-Poczobutt; physicists like Jędrzej Śniadecki; the famous historian and geographer Joachim Lelewel, whom you already know; and some excellent classical philologists taught at the University of Wilno. The city itself had become rich in Polish intellectual and cultural resources, and the animated center of a very vast region of the ancient Republic. Prince Czartoryski, although at this moment distant from the Emperor whose close friend and collaborator he had been for many years, still kept his prestige, which he could use to protect this beautiful hearth of Polish civilization.

The University was peopled by young people, the great majority of whom belonged to the nobility of the confines of the Eastern part of Poland. The landed nobility in this region differed substantially from the nobility of central Poland. The fact that it had for whole centuries been exposed to the danger of Muscovite and Tartar invasions and excursions, that for centuries it had fulfilled likewise a civilizing mission in that country, had left a special imprint on this class of men. Until now they have preserved a dignity, a kind of gravity and impressiveness which they have acquired in fulfilling that exposed mission of cultural and political leadership, at the same time possessing a political savoir-faire, a supranational and suprasocial comprehension of human affairs, that they had acquired by centuries of coexistence with national minorities and contacts with Russia.

They have always been, and they still are now—I speak of the average nobility—much more attached to their "nests of gentlefolk," to the earth, than the Polish nobility of central Poland, just because they had fulfilled a secular task of civilizing colonization: their "nests" had always been Polish cultural cells. On the other hand, they had absorbed the influence of the surroundings, of the non-Polish masses—a circumstance which enriched them and broadened their views. They represented, then, an excellent cultural and political alloy, based on long and venerable historical experience. They were much more simple and modest in their manners, in the tenor of their life—less fashioned after foreign models, less poseurs, much more serious, prudent, sincere, informal, without pride or pretense. They were characterized by a sort of nonchalance, always side by side with a very great personal dignity.

Mickiewicz found himself immediately in the best circles of the University youth of Wilno, and he soon took part in many social and literary activities organized by circles and societies of students. The young man had come with the aim of studying at the University in order then to embrace the modest career of a schoolmaster. In his childhood he had shown no superior faculty of mind, nothing distinguished him among his comrades. In Wilno the situation changed rapidly. We see Mickiewicz playing a role in the forefront, he is surrounded by young people who are profoundly attached to him and who become—and this is striking—his guardians, his "protectors," his vigilant "supervisors," who keep on observing him, guiding him with their advice, remonstrating with him, helping and seconding him.

They organized societies, the Philomaths and the Philaretes, whose ideals were expressed by three slogans: "Fatherland, Study, and Virtue." These societies, on the example of Masonic lodges, established an organization based on principles of hierarchy; patriotic moral virtues and intense literary labor played a very important role. Very soon Mickiewicz began to write, and he read his poems at meetings of these societies. He had worked a great deal and acquired vast erudition in history, classical philology, and literary history. (This good training at the University later facilitated his role of professor at the University of Lausanne and then at the Collège de France.)

His first poems, with some exceptions, followed the line of the Romantic school. He wrote *Ballads* and *Romances* in the style of Goethe, Schiller, and Uhland, but even in these works of his youth the young lion's claw appeared in the delightful and somewhat naïve "Lithuanian," in the picturesque energy of his language, in the plasticity of his images, in the national tone of his poetry, and in his mastery of Polish verse. His friends admire him more and more and "hatch" his talent, still from time to time permitting themselves very sincere and occasionally justified criticism.

But here came a great event in the young poet's life. He met the sister of one of his comrades—Maryla Wereszczaka, daughter of the deceased ex-marshal of the nobility of the District of Nowogródek. Mickiewicz was introduced into the house of the Wereszczakas in the country, on their estate of Tuchanowicze, in the summer of 1818 by his great friend Thomas Zan, who had been the young Wereszczaka's tutor. Maryla was nineteen years old at that time, a charming girl who took delight in savoring of the sentimental, romantic poetry of the time, the idealistic speculations on the union of souls and the fraternity of poetic spirits that she found in her French and German reading. Nothing could be more natural than that she should feel herself immediately attracted toward Mickiewicz, while *he* was smitten to distraction from the first meeting, with all the violence of his deeply passionate and hot-headed nature.

That passion became all the more feverish and ardent as the young man met insurmountable obstacles. In the first place, there was the social distance—the Wereszczakas belonged to a world which was by no means that of Mickiewicz, a poor young man aiming at the modest career of a teacher in high school. In the second place, she was engaged to a rich young gentleman, Count Puttkamer. With the growing reserve of the girl's family toward

Mickiewicz and with Maryla's obedience to the will of her people, which she never had the courage to oppose, although she became more and more attached to Mickiewicz, this love affair became a torture for the poet. He lived several long years in the climate of a love as powerful and deep as it was unhappy. After finishing his studies at the University he went to Kowno, where he was named teacher at a high school. There he led a very painful existence, more and more discouraged and more and more troubled by inner suffering. His poetry in this period became the story of this love. Alone, contracted within himself, having lost all hope of happiness forever—Maryla's marriage took place on the second of February, 1821—having lost his mother and gone through a grave illness—to which was added much trouble with the authorities of the Lyceum—Mickiewicz found himself in deep distress.

It was in this atmosphere that he wrote his *Forefathers' Eve*, the fourth part of which became for Poland a gospel of love. It is a mordant story of passion—before Mickiewicz no one in Poland had ever spoken such a language, with such great and penetrating sincerity. The poet unveiled the immensity of his unhappiness; the intensity of his suffering is such that his hero, whose anguish represents the living truth, finishes by suicide: he appears in the guise of a phantom, who relates all the extraordinary torment of his passion. Thus we have here Wertherism in full, the real Wertherism.

However, Mickiewicz's poetry also contained other motifs and aimed at other ends; the expression of the consciousness of latent inner strength comes into more and more relief; the poet detaches himself more and more from his entourage, he is more and more conscious of the distance which separates him from his friends. These latter were judging him according to their own measure— now the poet felt that disproportion, he also felt the rhythm of the progress that was growing stronger and stronger in him, the line of spiritual evolution appeared more and more distinctly, and the march of his moral being toward new destinies was fulfilled. Those two elements, those two traits—consciousness of his own strength and "movement"—accompanied by a third, which was the mystery of the "interior," of the intrinsic, of the "sacred fire" burning at the heart of his being and illuminating that being from the interior as the flame of a wick illuminates a lantern; those are the ideas that crystallized in him and persisted in seeking poetic images for their externalization.

They are also based on self-observation. And it is striking to see how faithful the poet will remain—down to his last work— to these principles of his moral existence and these images of his inventive genius.

In his poem of *The Navigator* we already have a beautiful image, inaugurating—one might say—this poetic cycle; the poet has a group of men appear on a rock beside the sea. They are his friends, who regard him with fright and stupor . . . He is ready to throw himself into the sea . . . The friends do not know that it is the storm which pushes him into the sea, "they see only light, while all around him the thunderbolt is striking . . ." They do not know what he feels . . . They will never be able to feel it:

> He who would judge me must not be with me but in me:
> I sail on farther—you go homeward.

Life will always remain faithful to that formula and to that image; the poet will navigate, will fly, will proceed, will march toward great goals and distant destinies; his contemporaries, his friends, observe him with fear or admiration but will never be able to rejoin him; they will remain fettered on the shore . . .

I should not fail to cite some other, later texts showing to what a degree the poet persisted in this path . . . Yes, the consciousness of his own strength, inner fire, and movement continue in the same way to pattern the world that the poet shows in his poetry. Movement—everywhere; in the sky it will be the movement of the birds, the movement of the clouds, of the stars; of the boats and sails, on the water; and on land, the horse, the rider, the hurricane, the wind going over the wheat . . .

In his *Ode to Youth,* written in 1820—one of his most beautiful poems, a poem that became an ideological program for his generation—he says, speaking of the young:

> He who in the cradle has torn off the Hydra's head
> Will throttle centaurs in his youth,
> He will rescue victims from Hell
> And for his laurels will go even to Heaven.
>
> Reach there, where vision cannot reach!
> Break what mere knowledge cannot break!
> O Youth! Like the eagle's is thy powerful flight,
> And like the thunder-bolt is thine arm!

He awaited his destiny, shackled to the dreary existence that he had to drag out at Kowno—a little provincial city without resources, without distractions, without anything that could animate a mind and soul ever greedier for the new, the unknown, the uncertain . . . He abandoned himself to some vain pleasures and immediately provoked the impatient criticism of his friends.

Destiny, however, intervened in an unexpected way. The Russian Government, more and more distrustful of the patriotic sentiments manifested by the youth of Poland, suddenly struck at its heart: the Philaretes and the Philomaths were arrested, put into prison, in the Convent of the Basilians at Wilno, Mickiewicz transferred from Kowno to the Convent, and the University closed several years later . . .

A new destiny opened up before the young poet and his friends: they were all consigned to the depths of the Russian Empire—sent to St. Petersburg and then, Mickiewicz and two of his friends, to Odessa; from Odessa he was then transferred to Moscow—some of his friends to Kazan, Orenburg . . . Now we are at a grave turning-point in the poet's life; here begins a period of almost five years, which I consider as perhaps the most important in his existence as man and poet.

When he left Wilno in the autumn of 1824, he was the author of two volumes of poetry, with which Russia was not acquainted. He arrived as an exile, for having taken part in some students' political activity, which the authorities had, by the way, exaggerated beyond measure. No one knew him in Russia, and, of course, Mickiewicz knew no one there. Although his arrest and imprisonment could not create in him any very sympathetic dispositions toward Russia, he reached St. Petersburg permeated with Slavophil ideas which had been in vogue earlier at Warsaw and in Poland. They went into eclipse toward 1824 as a result of the changes produced in the order of ideas by Alexander I; but at the period of his entering St. Petersburg Mickiewicz had none of that malevolence against Russia which characterized him later.

Again, let us remember, in 1824 Mickiewicz was only a modest schoolmaster, whose heart was gnawed by his unhappy love, and the author, as I have said, of two volumes of poems, a young man who had never seen anything outside his province. But he was educated, and well educated, particularly in the field of classical philology. The sumptuous Russian capital, one of the grandest and most beautiful in Europe, could not but impress the modest provincial. But, as I have said, this provincial was a genius, and moreover an educated genius.

He therefore opened his avid and curious eyes to all he saw and his genius analyzed and graded with astonishing rapidity the things he saw and the men he met. It was work, and this work made him forget his political wounds; the exile, all the while maintaining his distant and peculiar attitude of romantic "pilgrim," is little by little transfigured into a tourist, intelligent, greedy for sensations, and easily adapting himself to new circumstances. Here, once again, "movement" and the consciousness of his inner strength, which had no cause to fear anything whatsoever it might be, betrayed themselves in him and separated him from his friends. The "navigator" continued to advance, to develop, without the least fear of compromising anything or losing anything of his "inner flame" and his attachment to his native land.

He arrived on November 9, 1824, the second day after the terrible flood in St. Petersburg. He had plenty of spare time to frequent and—this is striking—he is immediately admitted to the most intimate circles of the Decembrists, to attend their secret assemblies where the revolutionary "Cruel Songs" of Ryleev are sung. Ryleev (who knew Polish well) translated one of the poet's ballads, and at the time of his departure for Odessa Mickiewicz brought away letters from Bestuzhev and Ryleev, recommending him to their friends. In his letter to Tumanski, Ryleev said: "My dear Tumanski, love Mickiewicz and his friends Malewski and Jeżowski. More I need not write—from their sentiments and way of thinking, they are our friends; Mickiewicz is in addition the favorite poet of his nation."[3]

Odessa caused an interruption in his Russian relations; he arrived there after Pushkin's departure and plunged into worldly Polish society. Beautiful ladies could not refuse him their tenderness, divining with their feminine instinct an ardent temperament under the Lithuanian mask of a cold and timid continence. He polishes his worldly education, his French; he writes erotic sonnets, full of elegance and suavity which he unites with an art that is peculiar to him alone and characterizes him again in *Pan*

[3] Tumanski—Russian poet.

Tadeusz. He "Petrarchizes" in his poetry and "Decameronizes" in the alcoves and the boudoirs. In short, his worldly and Don-Juanly education is accomplished. An excursion in the company of some Polish aristocrats over the charming strands of the Tauride (much more beautiful than the French and Italian Riviera) enriches his artist's palette; he composes his *Crimean Sonnets*, a marvel of poetic art which, incidentally, is the first work to make him known in Russia.

In December of 1825, Mickiewicz reached Moscow. In the first months of his long stay in that city, he saw no one other than his Polish companions in exile. But by the spring of 1826, two Russian officers, Colonel Pokhvisnev and Staff-Officer Poznanski, arrived from Poland and let the brothers Polevoy know about the personality of Mickiewicz. Poznanski read them some of his translations of the poems. His enthusiasm induced Nicholas Polevoy to go in search of Mickiewicz, and "after a few meetings," affirms X. Polevoy, "Mickiewicz became the intimate friend of our house." Once installed among them, he began little by little to get to know Moscow. And there again the extraordinary attraction of his person made him rapidly the object of universal interest, the "lion" of the literary evenings of Moscow. Finally Pushkin arrived at Moscow from his enforced seclusion in the country—it is well known with what ovations his entry into Moscow was acclaimed—and expressed an "irresistible" desire to make the poet's acquaintance.

This is what Sobolevski, the "Demon" (a name given him by Prince Vyazemski), wrote to Mickiewicz on a bit of paper during a literary evening at the Polevoys': "Do not forget to come, *kochany Adamie* ["dear Adam," in the vocative in Polish], I have reported your arrival to M. Pushkin, the gout will return to his head if you do not come." And Mickiewicz, in reply: "The plague and the famine on you, dear Demon! may the good Lord make you thin—I shall come, but I shall be missing a dinner with a charming lady."[4] A proof of good, gay, natural, human relations.

Princess Volkonskaya finally invites him to her salons where, surrounded by the finest of Muscovite society, Mickiewicz charms his hearers by improvisations the power and beauty of which make the heart pound and stop the breath. How many portraits the Russians have made of the poet-improviser! Down to the second half of the last century, that image of Mickiewicz, improvising before his friends, kept on seducing Russian imaginations; the great Russian painter, founder of the *Peredvizhniki,* Myasoedov, composed an admirable canvas, representing Mickiewicz at the moment of improvising in the salon of Princess Zeneida Volkonskaya. On this picture we see, beside the Princess herself and some beautiful ladies, Prince Vyazemski, Pushkin, Khomyakov, Pogodin, Venevitinov, Chaadaev, and many others.

The Princess' salon was the first in Moscow; this "queen of the muses and of beauty," as Pushkin said, attracted to her home the "Apollonian games." Mickiewicz soon became her friend, and this friendship by which he was distinguished was a stunning proof of success. He took part in picnics on horseback with Rozhalin, Polevoy, and Sobolevski in the suburbs of Moscow, he went with Pushkin and Sobolevski to see the haughty but hospitable Maecenas, "the descendant of Aristippes," Prince Yussupov, in his splendid *podmoskovnaya*—his estate near Moscow, Arkhangelskoye, where he visited the Prince's admirable library. He went for long sojourns in Prince Vyazemski's country, and used the agreeable leisure afforded him by the elegant hospitality of the proprietor of Ostafyevo to write poems.

And the women! Princess Vyazemskaya wrote on April 3, 1827: "Here is the coffee in question; be good enough to taste it,

[4] These two notes are written in French. (See W. Lednicki, *Przyjaciele Moskale,* Kraków, 1935, pp. 168-170. J. Sobolevski, a Russian, a friend of Pushkin, a very popular personality in the Russian élite of that time.)

and if it suits you it will be a great pleasure for me to send you more. As for the coffee-pot, it has been impossible for me to obtain the kind that I wished, for it has to be ordered; let me take care of that after the holidays. As I am by no means sufficiently disinterested not to exact some acknowledgement, I warn you in advance that, from time to time, I shall demand at the moment of your breakfast a light remembrance for her whose sterile votive offerings would have wished to be much less modest than that of contributing to the amelioration of your coffee; if they could be heeded, you would learn that, deprived of all egoism, all *mine* would have been for your happy return to your hearth. Accept the assurance of the sincere esteem in which I hold you."

And Princess Volkonskaya once wrote: "I beg of you, dear Mr. Mickiewicz, come to dinner tomorrow, unless you be among your compatriots, on Easter Day, for I yield you up only to them. We are strangers in the earth, we are all from the same country, and we shall celebrate Easter together as *brothers* and as fellow earth-dwellers."[5]

And all this took place in a society which at this moment possessed intellectual resources of extraordinary richness, at a moment when an amiable Muse had assembled on the fields of Russia a magnificent cluster of poets. The society in which it happened was quite some distance from all Polonophilia! On the contrary, at this very period between 1823 and 1826 all Russia was hostile to Poland in the highest degree; many Decembrists were brought to their act of revolt and certain ones among them even meditated regicide, under the sway of that hatred: they sought a way to destroy the plans of Alexander I concerning Poland and its border-regions. Scarcely one or two years had elapsed since Pushkin had written his anti-Polish poetry, addressed to Count Olizar! This vogue in Society, and this "crush" on Mickiewicz,

[5] See *Ibid., op. cit.,* p. 152. (Conf. *Psalm* 119:19.)

were attached to whom? To a modest Polish schoolmaster who
had suddenly found himself in the highest Russian society! These
facts are really compelling.

Let us hasten to say that in all this success there was none of
the stupid sort of pleasure with which at times Russians, as well
as Poles, receive every foreigner. Pushkin—that mordant critic,
that spirit who always knew how to choose an artist and intellectual with extraordinary precision, was by no means prone to bow
down reverently before foreigners—it is sufficient to recall his
bitter epistle to Prince Vyazemski on the occasion of the receptions given to the French writer Ancelot in St. Petersburg. Now,
that same Pushkin makes way for Mickiewicz and yields him the
precedence!

Aside from worldly triumphs, Mickiewicz had others. His
literary authority grew daily. Pushkin reads him his works, asking his advice and counsel; the Russian poet begins the translation of *Konrad Wallenrod;* Prince Vyazemski, Boratynski, Kozlov, Pogodin, Delvig, Venevitinov, Kireevski, Sobolevski—all the
best, in other words, that Russia could boast in literature—press
around him, coax him, address poems to him, translate his works.

In 1826, at the end of the year, he published his sonnets in
Moscow. In 1827, Prince Vyazemski translated them and published a long preface in the *Telegraph of Moscow,* and that preface
was from beginning to end an enthusiastic eulogy of Mickiewicz's
sonnets. He makes mention of the "oriental picturesque," of the
"luxuriant richness of his imagination," of the "expressive force
of this poetry," of the "veracious freshness of his poetic talk,"
of "the mastery and the art with which the poet has been able to
condense into the narrow frames of the sonnet, landscapes whose
grandeur is often gigantic."

Other translations appeared; the reviews published book-reports on *Konrad Wallenrod,* on the *Sonnets.* The *Telegraph* created a department of Polish literature, beginning it with the publication of an article by Dmochowski on Polish literature, borrowed from the *Bibljoteka Polska* and translated into Russian. A preface preceded that publication, in which the editor (Polevoy) complained of the ignorance in Russia of Polish literature, which is, as he says, "of such great importance," and belongs to a people that took notice "of enlightenment and civilization long before us"! A eulogy of Mickiewicz, ranged alongside of Byron and Goethe and opposed to "French writers of no importance," ends this notice. In 1829, Kireevski wrote his article on Russian literature, in which he paid the greatest homage to Mickiewicz. In 1829 also appeared the fine translation of the *Crimean Sonnets* by Ivan Kozlov.

That is not all. Mickiewicz, aided by his Russian friends, formed the project of organizing a magazine which should be dedicated to making Russian literature better known in Poland and Polish literature in Russia. That project was not realized, because of the malevolence with which Mickiewicz's request on the subject was received in St. Petersburg by the Russian bureaucracy. Finally his friends are seized with the idea of creating at the University of Moscow a chair of Polish literature, whose first incumbent would be Mickiewicz!

But Mickiewicz left Russia; Pushkin and many others took steps to help their friend obtain the right to cross the Russian frontier. The correspondence of von Fock, chief of the Third Section in the Ministry of the Interior, with General Benkendorf, demonstrates that even in those circles Mickiewicz was considered with a sort of sympathy and benevolence. On his departure his friends organized a farewell banquet during which they offered him a cup of gilded silver, on which their names were engraved.

This cup contained a leaf with a beautiful poem by Ivan Kireevski, the subject of which was the friendship which the Muscovite friends entertained for the Polish poet. Speeches were made . . .

On May 15, 1829, Mickiewicz left Russia. However, the Russian reviews continued to speak about him up till 1834—hence, even after the Insurrection of 1830-31. In 1941, Lermontov translated—he too—one of the *Crimean Sonnets*, and he borrowed from the Polish poet several images that he introduced into his poem *The Novice*.

But let us look a little into Mickiewicz's work of this period and into his inner life.

Let us begin with the *Sonnets*. I shall not touch upon the *Odessan Sonnets*, the erotic sonnets, although they contain delightful details. Suffice it to say that they were written in the climate of Mickiewicz's love affair with Caroline Sobańska, a woman who, though depraved, possessed very great beauty and irresistible attraction. Pushkin had been mad about her and could not forget her for years afterward, although his love for her was never consummated; perhaps for this very reason he could not emancipate himself from that sharp memory. Nevertheless, his letters and his poems demonstrate that she had awakened in the Russian poet a nostalgia all the greater in that this time "the mad violence of his desires" had not brought him victory.

Mickiewicz was more fortunate.

However, it is the *Crimean Sonnets* that I should like to run through here. They are a wonder; in my opinion we have there some of the most beautiful pages in the whole century's European poetry. The richness and beauty of the poetic expression, always sudden and unforeseen, always takes us by surprise and makes us marvel at the audacity of thought and the moral courage which produce the especial splendor of this collection.

Let us take the first sonnet,

The Akkerman Steppes

I sail a sea where waters never ran,
My wagon like a boat with plunge and dip
Cuts waves of green and floods of flowers, to slip
Past rosy isles of wild cornelian.
Night falls. No road or hill—My eyes must scan
The stars by which the sailor guides his ship.
That distant cloud, the Dniester's gleaming strip;
That star, the morning lamp of Akkerman.
We halt, flow still! I hear the cranes that pass,
So high the falcon cannot see. I hear
The butterfly that rocks upon the grass,
The slipp'ry-breasted serpent where it crawls.
So still it is, a voice might reach my ear
From Lithuania—onward! No one calls . . .[6]

What splendor . . . We have here, therefore, as always, movement—and then, that marvelous intensity of remembrance, of
nostalgia . . . It anchors him to the soil of Lithuania.

The poet continues his way. The sonnet, *The Voyage*, once
again carries us away by its movement . . .

Sonnet V, *The View on the Mountains from the Steppes of
Kozlov*, makes the stars march; it is the image that Lermontov
will love so; in fact, what more beautiful than a caravan of
stars . . .

Did Allah raise a wall of frozen foam?
Or for his angel hosts a cloud throne rear?
Or did the Divs[7] lift half a hemisphere
To keep the caravan of stars at home? . . .

The seventh, *Bakhchisaray in the Night*, sets the moon in
motion:

. . . The king of night is hastening home to lie
Beside his love. The harem of the sky
Glows soft with stars, eternal lamps that play

[6] See "The Slavonic Review," Vol. XVI, pp. 497-498.
[7] Divs—malignant genii in Persian mythology.

> Upon a cloud that swanlike on the bay
> Of heaven sleeps, bright-stained with sunset dye;
> Here shadows fall from minarets, and dark
> A cypress stands . . .[8]

The eighth gives still another charming variant of the movement of the stars, which are traces left in the sky by a look of nostalgia . . .

> Northward toward Poland stars in thousands glow;
> Why in that region are such myriads massed?
> Did your bright glance, before it died at last,
> Light sparks along the path it loved to go?[9]

The most beautiful, however, is the fifteenth . . . *The Road Along the Precipice of Chufut Kale:*

MIRZA AND PILGRIM

MIRZA

> Drop bridle, turn your face aside and pray!
> For in your horse's feet your brains must lie.
> Wise creature! Watch him measure with his eyes
> The chasm, and, kneeling, cling where best he may
> And hang there! Do not look! As soon essay
> To search the well of Cairo and descry
> Its bottom. You have not been winged to fly,
> So do not point! Keep even your thoughts away!
> For thoughts, like small crafts' anchors that are cast
> In plumbless depths, will fall but never reach
> The ocean's floor, and drag their ships to death.

PILGRIM

> I have beheld it, Mirza—seen the vast
> Abyss, and what I saw my dying breath
> Shall tell. For it there is no living speech . . .[10]

While in Russia, Mickiewicz had written a series of poetic,

---

[8] See *Ibid., loc. cit.,* pp. 499-500.
[9] *Ibid.,* pp. 501-502.
[10] *Ibid.,* pp. 505-506.

Byronic works of great charm, among which *Konrad Wallenrod*, *Farys*, and *Szanfary* are perhaps the most beautiful.

Farys, like the tenth of the *Crimean Sonnets*, is nothing else than a fugue, it is the song of the mad course of the rider galloping on his horse—very like Szanfary, where it is the *camel* that gallops.

The same motifs, similar images, suggesting direction toward something, and always that passion for movement, that Heraclitean element, for running, floating, flight; the same observations will appear later on in *Pan Tadeusz*, in the poetic painting of the flight of the clouds, of the sound of the horn through the woods, of the slow but irrevocable pace of the sun, of the flight of eagles and vultures in the skies, of the flow of waters into the river . . .

In the *Improvisation* it will be the flight of ideas, of thoughts climbing to the skies like eagles. It will be the poet's arms stretching toward the sky to grasp the stars . . . Leaving Odessa in 1825, he writes, "Let us fly away; God be praised, we still have wings to return. Let us fly, and let us never from now on lower our flight . . ."

Finally, in one of his last poems, he says:

> Rocks must remain erect and menacing,
> Clouds must carry the waters,
> Lightning must thunder and disappear,
> And I—must always flow on and on.

The citations could become innumerable. The other theme, that of inner strength and courage, is developed with the same precision and insistence. Let us take the poem, *Szanfary:*

The Arab seeks his friends among the wolf and the leopard (a friendship which Lermontov will take up again in *The Novice*), that people which knows only one law for offense—vengeance.

I am first to leap at the eyes of the enemy, but when it comes to sharing the booty, I stay apart—I act like the man of honor; none can equal the greatness of my spirit, and he who feels his superiority is worthy of staying all alone with it . . .

His poem, *Konrad Wallenrod,* is nothing else than a hymn to power, to superior and solitary moral force—(the theme of de Vigny's *Moses*). There we have the beautiful metaphor which summons up the falcon, who flies away in the skies, for the skies are his only element. There is another admission there, too: Woe to women . . .

> . . . Woeful it is to all women, he cried, to love madmen, whose vision
> Ever is fain to wander beyond the bounds of the village;
> Madmen, whose thoughts like the smoke from the fires will go drifting and flying;
> Men for whose hearts the contentment of home is not wholly sufficient.
> Such hearts, Aldona, are hives built too large to be filled with their honey;
> So they have also become a refuge and dwelling for lizards . . .[11]

But in *Konrad Wallenrod* appeared still another theme: the theme of the fatherland. This poem is the history of a man who had sacrificed all for the fatherland—his youth, his love, his personal happiness, and even his honor. It is by treason that he destroys his country's enemies, by fraud and lying. He will, then, pursue even moral peril—the annihilation of the soul for his country!

The poet comes to some sorrowful reflections:

> I know you *wajdelotas:* every strain
> Howls and forebodes mischance, like dogs by night;
> In songs of blood and fire is your delight,
> Leaving to us the glory and the pain.
> About the cradled child your traitorous song
> Twines like a reptile, cruelly to inflame
> His soul with poison—stupid thirst for fame,
> And hopeless dreams that for his country long.
> It dogs the footsteps of his youthful years;
> It ofttimes 'mid the feasting throng appears

[11] *Konrad Wallenrod and other writings of Adam Mickiewicz,* translated by J. Parish, D. P. Radin, G. R. Noyes, University of California Press, 1925, p. 52.

Like the avenging ghost of a slain foe,
To pour out blood where joyous wine should flow.
I unto songs too much have given ear—
I know thee, thou old traitor! Thou hast won!
War—that the poets glory in—is near;
Bring wine! The day has come! All shall be done.[12]

It is difficult to refrain from confronting this with a biographical text. It demands, however, an explanation. Mickiewicz was
always profoundly preoccupied with himself. Also, from his
youth, at Wilno and then in Russia, and thus at a particularly
happy period in his literary career and thanks to the atmosphere
of enthusiastic good will which his Russian friends created around
him at Moscow, he was customarily the object of the preoccupation of others. His Polish friends never stopped observing him
and guiding him with their counsels, desirous of making a national hero out of him: they strive to protect him against any
foreign influence that might be able to contaminate the integrity
of his national spirit. They preach intellectual asceticism and
also asceticism in the strict sense. At Moscow, Mickiewicz, young,
potent, happy, sure of his strength, gracefully defended himself
against these interventions: at that moment he was ideally typical
of the solidly free man whose freedom of action was guaranteed
by his knowledge of his own inexhaustible spiritual resources.

In 1827 he replied to the remonstrances of one of his friends
in this way: ". . . I have acquaintances here, and many persons
have attested their sympathy for me, several of them their friendship; so I should be happy to be able some day to pay them with
my recognition. 'Cursed be those who pay nothing!' . . . let me
quote the *Forefathers*. I frequent the salons, but I don't figure there
very much; it is not the desire that I lack, but the ability. If I could
dance well, or even middling well, I would be glad; if I could
play on the flute or the guitar, my joy would be still greater; if I

[12] *Ibid.*, p. 56 *(Wajdelota*—singer, bard).

could sing, that would mean even more to me; although I know
how to make compliments, I shall not be amiss in perfecting myself in this art. For in truth, let me tell you, one can dance, play,
sing, and be genteel without thereby being a parasite, without
ceasing to be useful to others, and that is the greatest recompense
for our efforts in all these little matters. Here is something else
just as true; if I were to return to our Lithuania, I should let
myself go like an unwound spring, and even if no one came to
bore me I should find some unhappiness to torment me myself.
I have begun to be gay among the Basilian Fathers, and tranquil
and wise in Moscow . . ."

It is a beautiful text! It brings into view a powerful man, master of his heart and his existence, a man essentially free . . . That
reminds one of a letter from de Vigny to E. Deschamps:

". . . Tell Jules de Rességuier to pardon his son at Vienna
for having yellow gloves and dancing, because *he* danced and had
gloves . . . when he was nineteen, too, and because at that you
and I danced . . . and because we are not of those whom La
Bruyère speaks of, who suppress from the story of Socrates the
fact that he danced—which was the case, and does not hamper the
Phaedo, which is not too bad . . ."[13]

Yes—Socrates and Mickiewicz had a right to dance!

Here, however, we reach another problem, that of the leader,
of the master and the usurper, a problem which likewise occupied
Pushkin and, after him, Dostoevski. We already have the following text in the *Forefathers*, in the part written in Kowno:

> There is but one spark in a man,
> Once only, in youth, does it flare up;
> Sometimes the breath of Minerva will kindle it:
> Then does the sage arise
> Over the dark tribes, and Plato's star

[13] *Ibid.*, letter to E. Deschamps on June 28, 1837. The letter of Mickiewicz is of
January 5, 1827, Moscow, to Jan Czeczott.

Shines through long ages.
If it is pride that lights that spark in the torch,
Then will a hero begin thundering, will clamber to the purple
By great virtues and by great crimes,
And make out of the shepherd's staff the scepter of the world,
Or pull down old thrones with a nod.

He develops it in the third part:

And thou dost glow like clouds that wander high
Yet know not what they do nor where they fly
Men! One of you, in chains, by thought alone
Can overturn or raise the loftiest throne.

And, speaking to God:

But I am a creator born;
My power hath come to me
From where Thine came to Thee:
Thou didst not seek it and Thou dost not fear
That of that power Thou shalt e'er be shorn.
So I, who have my strength, from Thee or otherwhere,
My swift and binding eye,
Fear not . . .[14]

These traits and that dynamism were connected with the poet's faith, a faith that was *par excellence* romantic, in the superiority of the irrational in human life and in the human personality. Already, in the *Ode to Youth,* the poet had expressed this faith with great emphasis, opposing those who are "wise by fury, wise by exaltation," those who possess the "wisdom of the heart," to those who represent the rationalism of the "eye-glass of the savant." Later on, in his *Forefathers' Eve,* he presented in his *Improvisation* a wonderful revelation of poetic inspiration, a unique page in literature, which provoked the admiration of Sarrazin: "He gives us the only image of inspiration that I know."

In 1833 he published in Paris an article entitled "On Reason-

[14] *Forefathers' Eve,* etc., by A. Mickiewicz, translated by D. P. Radin, published by the school of Slavonic studies in the University of London, p. 26.

able and Exalted Men." Here we have the same division; he alleges that, in times when "sick and sophisticated minds allow themselves to discuss everything, human wisdom, expelled from books and conversation, lives in the last refuge, in the hearts of men who feel" . . .

He also demonstrated in the same article how, at the time of the first partition of Poland, there were men who in the name of reason advised yielding one part of the country in order to preserve the rest . . . We have seen today, on the example of other countries, whither such calculations may lead . . .

This theory, this doctrine, or this belief was already developed in him in his youth when he had in his hands a little book, a kind of time-bomb, dynamic and explosive: *The Book of the Spirit,* by Helvetius. "These are the strong passions," Mickiewicz read in the chapter on the passions, "which, more enlightened than common sense, can alone teach us to distinguish the extraordinary from the impossible, which sensible people almost always confuse; because, not being animated by any strong passions those sensible people are never more than mediocre men . . . Before success, if great geniuses in every line are almost always treated as fools by sensible people, it is because these latter, incapable of anything great, cannot even suspect the existence of the means which great men use to achieve greatly. That is why those great men must always excite laughter until they excite admiration . . . The passions are, in fact, the little heavenly something which enlivens the moral world; it is to passions that sciences and arts owe their discoveries, and the soul its elevation."

Helvetius had stirred in Mickiewicz's soul forces and elements that already existed there. From the beginning of his poetical career he appeared as an essentially romantic poet, inspired in mind and soul. And in Russia he aroused admiration and astonishment as an inspired improviser. His name was on everyone's lips. Pushkin never spoke of him without the epithet, *"svyshev-dokhnovenny,"* "inspired from on high"—*"i svysoka vziral na zhizn."* All his Russian friends—poets like Boratynski, Prince Vyazemski, Kireevski; writers and historians like Aksakov, Pogodin, Shevyrev, even the famous philosopher Solovyev, stressed this same trait.

The same is true later in France: George Sand, Michelet, Guizot, Hugo, Sarrazin, Schuré, even Renan, and outside France Cavour and Mazzini—they all emphasized the inspiration and fervor of his metaphysical and heroic poetry, which at the same time possessed such realistic plasticity. The poet himself was soon aware of this quality, because very early the divinity of inspiration approached and touched his heart, as the seraph in Pushkin's *Prophet* (Mickiewicz's favorite among the works of the Russian poet) "touched his mind and his tongue." And Mickiewicz, who started in youth as a prophet of the future, later became, at the Collège de France in Paris in 1840, to use the words of Ballanche, "the prophet of the past."

Truth to tell, the poet possessed a wonderful power of suggestion—I call it his genius of personality—of which his gift of improvisation was the most essential and genuine manifestation. It is with this personal prestige that he seduced and captured the hearts and imaginations of his Russian friends in St. Petersburg and Moscow. But he also possessed great self-confidence and awareness of his dominating strength. He had nothing of the Usurper, of the Pretender, about him. He was a lord, and knew it.

And it is just this, I think, that explains the mystery of the immense impression produced by that personality on Pushkin. The personality and work of Mickiewicz operated with powerful suggestion on the Russian poet's imagination—that is incontestable. Probably his suggestion became and continued to act in him as a creative force, at least as a stimulant; moreover, this

Mickiewiczian element seems to act on Pushkin at moments when the poet faces problems that are particularly grave for him.

Such is that of the connection between "inspiration" and "work" in art, admirably presented in the "little tragedy" *Mozart and Salieri*, as well as in several lyric poems which form a kind of "Poetic Art" of Pushkin. We know that this counter-position, attached to what the Russians call "the psychology of the artistic creation," assumes in Pushkin an even greater scope and a more general sense. The chief problem which absorbed Pushkin was that of human personality: the irrational and the rational in the life of the individual. Another ramification, attached to the same trunk, is the antinomy of the two kinds of powers; Pushkin always shows them to us in contrast. One is immanent, innate, it cannot be conquered, it is "natural," over-flowing, firmly generous; it knows neither crime nor violence; its manifestations are spontaneous, it is effortlessly revealed, it is not organized, it *is;* and it assures to the individual who possesses it a special ascendant, that of incontestable authority. Decidedly, we have in Pushkin's "symbolic figures" an analysis of the psychology of the leader, a representation of the phenomenon of primacy.

To the recognized leader is opposed the usurper. The latter accumulates his efforts, prepares his power, is careful to watch himself and control himself; imagination replaces reality for the individual who, in spite of all his doubts, believes himself master of himself and of life; the knowledge of his power is enough, he fears the decisive test, he pushes it away, continually mobilizing his means for the struggle for power. At the moment of the trial the fancied leader is transformed into usurper.

That is one of the aspects of *Mozart and Salieri*, of the *Shot*, of the *Covetous Knight*. In *Boris Godunov* the characteristics are so fine and delicately shaded that one would like to ask which of the two is the real imposter, Boris or Dimitri. In *Poltava* we have a glorification of the "divine might" of Peter the Great; in *Eugene Onegin,* the contrast between the freedom and richness of the moral resources of Tatiana and the narrow egoism of Eugene; the same situation had already been outlined before in the *Gypsies.*

What connection has Mickiewicz with all this? None, directly, but Mickiewicz the improviser and Mickiewicz the one who "wants to dance" became for the Russian poet a kind of experience, an object of analysis, an example reinforcing and confirming the opinions that self-observation had brought him. This hypothesis becomes convincing when we see the Polish poet in Russian characterizations which I have already mentioned. For the most part, as in Pushkin's poetry dedicated to Mickiewicz (and in other works where the poet is mentioned), Mickiewicz appears adorned with epithets which are always and everywhere the same, and which create, if one may say so, a "track in stone," they are so invariable: he is, unalterably, the "prophetic poet," "poet inspired of the sky," looking at life from "heights," the prophet "to whom one listens greedily."

Mickiewicz's improvisations, it cannot be contested, made an immense impression on his hearers. Russians went into ecstasies as well as Poles. Prince Vyazemski affirms that ". . . all of us listened to him with shivers and tears"; Boratynski exclaims (kneeling), ". . . Oh, my God, why isn't he Russian!"; Pushkin: ". . . What genius, what sacred fire, what am I beside him?" We may suppose that these impressions did not pass without leaving traces in Pushkin's poetry. The *Egyptian Nights* try to analyze the phenomenon of improvisation, of the "creative transfiguration" of the improvisor at the moment of "the approach of the god of inspiration." The problem of the co-operation or the correlation of inspiration and labor, posed in *Mozart and Salieri,* is certainly not alien to the impressions left on Pushkin by the improvisations of Mickiewicz; the fact of having put this problem is in itself already significant. The poem written in 1834 and dedicated to Mickiewicz, is eloquent proof of it: Pushkin there makes concrete mention of Mickiewicz's improvisations. It is also a precious proof of the latter's singular prestige in Pushkin's eyes.

On the other hand, in this poem Pushkin adds some other traits: "pacific," "benevolent," "he frequented our chats," and "we shared with him our glasses and our songs." Prince Vyazemski underscores his ease, freedom, and suppleness: ". . . He was at home everywhere: in the scholar's study, in the salon of an educated lady, as well as at a table of merry companions . . ." Pushkin knew nothing finer in man than this very freedom and suppleness of soul, he repressed stiffness of every sort in life as well as in poetry. "Read Shakespeare . . ." he had said, "he never fears to compromise his character, and makes him speak with all the abandon of life, for he is sure, in due time and place, of making him find the language of his nature . . ."

Mickiewicz, the one we see in the letter about "the dance," "the flute," and "the guitar," was just the one to attract Pushkin's sympathy and curiosity. One is, then, permitted to believe that this friendship provided Pushkin with psychological observations and experiences that helped him in dealing with problems which had been at the back of certain of his poetic works. Let us add that the epithet, "inspired from the sky," is one that Pushkin had preferred only to his favorite national hero, Peter the Great—and to Mickiewicz.

We therefore have the right to claim that the *Egyptian Nights* are not only work of Pushkin's reflecting Mickiewicz the improviser. Perhaps he is clandestinely present even where nothing seems to signalize his presence. Pushkin, a poet whose soul was open to all that was essentially human, could not help having a deep admiration for the Mickiewicz of Moscow: with the beautiful generosity of which the Mozart of his "little tragedy" will always remain a highly poetic symbol, he bowed before his Polish friend, without fearing to "compromise himself."

Here we come to a very important problem in literary history —both Russian and Polish. Mickiewicz, although "happy" in Moscow, wished with all his might to leave Russia; "movement," the Heraclitean predominating element in this post, left him no peace. After many attempts Mickiewicz finally obtained authorization from the Russian Government to leave the Empire and go away abroad. He embarked at Kronstadt on the fifteenth of May, 1829, and went to Germany. After visiting Bohemia, where he met Czech men of letters; a stay in Berlin, where he attended the courses of Hegel; and a visit to Goethe at Weimar, Mickiewicz crossed Switzerland and established himself in Rome.

It was in Rome that he went through a religious crisis, which was, incidentally, only a sequence of the moral development which could already be seen in him in Russia.

At Rome he met many old friends from Russia—Princess Volkonskaya, Shevyrev, then his very close friend Sobolevski, many Polish refugees. It was there that he fell in love with a young aristocratic Polish girl, Mlle. Ankwicz, daughter of Count Ankwicz, and this love is closely related to his religious crises . . . A new fount of poetry gushed up in him.

But here the Insurrection of 1830 burst out, provoked by many political causes. Poland rose against Russia not only because of the abuses of the Russian Government in violation of the Constitution established in the Kingdom of Poland by the Congress of Vienna in 1815, not only for the cause of independence, but for the Polish "Marches," for those lands of Lithuania and Ruthenia over which the Poles had tried in vain to extend the Constitution of the Kingdom and which they now hoped to be able to detach

from Russia and join to an independent Poland. The Insurrection
was transformed into a real war, and the Polish chances were so
good that there were moments when the Russian Empire tottered;
Nicholas I admitted it in his private letters; and Pushkin, trem-
bling with fear for his country and with rage against Poland
and against Europe because of Europe's sympathy for Poland,
manifested in its newspapers, magazines, poems, parliaments—
everywhere, in France, England, in Germany, in Spain, in Italy—
compared this "terrible" year of 1831 to the year 1812![15]

Pushkin's letters in this period are full of fierce animosity
toward Poland, but in these letters also there often appears the
name of Mickiewicz, the "one Pole" who interested him and
whose fate is not foreign to him. That is a capitally important
point. When, after long combats with changing chance, Russia
finally, in consequence of errors committed by the Polish high
command and of her own immense military resources, emerged
victorious and Warsaw was taken, Pushkin wrote his celebrated
anti-Polish odes, representing a duel of the Russian poet against
European opinion; it is a song of triumph, full of the spirit of
satisfaction, profoundly nationalistic and imperialistic, representing a deep rupture of the poet—so European on the one hand,
so highly cultivated and civilized—with the West. It was unworthy of the great poet; he revolted many of his Russian friends,
who thought and felt differently; it is a publication marking a
sharp moral and political crisis in the Russian poet's soul.

In the Polish Insurrection, that Russo-Polish War of 1830-31,
Poland had mobilized great spiritual forces and shown them
clearly to the whole world. Public opinion throughout Europe
manifested sympathy for the Polish cause on one hand; on the
other, there was the ferociously and vulgarly imperialistic attitude of the majority of Russians, opposed by only a very small

---

[15] See Venceslas Lednicki, *Pouchkine et la Pologne*, ed. E. Leroux, Paris, 1928.

minority of the élite. As a result, that war, and especially its *finale* with the Russian persecutions in Poland after the capture of Warsaw, mark a new period in the development of Russia's moral and cultural relations with Europe. It separated Russia from Europe for a long time. This time, the rampart of European civilization, the *antemurale Christianitatis,* was the tomb that was Poland. Geographically nearer to Europe, Russia had become morally separated from it.

But what was Mickiewicz doing at that moment, at this fateful historic hour? He was in Rome. He had no faith in the Insurrection, and it was contrary to his feelings. But he felt that his duty was to take to the front. This internal debate took time; and here came about one of the most beautiful of human stories —a Russo-Polish story.

At the moment when Mickiewicz was passing through this inner crisis, provoked by the Insurrection, one of his great friends from Moscow, whom you already know—Sergey Sobolevski— had arrived in Rome. As Sobolevski had the good habit of writing a diary, it is his diary that posts us on these events. Arrived at Rome, he found Mickiewicz in a state of painful perplexity. What happened? Sobolevski helped him to regulate his financial affairs, and it was the same Sobolevski and other Russians, Prince Golitzin and his wife (originally Polish, it is true), who accompanied Mickiewicz during his journey from Italy to Poland, undertaken by the poet in order to rejoin the Polish armies! Sobolevski wrote in his diary, "so I have gotten my country one more enemy"! We must admit that there we have a beautiful example of the nobility of the human heart.

But the Russians would certainly have done this for no one else. It was Mickiewicz's singular attraction which partly explains this phenomenon. The proof of the justice of this opinion is furnished us by Pushkin; quivering with rage and hatred against

Poland, at the very moment when he was composing his famous anti-Polish odes and writing his "Polonophagous" letters—sinister letters—to Mme. Khitrovo, that same Pushkin confessed: ". . . Only a convulsive and general uprising could offer the Poles any chance whatever. The young people are right, therefore, but the moderates will carry the day and we shall have the Government (District, Province) of Warsaw, which ought to have been done thirty-three years ago. *Among all the Poles I am interested only in Mickiewicz. He was in Rome at the start of the revolt. I fear that he has come to Warsaw to attend the last crises of his country.*"

Mickiewicz did not, however, join the Polish armies. He went to Posnania, where he lingered over new meetings and friendships. By the time he was ready to cross the German frontier, everything in Poland was already over. He went through Dresden to Paris. It was at Dresden that he wrote the *Third Part* of his *Forefathers' Eve* and finished the *Fragment of the Third Part*— a series of historiosophic and satirical poems on Russia which he added to the *Third Part* of the *Forefathers' Eve* with a poetic dedication at the head—the famous poem *To Muscovite Friends.* He had, possibly, begun his Russian "Satires" while still in Russia.

For the present it is just these "Satires" which interest me. These "Satires," with the poem *To Muscovite Friends* (like a large part of the drama, the *Third Part,* of the *Forefathers' Eve*) represent a mordant historical critique on Russia and especially on St. Petersburg, which under his pen becomes the symbol of artifice, of Russian cultural subterfuge, the symbol on the other hand of political usurpation, the city of abuses and of sins— "the modern Babylon," a capital made of tears and suffering. St. Petersburg appeared finally, in these marvelous poems of Mickiewicz, as a fantastic and ephemeral city. Independently of Gogol and before Pushkin, before Dostoevski, Mickiewicz created an image of St. Petersburg which combines its prosaic and the fantastical qualities. In his "Satires," in spite of the marvelous picture of the "vision of enchantment," he gives a most realistic and eloquent picture of the prosaic vulgarity of St. Petersburg. Then appears the vision of the disintegration of the "airy city," and the disappearance of the "vision of enchantment" suggests the idea about the ephemerality of St. Petersburg itself.

The very founding of that dream city on the Chukhonian mud and marshlands at the command of Peter the Great, and also the St. Petersburg climate, stimulated the poet's imagination to a romantic and ironic stylization of St. Petersburg and the St. Petersburg period in Russian history.

Mickiewicz succeeded in creating a special atmosphere, a climate, which even today gives the "Satires" a rare strength of suggestion. At times—given the great historical events which have come after the *Forefathers' Eve*—the Mickiewiczian "Satires" seem to be astonishing prophecies of perspicacity and historical intuition! Such, for example, the poem, *The Monument of Peter the Great.*

> Two youths stood deep in talk one rainy night,
> Beneath one cloak, hand closely clasped in hand:
> One was that pilgrim from a western land,
> An unknown victim of the Tsar's grim might;
> The other was the famous Russian bard,
> Beloved through all the northland for his song.
> Although their friendship had not flourished long,
> They were united by a great regard.
> Their souls soared over earthly trials and woe,
> Like twin crags jutting from an Alpine peak:
> Though separated by a roaring creek,
> They scarcely hear the tumult of their foe,
> While each to each their towering summits lean.
> The pilgrim mused on Peter's awesome mien,

While gently thus the bard explained the scene:
"To the first Tsar, of mighty fame and deed,
Great Catherine here a monument decreed.[16]
So this gigantic image of the Tsar
Bestrides the bronze back of a mettled steed
And waits for space where he may ride afar.
But Peter could not rest on Russian ground;
His native land was small for such as he:
His pedestal they sought beyond the sea.
From Finland's shore they tore this granite mound,
Which, when the Empress speaks and waves her hand,
Floats o'er the sea and runs across the land,
And falls into its place at her command.[17]
The mound is ready now, and forth he goes,
A Roman-toga'd Tsar who rules by blows:
His charger gallops up the granite steep,
Rearing its body for a mighty leap.
        "In ancient Rome there shines in different guise
Marcus Aurelius, the people's pride,
Who first made his name famous far and wide
By banishing the nation's crafty spies.
When he has shamed the plunderers at home
And on the Rhine and the Pactolus' banks
Has overwhelmed the fierce invaders' ranks,
Homeward he turns his steps to peaceful Rome.
Fair, calm, and noble is that brow, aglow
With thoughts of all his people's happiness.
He lifts with dignity his hand, as though
His thronging subjects he were now to bless;
And on his reins he drops his other hand,
To check the zeal that in his charger burns.
You guess that in his path the masses stand
And shout: 'Our father, Cæsar, now returns!'
Amid the throng he fain would slowly ride,
With a paternal glance on every side.
The steed's mane stands erect, its fierce eye rolls;
But knowing that it bears a well-loved guest,

---

[16] The monument to Peter bears the inscription, *Petro primo Catharina secunda.*
[17] This verse is translated from a Russian poet whose name I have forgotten.
[Note of the poet. From Ruban, an obscure poet and journalist.—Tr.]

The father of unnumbered Roman souls,
It checks its ardent spirit's fiery zest:
The children can approach their father's knee.
Along the road the steed strides evenly—
It will advance to immortality.[18]
    "His charger's reins Tsar Peter has released;
He has been flying down the road, perchance,
And here the precipice checks his advance.
With hoofs aloft now stands the maddened beast,
Champing its bit unchecked, with slackened rein:
You guess that it will fall and be destroyed.
Thus it has galloped long, with tossing mane,
Like a cascade, leaping into the void,
That, fettered by the frost, hangs dizzily.
But soon will shine the sun of liberty,
And from the west a wind will warm this land.—
Will the cascade of tyranny then stand?"[19]

Let us add, finally, that the poem *To Muscovite Friends* contained very clear allusions to Pushkin, to his anti-Polish odes, and to his political attitude during the Russo-Polish War. As a whole, the *Third Part*, on this Russo-Polish plane, is a powerful protest made by the western spirit of freedom against the Muscovite spirit of despotism and oppression.

When these works of Mickiewicz were published, Pushkin received them through the intervention of the same good Sobolevski who had brought them to Russia, clandestinely of course, returning from his trip abroad. What happened? Pushkin now wrote one of his most beautiful and greatest masterpieces, the *Bronze Horseman.*

It would be useless to recall what has so many times been brought out, that the *Bronze Horseman* gives the impression of a dualistic work. It is a panegyric on Peter the Great, on St.

[18] The colossal equestrian statue of Peter, designed by Falconet, and the statue of Marcus Aurelius that now stands in Rome on the Capitoline Hill are here faithfully described. [Note of the poet.]
[19] See "The Slavonic Review," Vol. XV, pp. 295-296.

Petersburg, on the reformation of the Russian Empire and of the State; on the other hand, it is a refutation of the Czar, a repudiation of the Reform, a protest against the invasive supremacy of the State. Besides presenting in the Prologue a series of images of St. Petersburg, as a city of glory with its splendors and its pathetic beauty, the poet evokes a representation of St. Petersburg which is somewhat of a contrast: he depicts the tragic essence and unusual traits of the mysterious and moving capital of the Emperors of Russia.

We know that Pushkin had read Mickiewicz's St. Petersburg "Satires" (*Fragment* of the *Forefathers' Eve*) immediately before beginning to write his *Bronze Horseman*. We know also that he copied certain passages in Mickiewicz's poems with his own hand and that in the first part of his poem as well as in notes added to the poem he engaged in courteous polemic with the Mickiewiczian description of St. Petersburg.

But apart from this direct, though veiled, polemic, sufficiently clear, however, for any reader who knows the *Forefathers' Eve*— the entire poem is a reply to Mickiewicz. It goes without saying that this element of polemics does not exhaust the poetic sense of this singularly rich and peculiarly symbolic work. But that element is present: it is a reply, and it is a beautiful reply. More, it is chivalrous. These qualities become only more estimable when this poem is compared with the anti-Polish odes and when one recalls the mordant allusions the Russian poet had found on his own score in the *Muscovite Friends*. The poem is a reply to the *Monument of Peter the Great* of Mickiewicz, it is also a defense of St. Petersburg and of Peter the Great. Such is the essence of what might be called its official content.

However, while defending himself against Mickiewicz, Pushkin underwent the suggestion of his criticism, and the disconcerting vision of St. Petersburg—city of tears and abuses—evoked by

Mickiewicz penetrated into the *Bronze Horseman*. It was this element that made the *Bronze Horseman* definitely dualistic, indecisive; the action of the Mickiewiczian "poison" on the body of Pushkin's poem caused morbid and macabre traits to appear through the polished and resplendent façade erected in the Prologue.

Following this dualism, the literary role of this poem was also double. On the one hand, as a glorification of St. Petersburg and Peter the Great, even as a defense, the *Bronze Horseman* ends a long series of panegyrics of the eighteenth and the beginning of the nineteenth centuries, which sing the splendors and beauties of the Russian capital as well as the prestige of its emperors. On the other hand, the element of disaggregation introduced into the poem by the reading of Mickiewicz, inaugurates in Russian letters (with the new "impressionists" of Gogol) a new attitude toward St. Petersburg. Certain authors turn away from the capital of Peter the Great and go to seek their inspiration elsewhere, in the provinces and at Moscow (Goncharov, Turgenev, Tolstoy, Bunin); others (Dostoevski, Nekrasov, Merezhkovski, Bely, Blok) do continue, it is true, to situate their works in the frame of St. Petersburg, but they are above all haunted by the extraordinary, fantastic side, by the city's tragic essence, evoked by Pushkin and Gogol. In the minds of these authors, and that is after the *Bronze Horseman*, St. Petersburg becomes "the most fantastic city in the world." It is worth noting that certain visions of St. Petersburg to be found in the works of Dostoevski conform absolutely to those of Mickiewicz. There is no doubt of it. Mickiewicz was first among the poetical adversaries of St. Petersburg; he created a new vision of St. Petersburg by evoking its tragic essence as well as the fantastic aspect of the city. Beside him stands Gogol.

Chronology supports our point of view: The *Bronze Horseman* stands like a monument situated in a crossroads, a crossroads where the past and the future meet. The *Bronze Horseman* has two faces, one belonging to the past and the other to the future, but both look at Mickiewicz. The Mickiewiczian element, introduced into Pushkin's work, became a sort of Trojan horse, it destroyed the vision of the glory of St. Petersburg in that work, and so indirectly, through it, it gave an alarum to all Russian literature, which since then has continued to regard its capital with anguish and fright.

After Pushkin, it was Dostoevski's turn to take up Mickiewiczian motifs; it likewise befell Blok to come back to the same historiosophic subjects and themes—for both Russia and Poland.[20] Anyway, we have here a new proof of Mickiewicz's immense prestige and the importance of the role he played in Russia.

However, the *Third Part* of the *Forefathers' Eve* contains certain other elements that I should like to remark in order better to depict our poet's two essential traits: the energy of his self-confidence and again the Heraclitean element.

What does the *Third Part* of the *Forefathers' Eve* represent? It is the history of the Philomaths and the Philaretics, or rather the history of their arrest and their imprisonment in the year 1824. This story, in spite of the terrible consequences of the insurrection, became the poetic summa of Polish martyrdom. And what were the sufferings of young students of Wilno in comparison with the sufferings of Poland after 1830-31! This story, moreover, was written by a man who did not participate in the

---

[20] Cf. my studies: *Mickiewicz Dostoevski, and Blok*, in *Slavic Studies*, Cornell Univ. Press, 1943, pp. 75-98; *Russia and her Culture*, in "New Europe," New York, Vol. I, Nos. 10 and 11; *Blok's "Polish Poem,"* Polish Institute of Arts and Sciences in America, New York, 1944; *Poland and the World*, Polish Institute of Arts and Sciences in America, New York, 1943.

insurrection, who suffered accusations from his compatriots because of that indecision . . . In spite of this he wrote his story, he imposed his story upon the nation . . . he possessed the magnificent power of making his conception valid! And he certainly was no usurper—he was a lord, as I have already said.

We have many examples of this courageous self-confidence. For instance, in 1848, in the presence of Pope Pius IX, in a moment of emotion and excitement he caught the Pope's arm and cried out: "Do you know that the spirit of God is now in the smocks of the workers of Paris!" The Pope, shocked by his powerful voice, said to him, *"Figlio, non tanto forti, alzate troppo la voce."* Mickiewicz continued in a milder tone. That was the sort of man he was.

But let us take "movement" again. In the *Fourth Part* we have, as I have already said, the poignant lyric relation of the poet's love for Maryla. It is the story of a Polish Werther, it is the story of Gustaw; he appears before us as a being whose entire aims in life reduce themselves to his unhappy love.

He reappears in the beginning of the *Third Part*. And here begins the wonderful story of Gustaw, Konrad, and the Priest Peter.

Gustaw represented one phase of the poet's life, as we know—his individual pain; we are now in prison, for it is, as I have said, the story of the Philomaths and Philaretes. Suddenly there occurs a mysterious transformation: Gustaw is transformed into Konrad. Mickiewicz notes it:

Prisoner . . . (Rises and writes with charcoal on one side.)
D.O.M.
Gustavus
Obit M.D. CCC. XXIII. Calendis Novembris.

(On the other side.)

Hic Natus Est
Conradus
M.D. CCC. XXIII. Calendis Novembris.

Konrad parts with his personal sins and devotes himself to wider, national goals.

But this is only the first step in that evolution. Konrad, under the power of sudden inspiration, begins his improvisation. This *Improvisation*—one of the masterpieces of Mickiewicz's poetry —embraces many philosophical and religious problems.

But the *Improvisation* is not only a picture of poetical inspiration. The chief subject is contained in the talk between Konrad and God. This is not a talk, it is a monologue, as God is silent. It is a monologue of despair, and the essence of this despair is to be found—and here we have a theme which appears many times later in the writing of Alfred de Vigny in France and of Dostoevski in Russia—in the statement that love is not an attribute of God but of man. Konrad asks the Lord for an answer that would justify the sufferings of millions . . . The poet of course has in mind the sufferings of his nation. He is thinking about his love for the millions and asks the Lord to give him rule over the suffering millions . . . He says,

> Now is my soul incarnate in my country,
> And in my body dwells her soul;
> My fatherland and I are one great whole.
> My name is million, for I love as millions,
> Their pain and suffering I feel . . .[21]

Finally he takes an attitude of rebellion, as God is silent— the God "wise and cool," who is not "love" but "wisdom alone,"

[21] See *Forefathers' Eve*, etc., *loc. cit.*, pp. 28-29.

revealed in "books alone," "in limbs, bodies, metals, stone . . ."
He challenges God to a "battle for the heart of all mankind"—
but God is silent.

> Speak, or I thunder forth, and if I can
> Not shatter nature into shards, yet all Thy plan
> Of wheeling worlds and planets, every star,
> Shall reck, as I proclaim to all creation
> From generation unto generation
> That thou art not the father
> (Voice of the Devil) : But the Tsar . . .[22]

After his improvisation, Konrad was exhausted. But who had
an answer, who had a sign from God? Who obtained a vision of
future Poland? It was not Konrad, though he represented Mickiewicz himself. It was somebody else, who represented a further
step in the poet's spiritual evolution . . . Again that movement,
progress . . . It was the humble priest, Peter, with his humility,
resignation, faith, and Christian religious love . . . Mickiewicz
understood that reason is a prison, that the truth is outside, and
that man loves freedom more than certitude, that man prefers
to suffer at liberty rather than to be not free, and mysteriously
prefers his liberty with sufferings to his happiness. Here we have
the secret of the spiritual greatness of Mickiewicz, the author of
the *Improvisation* and of the *Ode to Youth*; as in the Mickiewicz
who was not afraid to dance, we see another greatness which
I have already termed the genius of his personality, so entirely,
completely free . . .

In 1832 he published a very beautiful book in prose, imitating
the style of the Gospel: *The Books of the Polish Nation and of
the Polish Pilgrimage.* These books bring consolation to the Polish

---

[22] *Ibid.*, p. 30. I have tried to show a possible relationship between the *Improvisation* and A. de Vigny's poems and some of the pages of Dostoevski . . . see *Alfred
de Vigny and the Slavs* in *Poland and the World*, New York, 1943, and *Mickiewicz,
Dostoevski, and Blok*, in *Slavic Studies*, Cornell Univ. Press, 1943.

émigrés of 1830-31 as well as to all Poland. They teach Christian
love and patience, they propagate the idea of Christianized politics, they presage a new era in which a new Poland will be born
again . . . But this era cannot be obtained until the ideal of
man's inner freedom is attained, by the Poles themselves as well
as by foreigners.

These *Books* aroused the enthusiasm of the whole world—
Montalembert translated them into French, Lamennais imitated
them, they were translated into every language and cast an aura
around the name of Mickiewicz . . .

Between 1832 and 1834 he wrote *Pan Tadeusz*, his greatest and
most beautiful work, the most beautiful masterpiece of Polish
poetry—and, according to the opinion of Germans, Danes,
Frenchmen, Englishmen, Russians, and Italians, the one modern
epic in the whole world. Brandes said "that it is the only work
of the nineteenth century which approaches the spirit of Homer,
achieving that grand and costly naïveté which has become so
rare in modern times."[23] M. Louis Gillet: "It has fallen to this
Slav, born on the Marches of old Poland, to write the one work
which, since the *Odyssey*, breathes most naturally the broad style
of Homer."[24] This Polish masterpiece has been compared with
Ariosto, with *Don Quixote*, and on the other hand the German
critic Fr. Muckermann says, *"Es ist da nicht mehr Klassik und
nicht mehr Romantik, es ist da in der Form schon etwas so
Eigentuemliches, dass es mit Worten gar nicht zu schildern ist."*[25]
But what is particularly striking in this *Pan Tadeusz* is the vigor,
the health, the strength, the *joie-de-vivre*—that robust climate of
the work, which permits Borowy to compare it to the work of
Dickens: "The truth is that Mickiewicz's poem, like Dickens'

[23] Cited by W. Borowy, *Mickiewicz's "Pan Tadeusz,"* "The Slavonic Review," Vol.
XIII, pp. 400-401.
[24] *Ibid.*
[25] *Ibid.*

novels, is vigorously healthy and emphasizes what great elements of joy there can be in life."[26]

The poet's first intention had been to write a sort of pastoral on Polish country life of the time of his childhood, something in the manner of Goethe's *Hermann and Dorothea*. But he soon changed his plan, and the path he took was the way of Scott's historical novels, "until," as Borowy says, "at some moment it was opened to Quixotic and Homeric perspectives and became what it is."[27]

But the element of irony ought not to be forgotten. And that is why—in the words of Henri Pourrat—"What gives so much charm to *Pan Tadeusz* is just that, this malice, this verve, and what far exceeds verve, a sort of happy enthusiasm, fine and smiling.[28] Yes, there is irony, there is "the smile of Mickiewicz, as mysterious as that of Mona Lisa," as has been said. And that irony, that smile, are universal.

Nor ought we to forget that it is a poetical work, and therefore, to tell the truth, untranslatable. All the translations, even those in prose, those of Cazin in French and Noyes in English, give only a weak idea of the beauty of this work. The whole world that the poet's words call into being, all that adorable vision of the truth of human life, of the countryside, of the general atmosphere of the country—all that is a poetic dream, fine as a cobweb and translations tear that cobweb.

Here, likewise, we have movement—movement in nature; how many, many ravishing images!—but movement also of souls, transformation, *transubstantiations* . . . It is precisely there that Mickiewicz appears most himself. The story of Jacek Soplica and of his transformation, "elevation," is a grandly and deeply intimate story, although the exterior facts of which it is made

[26] See *ibid.*, p. 400
[27] *Op. cit.*, p. 403.
[28] *Ibid.*, p. 410.

differ absolutely from the real life of Mickiewicz. But we have there the love affairs of Mickiewicz and of Maryla; we have likewise the complex of insurrection and expiation . . .

This true, real expiation began just after *Pan Tadeusz*—incidentally, in new conditions of life for the poet. On July 22, 1834, Mickiewicz married Celina Szymanowska, daughter of the famous Polish pianist Marie Szymanowska, whom he had known very well while still at St. Petersburg. He now underwent a phase of particularly intense spiritual concentration. He found himself under the suggestion of the writings of J. Boehme, and above all of the eighteenth-century French philosopher Saint-Martin.

An inner labor was accomplished in him, the secret of which was unveiled by the poet's famous letter to the Abbé Kajsiewicz; in that letter the poet insisted on the value of the inner man, on truth. "The word of truth falls gently and slowly," he said, "it reposes long in the soul before shooting buds, its fruit will be love and peace . . . On the other hand, the word of lies precipitates itself noisily and leaves after it wounds and death . . . The labor of conscience is a labor of digestion of the soul . . . Do not think that the word of truth will deliver you from temptation and struggle . . . The greater one is, the easier and deeper may the fall become . . . All our outer strength depends on the inner struggle and inner victory . . . A country and a man fall when they are inwardly impotent . . ."[29]

These thoughts—Tolstoyan *avant la lettre*—were definitely crystallized in him, but they were not new for him. We well know that it was this "sacred fire," this "inspiration from beyond" that Pushkin had so admired in him, that had always been the secret of Mickiewicz's faculty of radiance everywhere. He had always been attracted by this mystery of a man's inner power.

[29] See *Sto lat Myśli Polskiej*, etc., Vol. III, p. 117.

Already in the *Forefathers' Eve*—in the *Forefathers' Eve* of Kowno, he had said,

> Sometimes this spark lights up the eye with a heavenly divinity,
> This flame then is consumed in itself,
> It burns for itself,
> Like a lamp in a Roman tomb.

He continually returns to this same metaphor—memory, remembrance, for him will become a lamp, a vigil that will never be extinguished . . .

In *Konrad Wallenrod,* for example,

> But still the sparks of youthful ardor glow
> Deep in my breast, and often kindle there
> The flames that warm my soul and brighter show
> The scenes of old. For memory, like a rare
> Crystalline globe of intricate design,
> Though filmed with dust and scratches, if one set
> A candle in its heart, again will shine
> With limpid color; once again will throw
> On palace walls a fair and delicate net,
> Though somewhat blurred and darkened, radiant yet.[30]

In the *Crimean Sonnets* the sun appears as the "lamp of Akkerman," as the "lantern" of Allah . . . the "lamp of the worlds" . . .

Such also will be the image of the human faces appearing in his Russian "Satires"—

> I meet the men who dwell within this land,
> Broad-chested, great of strength, a stalwart band;
> And, like the trees and creatures of the North,
> They pulse with life and health that knows no pain:
> But every face is like their home, a plain,
> A waste, on which no inward light shines forth.
> Their hearts, like underground volcanoes, throw

[30] *Konrad Wallenrod,* etc., p. 37.

Upon the cheeks no flame of fierce desire.
Their moving lips reflect no ardent glow;
No wrinkled brows fade with the dying fire
Seen on men's foreheads in more favored lands,
O'er which have passed, through many weary years,
Such strong traditions, sorrows, hopes, and fears
That in each face a nation's history stands.
And here the eyes of men are large and clear,
Like their unstoried towns; no storm-tossed heart
Makes anguished glances from their pupils dart
Or hopeless sorrow in their depths appear:
Viewed from afar they seem austere and great;
But near at hand, empty and desolate.[31]

Memory will also—often—become suffering:

O sea, among thy happy creatures, deep
Below, a polyp slumbers through the storm,
Its long arms ever lifted, poised to dart.
O thought, the hydra, memory, asleep
Through evil days, in peace will lift its form
And plunge its talons in thy quiet heart.[32]

And *Konrad Wallenrod* is not only a song of power, it likewise is a song about memory, reminiscence—the poet is obsessed by the strength of memories, and it is they which become in him that luminous clarity lighting his being . . . And as for *Pan Tadeusz*, that bright vision of the past, it becomes not merely a little lantern of memory, but an immense fresco which the memory exposes to view . . .

Let us return, however, to the Parisian period in Mickiewicz's life.

After *Pan Tadeusz*, Mickiewicz abandoned his art—just like Gogol, like Tolstoy. He devoted himself entirely to the service of the national cause, and from now on he will live by acts alone . . . Poetry becomes life, or rather life becomes his new poetry.

[31] "The Slavonic Review," Vol. XIII, p. 483, transl. by G. R. Noyes and M. B. Peacock.
[32] "The Slavonic Review," Vol. XVI, p. 498, tr. by F. P. Radin.

We see him now in Paris directing his magazine, *The Polish Pilgrim*, and writing articles in it; we see him in his capacity as professor at the Collège de France from 1840 to 1844.[33] He gives a course, in which he displays fine preparation, deep erudition, and penetrating comprehension of Slavic civilizations and literatures. He accomplishes the difficult task of a pioneer in the field of Slavic philology, he gives formulas and interpretations several of which still live today. As a Pole, he becomes, at this chair in the Collège de France, a veritable intellectual and spiritual ambassador of Poland at the universal hearth of letters and arts which Paris was at that moment.

After four years of work, he abandoned his chair. Two events which took place in Paris just before the beginning of his course eventually exercised a peculiar influence on him, and led him far from his professorial task. On December 15, 1840, the ashes of Napoleon arrived in Paris. The same day saw Andrzej Towiański, a Polish mystic, arriving from Wilno on his little Lithuanian horse, with the sole aim of being present at the ceremony. After two days Towiański returned homeward, but in a year he was again in Paris. Soon Mickiewicz found himself under the man's influence. Towiański's mysticism, developed in Rome, and his romantic cult of Napoleon as a man of destiny found an echo in the soul of the poet and prepared the way for his mystic doctrine. Mickiewicz began to teach this doctrine in his course and to preach the cult of the Emperor. It was under the reign of Louis Philippe. Mickiewicz finally had to abandon his course.

Now he devoted himself to new human and religious enterprises. He had sacrificed his chair for his Polish Legion . . . There were no bounds to his spiritual activity, and no peace for his Heraclitean soul . . . One of the most beautiful moments in

[33] See W. Lednicki, *Mickiewicz at the Collège de France, 1840-1940*, "The Slavonic Review," Vol. XX, 1941, pp. 149-172.

his life was this very story of his Polish legion. This legion was an incarnation of poetry in life. The poet was by now no longer young; at his chair in the Collège de France he had preached his ideas on the necessity of spiritual effort and the necessity of sacrifice, on the "Christianization" of public life; now, when the news came of the Italian Revolution, he went to Rome to organize a Polish legion whose task should be to fight for the freedom of the Italian people as well as for the freedom of Poland, following the traditions of the Insurrection of 1830-31, which had engraved on the Polish flags the beautiful Polish motto:

> "For your liberty and ours."

He made a magnificent "pilgrimage" of propaganda across Italy, going from one city to another and speaking to crowds of Italians, animating them by that inexhaustible sacred fire which was never extinguished in his heart. He succeeded in organizing his legion, which took part in the Italian war.

After that glorious episode we see him once more in Paris, this time at the head of a new journal—*La Tribune des Peuples,* in which he published articles always animated by the same spirit of independence and international brotherhood. The *Tribune* was liquidated at the moment when after the Revolution of 1848 France found herself in a period of Reaction.

In 1852 Mickiewicz, who had always kept his title as Professor of the Collège de France, received his definite dismissal. Supported by Prince Jerome Bonaparte, he was named librarian of the Bibliothèque de l'Arsenal in Paris . . .

But that was not the end of his laborious path; the culminating point was always before him, this continual climb never stopped . . .

This culminating point was Constantinople, Mickiewicz's Missolonghi . . . In 1853 Turkey declared war on Russia . . . Prince Adam Czartoryski, who since the Polish defeat of 1831 was in Paris at the head of "Polish affairs" in Europe and guided the international policy of émigré Poland, had long been organizing Polish political activities in the Balkans . . . At the moment when the Crimean War was declared, Czartoryski and his nephew, General Count Władysław Zamoyski, took steps to constitute a Polish division of infantry and of cavalry under the orders of the English generalissimo. England furnished the pay, France the uniforms and the arms, Turkey the victuals and the horses. Poland—as always—furnished her blood.

During this time an old diplomatic agent of Czartoryski, the novelist Michał Czajkowski, organized under the name of "Cossacks of the Sultan" two regiments of Ottoman Cossacks who distinguished themselves in the defense of Silistria. Difficulties arose between him and Zamoyski . . . The French Government then sent Mickiewicz to establish accord and hasten the organization of the Polish contingents. Mickiewicz arrived at Constantinople with another new project—to organize in addition a legion of Jewish volunteers . . . At this moment cholera broke out in Turkey. The contagion took Mickiewicz. He died in Constantinople on November 26, 1855.

Mickiewicz led Poland into the broad fields of Europe and assured her undying prestige on the continent. This conception of an independent Poland was closely bound up with his idea of the moral regeneration of Europe and Poland . . . Here again appears the principle of movement, evolution, progress, transformation, and transfiguration.

There was no place for Poland in the Europe of the "Old Testament." In suffering, Poland awaited and prepared the coming of the reign of the "New Testament," and prepared herself for it. And that was the theodicy of her martyrdom; that is the essence of Polish messianism. This essence is real even in our days. The Europe of the last twenty years was not a good Europe, it was not Mickiewicz's Europe. Neither was it quite his Poland.

I am convinced that, in spite of the decisive role of geographical, political, and economic factors in the life of nations, the present war is conducted not for dollars and pounds, as Hitler says. It is waged for intangible values which have nothing to do with money. These things for which we are fighting are summed up in one simple quotation which I read in a letter of Mickiewicz: "Goethe said, *'Was ist am heiligsten? Das, was die Menschen verbindet.'* " And this was that the poet preached in his poetry; at the Collège de France, even when he felt waves of indignation and sorrow in his heart; this was what he preached by his legions, by his death. That was his task as a Pole, the historical Polish task, his task as a Slav, his human and his divine task. His whole life, his whole work was and still is a Polish introduction to universality, as he, Mickiewicz, was, owing to a favoring Fate, the Ambassador of Poland to the United States of Humanity.

This spiritual Ambassador of Poland ended his days, as I have said, in Constantinople. Not long before his death he told one of his friends about his visit to Smyrna:

"I was informed that Homer's grotto was in Smyrna; but I was not anxious to see it. I was looking, gazing at something else. There was a great heap; everything was there: sweepings, filth, bones, broken glass, soles of old slippers, feathers. That was just what pleased me, because it was absolutely like what one sees before a tavern in Poland. Probably my own son would not understand what sort of things I saw there, and he would no doubt prefer to go to Homer's grotto."[34]

It was a new Homer who stood there, a Homer who did not wish to see the real Homer's grotto—it touched him no more.

At that moment he was a Ulysses who gazed at the heap of filth, as he found in it a morsel, a patch of his real Ithaca . . .

His Poland was in his heart and, as his heart was large, his Poland was large as well. He died with his Poland in his heart. And we now, we Poles again have more of Poland in our hearts than in reality. Again we stand before a heap of rubbish. How terrible to think that we through the ages have been carrying our culture in rags and tatters, carrying our poor, eternally shattered Ithaca in the hearts of generations! But we will live with our Mickiewiczian lamp in our souls—a day will come when this lamp will become a torch, a torchlight for others too . . .

[34] See *Mickiewicz at the Collège de France, loc. cit.*, pp. 170-171. For a more detailed treatment of Mickiewicz and especially of his relations with Russia the reader is referred to my studies: *Przyjaciele Moskale*, Kraków, 1935; *Jeżdziec Miedziany Aleksandra Puszkina*, Warszawa, 1932; *Mickiewicz en Russie*, "Revue de l'Université de Bruxelles," 1929; *Pouchkine et Mickiewicz*, "Revue de Littérature Comparée," Paris, 1937, from which are taken most of the quotations in the text.

VI

The Uprooted (Part One)

ON AUGUST 15, 1831, the Russian armies were approaching Warsaw, which was to fall into their hands on September 7 after a bloody struggle of a whole year's duration between Poland and Russia. At this moment the Polish National Government, in order to interpret to Europe the sentiments of abandoned Poland before it disappeared, addressed the following message to its western agents:

"Truth, seen whole, has appeared before our eyes. We no longer count on the support of the great powers, who could and who would not, who still can and who will not, save us. We can no longer place any faith in the promises which they have made to us and which they belie by their conduct . . . England and France, then, would not have employed us for the occasion except as an instrument fit to serve the course of their interests. England would not have lulled us with a few illusions except in order to have one more method of establishing the independence of Belgium. And France would not have made promises to us except to win a majority in the Chambers. Would faith, then, be wholly banished from cabinets, and the words of a French and English minister be nothing but worthless farthings? . . . If

France and England abandon us today and fail to justify the hopes that they have aroused, our ruin will have been brought about, not by the fury of Russia, nor the hostility of Prussia, nor the indifference of Austria, but by the self-styled sympathy shown us by France and England . . ."

"If the cabinets lack the courage to help us, let them at least possess enough to acknowledge their barbaric indifference toward our cause. And if they have ignored the duty imposed on them by prudence, morality, and humanity, the Poles will know how to follow him who prescribes to them the sanctity of their rights and the love of their country."[1]

A new tragedy of Poland, and perhaps the most grievous of all, was over. If the Partitions of Poland could have been considered by the Poles themselves a partial consequence of the faults and errors of the past, *this* time the Poles—the whole nation—had nothing for which to reproach themselves: during the period between the last Partition and the Insurrection of November, Poland had sacrificed all her material efforts and all her moral resources, as well as her blood, for the cause of freedom—for her own freedom and that of others.

On the other hand, never had the moral bonds been stronger and more intimate between Poland and the West, between Poland and that European civilization which these Latin Slavs cherished with such beautiful ardor and beautiful devotion. Since the end of the eighteenth century the Poles had traveled all the battle-fields of Europe and America; they were allied to every great cause in Europe; the name of Poland reverberated in the whole world's poetry—the Wordsworths, Campbells, Keatses, and Byrons in England, the Bérangers, the Barbiers, the Hugos in France, Espronceda in Spain, the Italians, and German and Austrian poets without number sang the extinct glory of Poland and

[1] See H. Grappin, *op. cit.*, pp. 249-250.

shed tears over her martyrdom. It was a continuation of an anti-
Russian and pro-Polish poetic tradition established by Byron in
Europe.

I am not going to quote the English poems and articles written
in England and the United States.[2] Let it suffice us to mention
here a few European texts, German and French—of which the
former are particularly eloquent.

Among the crowd of German and Austrian poets who published
hundreds of poems in admiration of Poland at that moment, it is
Count August von Platen who especially merits our attention; he
addresses twenty-three poems to the Polish cause and to Russia.
The Russo-Prussian Entente cuts him to the quick, wounds his
knightly pride:

> Hohenzollerns edler Stamm,
> Werde Deutschland Wehr und Damm!
> Aller Knechtschaft Widersacher
> Sind die grossen Wittelsbacher:
> Beugte Habsburg bloss den Nacken
> Vor Kosacken?
> Aus Europa muss hinaus
> Jeder absolute Graus!
> Moskowiten oder Tuerken
> Wollen uns entgegen wirken?
> Kehrt nach Osten eure Thaten,
> Asiaten![3]

[2] See *Pouchkine et la Pologne,* as above; *Poland and the World,* as above; E.
Privat, *L'Europe et l'Odyssée de la Pologne au XIX siècle,* Lausanne, 1918.
[3] See *Pouchkine et la Pologne,* as above; p. 79.
(Noble race of the Hohenzollerns
Become to Germany a bulwark and dyke!
The great Wittelsbachers
Are the opponents of all slavery
Does Hapsburg bend his neck only
Before Cossacks?
Out of Europe must go
All the rubbish of Autocracy!

And Béranger said the same thing in the *Chant du Cosaque:*

> Tout cet éclat dont l'Europe est si fière,
> Tout ce savoir qui ne la défend pas,
> S'engloutira dans les flots de poussière,
> Qu'autour de moi vont soulever tes pas.
> Efface, efface en ta course nouvelle,
> Temples, palais, moeurs, souvenirs et lois.
> Hennis d'orgueil ô mon courier fidèle!
> Et foule aux pieds les peuples et les rois.[4]

The Chambers and Houses of Parliament at Paris and London quivered with indignation and anger, the journals and reviews in Europe and America were filled with articles, manifestoes, messages, addressed to the "heroic" and "martyred" nation; anti-Russian manifestations took place in the streets of London, Paris, and even in Austria and Germany. The peoples of Europe followed the "peripatetics" of the Russo-Polish struggle with breathless attention, and the fall of Warsaw plunged all Europe into blackest mourning. Even in Russia there were some men who felt distress, like him the poet speaks of, who "at the moment of Warsaw's fall, burst into sobs like a Jew bemoaning Jerusalem."

With what irony must the Poles have contemplated the declarations of English and French statesmen, like Grey, who said, "In

---

Moscovites or Turks
Will they check us?
Move your doings to the East
You Asiatics.)
   [4] *Ibid.*, p. 74.
(All this brilliancy of which Europe is so proud,
All this knowledge which does not defend her,
Will be engulfed in the clouds of dust
Which your footsteps will cause to rise around me.
Wipe off, wipe off, in your new course
Temples, palaces, customs, memories and laws,
Neigh with pride, O my faithful steed!
And trample down with your feet peoples and kings.)

the present circumstances we must wish that Russia's hands may
be free as soon as possible and that your insurrection be sup-
pressed with the least possible delay." Or Palmerston, who declared that Great Britain had no reason to be disagreeable to its
"good and faithful ally," Nicholas I. Or the Duc de Mortemart:
"You are deluding yourselves about us. Our situation is quite
critical. The new government is not yet solidly established . . .
We cannot wage war on your behalf . . . Your hour has not yet
sounded. You must be reconciled to the Czar . . ."[5]

And finally, Sebastiani, with his immortally famous sentence:
"order reigns in Warsaw!"

This Polish Insurrection of 1830-31 was a drama of enormous
historic import and significance. A nation which for centuries
had been devoted to the "defense of the West," and which considered itself called upon to fulfill the task of the missionary
preaching the gospel of western civilization, had been voluntarily and deliberately sacrificed by that civilization—and for
purposes completely opposed and alien to it.

On the other hand, as I have already said, Russia, which, thanks
to the Partitions and later after the repression of the Polish Insurrection, had become geographically nearer to Europe, was
morally separated from it, for precisely the same reason. That
can be best seen in Pushkin, of all Russian poets the one par
excellence European, who represents in his genre a unique phenomenon for Russia precisely because of the profoundly intimate
union between the Russian national genius and the genius of
European civilization which he achieved in his wise and harmonious poetic work. That poet could not resist the ordeal: his
famous anti-Polish odes evince a flagrant moral break with
Europe by Russia. From that moment, one may say, "the

[5] See H. Grappin, *op. cit.*, pp. 244-245.

Polish question" in Russia became a political problem, the essence of which never ceased to be profoundly moral.[6]

The elite of French society understood that immediately; in 1833, Ballanche wrote in the magazine, *Le Polonais—Journal des intérêts de la Pologne:* "At this moment France, like Italy in the fifteenth century, is being enriched by several emigrations which differ widely in character but which will all be appreciated by history some day. The Polish emigration is distinguished among them by its importance, by the intensity of its unhappiness . . . The destinies of Europe are being reconstructed under the shelter of that living tomb [Poland]—which continues to protect us . . . *The anathema which issues from the bloody ruins of Poland excludes Russia for ever from the brotherhood of Europe.* I advise the director of this collection of articles to call it hereafter *Journal des intérêts de l'Europe.*"

This Polish emigration was a historical phenomenon really unique in its kind. It was a whole world in exile, almost an entire nation which was not willing to give itself up, which did not accept defeat, and which hoped to be able to continue the struggle and resistance with Europe's help.

While in Poland the three parts of the mangled Republic were weighed down by the oppressing regimes of Russia, Prussia, and Austria, an immense mass of Poles left the country and established itself in Europe. The army does not give up its arms but goes abroad; with the army go the Government and the Parliament, the intellectuals, priests, men of letters, scholars, private citizens and officials, politicians—red and white—women, children . . . Yes, it was a procession, a "Funeral March" of a whole people, but it was also a Polonaise . . . In its way, it was a March of Triumph . . .

[6] See V. Lednicki, *Pouchkine et la Pologne,* etc.

To begin with Germany—Prussia! At that moment this was
not the Germany of Bismarck or Hitler, it was the country of
Schiller and Goethe; the patriotic and national ideal did not yet
know the corruption that has since come to taint them so deeply.
Even the Prussian generals and other officers who had to concern
themselves with the Polish troops interned in Prussia often showed
much sympathy, to such an extent that the Poles offered the
Commandant of the Fortress of Weichselmende, for example, a
silver goblet as a souvenir. General Zoeppelin was no less humane;
and grateful Poles also bestowed gifts of recognition on such men
as Lieutenants von Buttler, Khall, Magen-Hoffer, and von
Goltzov.[7]

In almost every German city—Braunschweig, Beyreuth, Bre-
men, Frankfort, Gotha, Karlsruhe, Kiel, Mannheim, Munich,
Mainz, Stuttgart, Tubingen, Jena, Wurzburg, Leipzig, to name
but a small part of them—committees of *Polenfreunde* were
immediately formed, and collected money, clothes, shoes, medicine, victuals.

The Germans organized demonstrations, masses, concerts, receptions, balls . . . Societies of music, like Geward-Haus Eu-
terpe, and others in Leipzig, organized musical evenings in honor
of the Poles. The *Literarische Museum* published Mosen's famous
poem *Die letzten zehn vom vierten Regiment* with music by August Schuster—to be sold, the proceeds to go to the Poles. And
how many pro-Polish pages were published by the review, *Unser
Planet,* and the daily *Leipziger Tageblatt!* In 1832 the New Year's
issue was entitled:

> Seht ihr dort das Rot in Osten?
> Das ist Polen's Heldenblut![8]

[7] See Lubomir Gadon, *Emigracya Polska,* Vol. I, Kraków, 1901, pp. 50-51.
[8] Do you see there the redness in the East?
This is Poland's heroic blood!

Everywhere re-echoing, in every German kingdom and principality, are the enthusiastic cries, *Hoch Polen! Es leben die Polen!
Hoch das Vaterland Polen!* Theaters, with spectacles—*Kościuszko
on the banks of the Seine,* musicales, illuminations—and all that
at Muelheim as well as at Gotha, at Tubingen as well as Ulm, at
Dresden as at Worms, in Germany as well as in Bohemia and
Austria. The *Polenlieder*—more than two hundred of them—
populated German poetry; Poles were received, feted, and acclaimed as the *Sturmvogel der Revolution.* All Germany, despite the policy of Prussia as Russia's ally, understood that the
fall of Warsaw and the defeat of Poland meant the wreck of the
ideal of freedom and the collapse of the rampart of European
civilization.[9]

It would be vain to strive to list all the symptoms of sympathy
in France; the ten thousand Poles who were in France became
the immediate object of positively frenzied worship and admiration.

As in Germany, but even more so, the theaters played dramas
whose content was always the same—the apotheosis of Poland
and the banishment of Russia; nor were these themes abandoned
by the magazines and reviews. Yes, La Fayette had well exclaimed in the Chamber of Deputies: "Messieurs, all France is
Polish, from the veteran of the Grand Army who speaks about
his Polish brethren to the children in our schools who send us
daily the product of their small savings to assist the Polish cause.
Yes, all France is Polish."[10]

These words were spoken before the defeat. We are also acquainted with other words—those of Périer, who said, that
"France concedes to no people the right to force her to fight for

[9] See *ibid.*, pp. 50-59.
[10] See E. Privat, *op. cit.*, p. 129.

it; French treasure and French blood belong only to France."
A sad reply, it has been said, to make to the fidelity of a Poniatowski!—of that Prince Poniatowski who, since his death at the
Battle of Leipzig, had become the symbol of honor . . . That
is why, after the fall of Warsaw, the indignation of the French
became still greater—above all, when Thiers, in order to defend
the government's policy of opportunism, made no scruple in
trampling the murdered body of Poland by calling her "a people
of adventurers."

Barthélemy was the man who sang the indignation of all France
when he wrote:

> Noble soeur Varsovie, elle est morte pour nous,
> Morte, fusil en main, sans fléchir le genou,
> Morte en nous maudissant à son heure dernière,
> Morte en baignant de pleurs l'aigle de sa bannière,
> Sans avoir entendu notre cri de pitié,
> Sans un mot de la France, un adieu d'amitié.
> Cachons-nous, cachons-nous, nous sommes des infâmes!
> ... Ne parlons plus de gloire et de nos barricades.
> Que le teint de la honte embrase notre front!
> Vous voulez voir venir les Russes? Ils viendront.[11]

Society rushed up from everywhere to hail the Polish émigrés
and make their existence easy. The situation was similar in
Italy, Switzerland, Algeria, Spain, England, and, a bit later, in
the United States.

The émigrés had left the country with the determination to

[11] *Ibid.*, p. 130.
(Noble sister Warsaw, she is dead for us
Dead with a gun in hand without bending her knee,
Dead while cursing us at her last hour
Dead while bathing with tears the eagle of her banner
Without having heard our cry of pity
Without a word from France, a farewell of friendship.
Let us hide ourselves, let us hide ourselves, we are infamous!
Let us speak no more of glory and of our barricades.
Let the color of shame inflame our face
Do you want to see the Russians coming?
They will come.)

continue the struggle and the hope of finding allies for the Polish cause. Today we know that they were in error; the European governments, French and English, were determined to keep strictly neutral toward the Russo-Polish conflict, despite the manifestations of sympathy for the Polish cause on the part of French and English society and the political activity having intervention in mind—particularly intense activity, which the Polish émigrés displayed incessantly from the time of their arrival in Paris and London. At the start of their exile, the émigrés considered their stay abroad a temporary one; they counted on a rising of all the peoples, and the manifestations of sympathy that they met everywhere fortified this faith.

Some among them pinned their hopes on the success of the diplomatic activity that certain Polish groups continually practiced, as we have said, on the cabinets of Paris and London. That is why the great mass of this immense emigration at the start of its exile believed itself only provisionally established abroad. It pushed no roots into the soil of exile, it did not form more intimate relations with foreign society, it did not endeavor to adapt itself to the new conditions of its life—to conditions which were to become permanent . . . Many among them were ignorant of foreign languages and had no métier at hand which would have enabled them to create for themselves a more or less normal existence. As quickly as possible, they organized committees, associations, political clubs, magazines and reviews of Polish propaganda and newspapers in Polish to propagate among the Poles ideas and conceptions of Polish and international policy. They were very soon divided into groups and parties, into opposing camps, debating Poland's future and . . . likewise, the recent past: the responsibility for the new catastrophe.

Finally, this crowd of Poles, in France as elsewhere, retired within itself during the first years of the emigration, forming a

world apart, a world that was profoundly unhappy, restless, more
and more impatient with time, which advanced without advancing
the events longed for in the profound distress of every Polish soul.

The true drama, however, the crux of the drama, began when
all doubt vanished that the cause was, if not definitely lost, at
least uncertain and hopeless for an indefinite length of time. It
was then that all these groups—societies, unions, federations,
committees, all these "red" and "white" parties, aristocrats and
democrats, of Poles and Lithuanians, of military men and civil-
ians, began to deliberate questions of responsibility, faults committed, and the guilty ones. Reciprocal accusations were made,
in most of the cases unjust but justified, to a degree, by the terrible conditions in which this singular collection of people was
living. It was then that the past—so recent but yet veiled by the
smoke of the rifles of 1830-31 and by the tears of poor exiles as
well as those who remained in "the tomb," there in Poland
martyred by Nicholas I—it was then that this heroic past became
the object of criticism and recrimination.

The insurrection had certainly been waged by the moderates.
These moderates were always the same Polish nobility, the
szlachta, ever responsible for the destiny of the country. It had
made the movement national; it had not made it social, it had
not made it popular, it had not strengthened it by giving satisfaction to the masses. It had been, as always, full of devotion, of
heroism, and ready for very great sacrifices; but, for fear of
"flabbergasting" the foreign cabinets, it had not attempted to follow the traditions of Kościuszko and the Constitution of the Third
of May; it had not advanced the agrarian reforms promulgated
in the Constitution of the Third of May.

The democrats reproached it with that; they believed that instead of tying up the Polish cause with the whims of diplomatic

chancelleries they ought to associate it with the cause of the peoples, with the general revolution of Europe against the Holy Alliance of the princes. The first step, according to them, ought to have been to confer property to the soil on the peasants of Poland; that was the only way in which the revolution could have become national in the broadest acceptation of the term, it would have become an armed democracy that would have fought for its patrimony and would have overthrown all obstacles.

The "whites"—the aristocrats—grouped themselves around a man whom the poet had called "the last of Polish gentlemen"; whom others had compared to "a boat that everyone uses to cross the dangerous current but pushes away on arrival at the other bank"; whom Mochnacki, hero of the Insurrection of 1830 and its first historian, had represented as a patriot who was irreproachable and ardent but always wavering on the wavering stage of the contemporary history of Europe and Poland.

This man—this great uprooted Pole—had arrived in London on December 22, 1831. A modest hack stopped before the door of the boardinghouse in which lived one of Poland's most ardent patriots, a veteran of the struggle for independence, the old Ursyn-Niemcewicz; two men got down from the carriage . . . Very late at night the old Niemcewicz inscribed in his journal: "This evening Prince Adam Czartoryski arrived without any servant, with only one little bag, deprived of all his goods . . . What a trick of fate. When I come to think of it—at the time when I was his father's aide-de-camp, fifty years ago and we reviewed the Lithuanian Army, our retinue numbered three hundred horses and fourteen camels to carry our tents. Today the son is in complete destitution; but he is surrounded with glory, and feels his country's misfortunes much more strongly than his own."[12]

He was a great personality. Successor to the royal ambitions of his illustrious family; friend of Alexander I, lover of Alexander's wife; object of the hatred of Paul I and the jealousy of the Russians; the Czar's ambassador to Sardinia; member of the Imperial Council of State; Alexander's Minister of Foreign Affairs; avowed enemy of Napoleon; Freemason and good Catholic; ardent patriot; apostle of an entente and the union of all Poland with Russia; responsible for the decisions of Vienna in 1814-15 —from 1818, he strives in France and England to promote co-operation with Poland, and finally, after the death of Alexander I, becomes the center of stealthy and subterranean opposition under Nicholas I, to find himself put by the events of 1830-31 at the head of the Polish revolutionary government, proclaiming the dethronement of Nicholas I from the throne of Poland and waging war against Russia.

Condemned to death by the Czar, deprived of his immense fortune in Lithuania, Poland, and Podolia—all his goods were confiscated—separated from his family, he arrives in London in 1831 after the defeat, to establish himself definitely in Paris from the year 1833. His wife and his children, having saved the little money that remained to them at Cracow, rejoin him; in Paris at l'Ile Saint Louis he buys an old town-house, l'Hôtel Lambert, and becomes the head of one great current of opinion, of one Polish party—to represent in Europe, however, the entirety of Poland, to take on himself the duty and the responsibility of speaking in the name of his country.

The Hôtel Lambert became a sort of unofficial court, and the Prince, a king of Poland. The Hôtel Lambert represented everything great, illustrious, influential, in Paris—and so, in Europe.

[12] See L. Gadon, *op. cit., loc. cit.*, p. 192.

To the Benefit Balls arranged at the Hôtel by "Polish Ladies" came all the intellectual, political, and worldly élite of Paris. And everything was stamped with grandeur, dignity, and grief; take Alfred de Vigny's *Wanda,* and you will see how sad the "stories," related at those balls, were. It did not matter whether they were "Russian" or "Polish."[13]

The most lively and active Polish figures in that great Parisian political salon were Niemcewicz—novelist, poet, author of comedies and memoirs, traveler, citizen of two worlds; the Generals Bem, Umiński, Kniaziewicz, the Counts Zamoyski, the Princes Sapieha . . . Mickiewicz appeared there beside Chopin and Słowacki.

"This perfect Anglomaniac," writes his brilliant biographer, M. Handelsman, "this liberal Tory of the eighteenth century . . . aspired to a rejuvenated and modernized Poland—he was indeed the promoter of a just solution to the peasant question in Poland since 1814—but he always reckoned only with the mentality, the interests, and even the prejudices of one single class, that of the great Polish nobility. Personally free from all preconceived ideas, of an independent mind, he was not able to defend his entourage against the influence of ideas, apparently victorious in France, the future of which was to be so fatal at a certain epoch but which seemed to them forever reaffirmed."[14]

His essential method was diplomacy. By this means he and his party desired to reconstitute a monarchical Poland with foreign support. He had agents in every capital in the world, accredited, after a fashion, to certain cabinets. He had brochures, articles, and informative pieces published, the aim of which was to enlighten Europe. He had, moreover, been the initiator of all the

[13] See "Alfred de Vigny and the Slavs" in *Poland and the World,* New York, 1943, pp. 87-92.

[14] Marcel Handelsman, *Les idées françaises et la mentalité politique en Pologne au XIX siècle,* Paris, Alcan, 1927, pp. 152-153.

useful works of the emigration, of a society for scientific studies, of a literary society, of the Polish Library on the Quai d'Orléans in Paris, of schools, of works of charity, of committees for closer relations between the Polish refugees and the nationals of the country where they reside . . .

But—this moderate, this perspicacious man with a rare richness of political experience, tempered by his spirit of legitimism, "let himself be used, on the other hand, as protector of all the riskiest projects of military organization of Poles in the service of Portugal, Spain, Egypt, Turkey, or Belgium." His diplomatic activity was tireless in the search for instruments that might serve in the struggle against Russia, and his plans sometimes took on truly gigantic energy. "He . . . tried to bring about an Anglo-French alliance against Russia . . . When the Anglo-French Alliance against Russia did not materialize, he renewed his erstwhile plan of organizing the Southern Slavs, with Poland as a nucleus, under Turkish hegemony. Turkey's sovereignty and integrity in turn were to be guaranteed by Western powers. This grandiose scheme was financed by contributions coming from Poland and through the generosity of Lord Dudley Stuart." He established in Constantinople an Eastern agency which co-operated with Serbia, Bulgaria, and Rumania.[15]

He placed some hope in the possibility of a French-Prussian-Polish war against Russia. He studied the possibility of breaking up Austria and wanted to create a strong Slavonic bloc and at the same time he wanted to reconcile Hungary with the Slovaks, Rumanians, and Serbs. He tried to restrain the Southern Slavs from anti-Italian, anti-Magyar action. "In the same year, 1848, Prince Czartoryski extended his diplomatic activity into the Scan-

[15] Comp., *Great Men and Women of Poland*, ed. by J. P. Mizwa, New York, 1941, pp. 169-183 (*A. Czartoryski* by M. Handelsman).

dinavian north and, counting upon the possibility of a Finnish uprising, visioned a defensive-offensive alliance against Russia between Poland on one hand and Sweden and Norway on the other."[16]

The events of 1848-49 did not stop him; he continued his activity in the Bosphorus, anticipating a general European war.

These varied plans, conceptions, and activities do not represent all the gigantic ensemble of enormous political labor executed by the Prince down to his last day—July 15, 1861. I should have to mention his periodical *Polish News,* in which he expounded the necessity for the emancipation of the peasants in the northeastern provinces of Poland; his Bureau of Polish Affairs, whose influence with the aid of the Havas Agency, spread into the French, English, and German press, penetrated to Poland through the Prince's emissaries. I should have to cite still other magazines, dedicated to the study of revolutionary and insurgent movements in general, the main object being the systematic, "scientific" propagation of a new Polish insurrection.

Finally, by way of preparing the ground and strengthening the nation, Czartoryski took under his protection the movement in Posnania led by Marcinkowski, which looked to the economic and social rebirth of the country. The Prince's goal was to forge an organic national force based on the co-operation of all classes and on unity of direction. He developed his ideas on this problem in his special pamphlets and in the magazine entitled *The Third of May.* This movement, led by the "bourgeois" Marcinkowski in Posnania, succeeded in organizing in that part of Poland a powerful concentration of social, economic, and national forces. Analogous movements took shape in Warsaw and in Galicia; in Warsaw it was the magazine, *Library of Warsaw,* founded in

[16] See *ibid.*

1841, that became its center; in Galicia Prince Sapieha, the nephew of Prince Czartoryski's wife, became the champion of the economic renovation of Galicia.

What a grandiose task, and what immense scope! What if he *did* waver on the wavering stage of Europe, this "last gentleman of Poland"—he wavered well. Certainly, there was in him a particularly profound and potent complex: the Russian complex, which formed the dualism of his life. The more he had worked in the first part of his life for Russo-Polish understanding, the more he worked later for the struggle against Russia, having lost all his previous illusions. It was not Poland that removed them, it was the Russian monarchs—Alexander, who betrayed him on several occasions, the Grand Duke Constantin, with his Polish policy, and finally Nicholas I—the true butcher of Poland. One cannot, however, but be seized with admiration on the perusal of his *Essay on Diplomacy,* published in France in August, 1830, in which this great Polish statesman developed his political ideas and conceptions, which are only today receiving—we hope—true historical sanction. He said there that "the world can survive only if it lives in peace; and peace is possible only through an effective league of nations fully recognizing and guaranteeing national rights to each member." You will say: then how could this pacifist and legitimist have devoted himself to the idea of insurrection and war? True pacifists and true legitimists do not shrink from revolution or war when it is a question of struggling against usurpation and violence.

The democratic side, that of the Reds, comprised above all the young men, students, journalists, officers. But at the center of this group were the old and famous historian-geographer Lelewel;

Louis Mierosławski, who organized in Posnania the Plot of 1846
which preceded the Revolution of 1848; Mochnacki, man of letters and author of one of the first and particularly interesting histories of the Insurrection of 1830-31; Worcell; Zaliwski, who
in 1833 organized a war of partisans against Russia, in Poland.

This party entered into relations with secret societies in Europe, especially in Italy, with Mazzini. *Young Europe* affiliated
itself with *Young Poland;* it was with them that La Fayette in
1831 founded his Franco-Polish Committee, and his Polish-
American Committee in which we see Samuel F. B. Morse and
James Fenimore Cooper! A National Polish Committee was
founded, and the Polish Democratic Society . . .

All these initiatives led the democrats to great disaster; their
activities in Poland provoked unprecedented reprisals; abroad
—the Russian Court intervened, and many of them were obliged
to leave France, with Lelewel at their head. Little Belgium gave
them the asylum which France, under the pressure of Pozzo di
Borgo, the Russian Ambassador, would no longer accord them.

But, on the other hand, these revolutionary activities, sometimes noisy, often incoherent, badly organized, anarchic, many
a time guided by personal ambitions, based on rancor and hatred
toward the "whites" and the "aristocrats," linked these Polish
groups with foreign centers of radicals, as I have said—with the
Italians, the French, the Germans, the Russian revolutionaries
who themselves also owed much—as Russian historians have
recognized—to the Polish exiles, having found in their milieus
new inspiration, ideas, and energy.

The mass of these uprooted emigrants represented a whole
world; now in this world there was everything, as in all worlds,
there was good and there was bad.

Quarrels, duels, animosities, calumny, accusations and conflicts of every kind surged up in it; but, as we now know, nothing

seriously bad, nothing ugly or criminal was produced. We know, for example, that the Sureté in France failed to find any provocateurs or confidantes among the Poles; that from the moral point of view this multitude lived decently, honorably, although often pursued by poverty. There was disorder, lack of discipline, lack of leaders; above all, the generals, with some few exceptions, were not equal to meeting the situation in which fate had placed them, and great political ambitions developed among them, a phraseology often insupportable because of its grandiloquence and its buffoonery, lack of education and of political preparation, an irritating Polonocentricity, exaggerated opinions of Poland's role and above all of the emigration. Of course there also existed here some dishonest men, imposters, adventurers, sharpers—but they were not numerous, and they did not destroy the general esteem that this mass of Poles succeeded in winning for itself abroad among the nationals of the lands where it lived. Quite the contrary, the Polish exile became an imperishable symbol of probity, courage, and dignity.

"Unable to act in a real way," writes Professor Marcel Handelsman, "in the expectation of a favorable moment that receded further and further into an uncertain future, the refugees had only one real goal before them, that of formulating a program for the nation which should contain the true, unique, infallible means of delivering it from the misfortunes that surrounded it. And as there was no possible way to control the worth of all these programs, as life incessantly overthrew every one of our enemies' (frequently chimerical) forecasts, they grew so much the more obstinate in their position, they shut themselves up still more narrowly in their little churches, they did nothing but sharpen their ideas to precision. For the one field which was at their entire disposal was that of ideology."[17]

[17] See M. Handelsman, *Les idées*, etc., p. 112.

Indeed, it was precisely in that field that great miracles occurred. These "uprooted people"—the true, first great uprooted people of modern times—not only furnished their own country an ideological basis on which it could wait and prepare itself for the hour of deliverance but also became, for many foreign minds, a source of inspiration and . . . optimism. They became more than that; foreigners sought to plunge themselves into this Polish emigration—into this world of uprooted people in which they persisted in pushing roots! Take Montalembert, for example, who found in Polish surroundings "a moral prop, a strength of resistance, religious ideas and a personal sympathy which was so necessary to him at an era of moral crisis." "I owe them," he said himself, "one of the greatest boons in life; the honor of knowing and understanding the grandeur and the beauty of lost causes." And on July 12, 1834, he wrote the following words: "I beg the person I address to count on me on any occasion, to use me in any way and to any extent he wishes, and to be firmly convinced that after God, it is Poland and her future that occupy the first place in my heart."[18]

It would not be difficult to find texts of like eloquence in Michelet, Lamennais, Delavigne, Hugo, and many others. What interests me here, however, in the first place, is to see where and how these uprooted people pushed their roots, and what gardens, fields, of human thought they found in which to plant the roots of the entire Polish nation.

The role of our great poets and some others here has been quite surprising. They were all in the emigration; one might say that the greater part of our literature in this era developed abroad, especially in France. The three greatest Polish romantic poets— Mickiewicz, Słowacki, and Krasiński—were in exile.

Mickiewicz, the greatest of them, arrived in Paris with two

[18] See M. Handelsman, *op. cit.*, pp. 173-174.

books that he had just finished in Dresden and in Rome, with the third part of his *Forefathers* and with the *Books of the Polish Pilgrimage and of the Polish Nation.* The attitude he took was that of taking the defense of the "madmen," those who had dared to risk and thereby had won the title of great men, and to profess proudly that the name of Poland was indissolubly associated with the idea of sacrifice for the cause of universal liberty and equality. He said something else when speaking of the miseries of exile: "He who stays in his fatherland and endures slavery in order to preserve life loses fatherland *and* life. But he who leaves his fatherland to defend liberty at peril of his life will save his fatherland and will live eternally . . . The Pole says to the nations: a man's fatherland is wherever there is evil to be resisted."[19]

He said something still more significant: "There are some of you who say: 'Let her (Poland) rather lie in slavery than that she should awake an aristocracy'; and others: 'Let her rather so lie than awake a democracy'; and others: 'Let her rather so lie than have such boundaries,' and others say: 'Other boundaries.' These are all doctors, not sons, and they love not their mother, the Motherland. Verily I say unto you: Do not inquire as to what shall be the government in Poland; it sufficeth you to know that it shall be better than all that ye know of; neither question about her boundaries, for they shall be greater than they have been at any time. And each of you hath in his soul the seed of future laws and the measure of the future boundaries.

So far as ye enlarge and better your spirit, so far shall ye better your laws and enlarge your boundaries." . . .[20]

All that was a magnificent program; it represented an heroic climb of national thought to the heights of universalism. Mic-

[19] *Ibid.*, p. 96.
[20] Comp., *Konrad Wallenrod and other Writings of Adam Mickiewicz*, etc., University of California Press, 1925, pp. 175-176.

kiewicz became, in truth, as I have already said, our Ambassador to the United States of Humanity!

But man cannot be "mad" and heroic all his life, especially when he is alone, abandoned by everybody, when he is an exile without hope of ceasing to be one. "Emigration," said Lelewel a little later, "is a great misfortune. It is a great misfortune to be torn from one's native land, from one's cottage, from one's family, father, mother, brothers, relatives, friends, compatriots, from all those who have stayed in the country—to have no assistance, friendship, or news from them. It is sad, and that makes you repine . . . The exile is outside the law; everywhere and every day he undergoes suspicions, disagreements, quibbles, irony, and offense. He is the object of blackguard actions, of violence on the part of higher authorities and of subalterns; he is not distinguished from swindlers and malefactors. For him there is nowhere any asylum or any tranquillity or any certainty . . . Exile is an inexpressible misfortune. One has to know it to appreciate its misery."[21]

"Fatherland—you are like health; how much you ought to be appreciated, only he will know who has lost you . . ." That is how Mickiewicz begins his *Pan Tadeusz*, written in Paris.

With this work Mickiewicz gave Poland—Poland in exile as well as eternal Poland—a book that became for it what no book in the world has ever been for any nation. He gave the exiles a living image, the indestructible image of the fatherland. It is the first garden in which the Poles—first of all the exiles, the "uprooted ones"—can plant their roots.

This "garden" was the soil, the land, the sky, the trees, the

[21] See M. Handelsman, *op. cit.*, p. 95.

fields and prairies, the dwellings of the squires and the peasants' cottages; it *was* relatives, brothers, sisters, the family . . . The evocation with exquisite simplicity and modesty, of a life common to all, of the ordinary life, everyday life, of everything that makes for instinctive happiness, natural felicity in man's existence . . . To live and breathe the air of your country, to scent all its odors and all its perfumes, to embrace with your gaze the clouds of your sky and the color of the verdure of the woods, to know and recognize all the shades of the soil—its sand and its mud, its flowers and its herbs, its foliage, its orchards, its truck gardens, its flower gardens . . . The morals, habits, characters, types, various social layers, Poles, Lithuanians, Jews, and even the Russians that Mickiewicz introduced, for he evokes the image of Poland after the Partitions—it is the year 1812 he describes, that year full of hope for the Poles, that year full of unspeakable glory and beauty . . . All that stands in this book like the radiant vision of a sun-bathed dream!

As you know, the poet had left his country at the age of twenty-five and never returned to it again. So it was after ten years of complete separation, in Paris, on the "pavements of Paris," that he yielded himself up to the magic of his art and his memory . . . art and memory that were unique, irreplaceable, incomparable . . . The poet has omitted nothing, forgotten nothing . . . He has reproduced all the noises and all the sounds of the forest, all the songs of the fields, those of man and of birds, all the voices of the marshes and all the rustles of the prairies . . . His eye was no less attentive than his ear; no one has outlined, better than he, the movement of clouds and the flight of birds in the sky, the windings and rewindings of the forests, the undulations of the wheat under the buffeting of the wind, the play of shadows and glimmers of the sky on the earth, the wrinkles and tints of human faces, gestures, the bodies of men and women.

The poet plunged into the "common" soul of his people, in its language, in its beliefs and its traditions. His poem—an *Odyssey* rather than an *Iliad*—is a masterpiece of poetry whose most beautiful secret and most moving mystery is benevolence, goodness, comprehension, the sympathy of the artist for life—for the ordinary, daily, delightfully customary life of man. Here there is no heroism, no elevation and folly of the soul; no one "wise through passion" and rich through sacrifice and resignation; here is no pathetic, ornamental richness in the style of the *Crimean Sonnets* with their Oriental wisdom, accompanied by romantic curiosity, with their philosophy of nature and their philosophy of passion . . . No historiosophy—none of the philosophy of history that we find again in the *Forefathers' Eve*. No erotic lyricism—works of the poet's youth . . . Here everything is simple and clear, modest, ordinary, everything is essentially human and Polish—because modest and ordinary . . . The men and women are simple, robust, and sane, like the trees that surround them and the century-old houses they live in, they are like all those innumerable vegetables and fruits that the poet depicts for us, like the birds, the animals, the herds of cows, the frogs, the insects, the mushrooms . . . In the limpid clarity of nostalgic memories, as if under the rays of the setting sun, this land and this life appear in an unique splendor, in the splendor of the last hour, in the eternal splendor of memory that nothing can ever destroy . . . For a century this vision nourished souls of our countrymen, and no one, no power, will ever be able to take it away from them.

If the *Forefathers' Eve* and the *Books of the Polish Nation and the Polish Pilgrimage* became a sort of balm for Poland at the moment of their appearance and long after, *Pan Tadeusz* became a sort of communion, a national eucharist. It was an act of communion with the earth: the poet replanted us all and continues to do so, notwithstanding that this act of the poet was only poetry.

But the poetic roots are sometimes stronger than those which can assure us life. The roots through which Mickiewicz attached our soul to our native earth, to the fatherland, are in truth as powerful as those which childhood plants in every man's life: no one can ever tear them out of our hearts and detach them from that of our fatherland. Thanks to him, we shall never be uprooted —whatever our destiny may become.

On October 30, 1849, crowds thronged to the Temple of the Madeleine in Paris. A great Pole had died thirteen days before. An "uprooted one"—one more "uprooted!" It had taken thirteen days to prepare these solemn funeral rites. M. Daguerry, the Curé of the Madeleine, took two weeks to obtain permission to have ladies sing in his church. Without that, it would have been impossible to give Mozart's *Requiem*—and that is what the defunct had demanded. The orchestra of the Conservatory performed, directed by Girard. The soloists were concealed by black drapery, behind the altar: Pauline Viardot-Garcia and Mme. Castellan, Lablache, and Alexis Dupont. Lefébure-Wély was at the organ. At the offertory, he played two preludes by Chopin: Number 4, in *E Minor*, and the Sixth, in *B Minor*,[22] composed at Majorca in that twilight where Chopin had seen death while the rain fell in squalls on the Chartreuse de Valdemosa.

The church was full of Poles and Frenchmen. All the eminent people in musical and literary circles were present. When the

[22] See William Murdoch, *Chopin—His Life*, The Macmillan Company, New York, 1935, p. 389.

coffin descended amid the multitude for the first time the *Funeral March* of Chopin, orchestrated by Reber, sounded forth. The cordons of the pall were held by Prince Alexander Czartoryski, Franchomme, Delacroix, and Gutmann. Meyerbeer and Prince Adam Czartoryski walked behind the hearse. They all walked as far as the Cemetery of Père Lachaise, where the uprooted one was interred. But only his body—his heart was sent to Warsaw, where it has since remained, in the Church of the Holy Cross.

No speech was pronounced. Only a friend's hand was seen to throw on the coffin that bit of Polish earth which had been delivered to the deceased on November 2, 1830, when he had left Poland forever.[23]

When Schumann learned the news of this death, he penned his desolation in moving words: "The soul of music has passed away from the world." "In art the soul is what matters," Delacroix had said. "The life of Frédéric Chopin was completely reserved," wrote one of his most brilliant and inspired biographers, Guy de Pourtalès; "the life of Chopin was completely reserved and no hand was able to pluck it, but it was so much the more charged with perfume. Everything he did not give up, his love which no one took, his bashfulness and his timidity, that continual fever for perfection, his elegance, the nostalgia of exile; and, up to the moments of his communication with the unknowable, all that remained in full potency in his work. Such, even today, is the secret of his strength. Music received what men and women disdained." But in this work—to our own day— "burns the mysticism of a nation."[24]

Son of a French teacher of peasant origin, emigrated to Poland and deeply Polonized (he took part in the Kościuszko insurrection[25]) and a modest bourgeois Polish woman, Justine Krzyża-

[23] See Guy de Pourtalès, *Chopin ou le Poète*, N.R.F. Paris, 1927, pp. 244-245.
[24] *Ibid.*, pp. 243-244.
[25] See W. Murdoch, *op. cit.*, p. 9.

nowska, Frédéric Chopin passed all his childhood and all his adolescence in Poland, where he was born in Żelazowa Wola, near Warsaw, on February 22, 1810. He left Warsaw on November 2, 1830, three or four weeks before the Insurrection. After concerts in Vienna and Munich, he found himself toward the end of September in Paris, where on October 17, 1849, he died in his apartment (Place Vendôme) at the age of thirty-nine.

It would not become me to trace his biography for you here, and still less, the evolution of his art. You know, perhaps better than I, what made up the great, irreplaceable and inimitable qualities of that art: his exquisite sensibility, the richness of his melodies, the special tone of his piano, the extraordinary power he gave to that instrument, his elegant style, the profoundly nostalgic essence of his music. "Like Heine in verse, he wrote in music very freely and without any particular care for formulas established by tradition," Hugo Riemann tells us. And it is not only in the total effect, but down to the smallest details, that his music is new and original;[26] he is the creator of a special genre, of a pianistic style which Liszt adopted and extended without really perfecting it . . . It is in the richness of his ideas and the variety of workmanship that one must seek the key to the mystery that surrounds Chopin's work.

Grove considers that no imitation of Chopin is either possible or desirable—"he was a great inventor not only as regards the technical treatment of the pianoforte, but as regards music *per se,* as regards composition." In fact, of course, never before had the piano had that penetrating, persuasive, and captivating power; never afterward did it attain the same beauty and the same highly aristocratic character.

We know how much is owed to him by Schumann, who adored

[26] Schumann said: "He plays just as he composes, that is, uniquely." (W. Murdoch, *op. cit.*, p. 182.)

him with an adoration expressed with voluptuous sincerity in the
Carnival; we know how far Grieg and Smetana are in his debt;
we know that without Chopin there would have been no Liszt,
Tchaikovsky, Scryabin, Rachmaninov, Debussy, Paderewski, and
Szymanowski, such as we know them. We know that the Russian
national or nationalistic school—Rimski-Korsakov, Moussorgski,
Borodin, Lyadov, and others, admired him and dedicated works
to him. We know that he was the true creator of two currents, of
two styles in music—romanticism and nationalism.[27]

Beside Copernicus, Chopin is our greatest universal genius.
He changed the music of the world, bringing it new musical ideas,
new forms, new tones, new melodies, new rhythms and new
accents. But we know, likewise, that that music is intimately and
deeply Polish; we know that it has become the most powerful, the
ideal expression, of the heroic history of the Polish nation, of its
glories, of its soul, of its sorrows and its sufferings.

Schumann had already divined and felt that: "if we could look
at the very bottom of the causes which gave rise to certain (of
his) compositions, we would learn dreadful things." At another
time he said: "Cannon hidden under flowers; if the Autocrat of
the North knew what an enemy threatens him, even in the simple
melodies of Mazurkas, he would ban this music."[28]

The artist succeeded in wedding folklore and history, nature
and civilization, and in raising the national to the universal, in
imposing on the whole world the style of his art—so original, so
personal, so Polish.

His études, his preludes, his rondos, his mazurkas, ballads,
impromptus, scherzi, his sonatas, and his polonaises—all his
works—and even his waltzes and his nocturnes—are imbued,
impregnated, with Poland. His music is amorous toward his

[27] See W. Murdoch, *op. cit.* (Chapter VIII, pp. 119-122.)
[28] See E. Privat, *op. cit.*, p. 187.

country, like a woman who adores her lover—as the world is
amorous of Chopin. And when one considers that to this day his
Nocturnes are an indefatigable expression of passion and nostalgia, that his *Waltzes* are for each of us the translation of our
most beautiful memories, that those *Polonaises* carry away the
soul of every listener into the majestic trains and grandiose defiles
of the history of Poland, that, finally, his *Funeral March* is still,
after so many generations, continually accompanying thousands
of men to the grave all over the world—one cannot help being
struck with the miraculous potency of this uprooted Pole who
opened to Poland, with his delicate white hand, the hearts of
human beings in every country in the world. He immersed the
Polish soul in the universe. His musical key became a key open-
ing double-barred locks, locks which no other key could ever
open.[29] His art is filled with an ineffable perfume distilled from
the spirit of his suffering fatherland, which he thus elevated to
the world of universal symbols. This "uprooted" man—with his
perfect hands—gathered up the tears from the poor earth of
Poland, he gathered them and set them in the sky, where they still
continue to join in the music of the spheres and to move even
those hearts most obstinately shut against our cause. As Schumann said, "He was the boldest and proudest poetic spirit of the
time."

[29] Comp. W. Murdoch, *op. cit.*, p. 390: "Chopin loved his country, and because of
that love he was able to give it a national heritage. His poetry did not belong to
one man; it belonged to a nation bereft of its freedom. He was endowed by his
genius to express the soul of his people; and by his music he has helped more
than any of his compatriots to preserve the ideal of his country. He lived and died
a patriot."

VII

The Uprooted (Part Two)

1. JULJUSZ SŁOWACKI

THERE was something truly pathetic in the transfer of the ashes of Juljusz Słowacki from France to Poland in 1927.

The Polish ship which carried that relic so dear to Poland trailed a long, broad wake behind it.

Poland took her poet back from the Cemetery of Montmartre in order to entomb him in the old Wawel of Cracow, in the Cathedral of the Wawel where the kings of Poland and the princes of Poland repose and where Kościuszko, Prince Józef Poniatowski, and Mickiewicz sleep beside them. "It is a rare gesture," a Frenchman said; it is even, let us say, a bit difficult to grasp for a foreigner, given the fact that the work of the Polish poet was little known outside of Poland, even in France. That "rare" gesture was symbolic—modern Poland seemed to be desirous of installing the moral reign of him who had been author of the *King-Spirit*.[1]

In Warsaw, too, it had been said: "The homage paid to Słowacki contains the recognition of the tyranny of the Spirit and

[1] See Venceslas Lednicki: *Jules Słowacki (1809-1849)*, "Revue de l'Université de Bruxelles," 1927.

241

of its right to summon to daily toil for the good of the community those who are most highly placed in the hierarchy of the Spirit."[2]

At a certain period in his life (a very brief one—born in 1809, the poet died in 1849), Słowacki did not accept Mickiewicz's optimism in the evaluation of Poland's past; he was also very dubious about Mickiewicz's faith when the latter, all alone, guaranteed a happy and redeeming future. He was full of skeptical pessimism as judge of his people's present; he accused it of a sort of weakness in acting and struggling . . . What severity, what haughty exaction! After all the nation had done and after all she had suffered!

However, the suggestive strength of Słowacki's talent, the ardor of his poetic temperament, and the violence of his polemical eloquence made him for many Poles the man who would in time replace the "master." Forgetful of the patent *activism* of Mickiewicz's poetry, the champions of this opinion saw in Słowacki alone the songster "who made his call to action by the free spirit which, alone, should conquer the right to the free form." That is why, at the period when Mickiewicz became in a way the poet of the past, Słowacki was always one of the first on the road of the future. He was the guide of all those who, after the catastrophe of November, kept on looking for new battlefields; he was the guide down to the hour of freedom . . ."[3]

In the second half of the nineteenth century Słowacki suddenly became Poland's guide and master in the field of "pure poetry" also. "Young Poland"—a school representing the Polish modernists—seeks inspiration in the poetry of Słowacki, who has become for this school its absolute master . . . "Scarcely had he died," it has been said, "when Słowacki was suddenly revealed as the poet of the future, and never since has he ceased to be so and

[2] *Ibid.*
[3] See *ibid.*

become so. All the subsequent flights of Polish poetry and literature issued from him . . ."[4]

I propose to present here only a fragment of Słowacki's great poetical work. The fragment is as beautiful as it is characteristic of him. Słowacki's work presents an infinitely complex aspect, but there is in it a peculiarly powerful element: I mean the subjective element and imagination. The poet's principal law is the will of his ego, the free will which knows no barrier.

According to the just observation of one critic, the heroes of Mickiewicz, Garczyński, and Krasiński, despite their exaggerated, irreducible individualism, definitely find Archimedes' point outside themselves and submit their own desires to the yoke of the "categorical imperative" of the common right. That is not the case for Słowacki. Kordian, the hero of one of the poet's dramas, the story of which I propose to relate, cannot renounce his own ego, he cannot identify himself with the "millions" and "love the millions and suffer for them." He remains alone . . . even at the height of the struggle he finds himself powerless to detach himself from his ego: "he feels grief in every hair, he feels death in every hair . . ." And this sensation, one would say, absorbs him entirely. There is a way, however, to find very significant correctives to Słowacki's "theory" of individualism. That is just what I propose to do tonight.

The problem of action arose for Słowacki; and arose as a moral duty. Those who wish to lull the enslaved and vanquished nation by chimerical dreams are wrong, the poet's obligation is to lead his people toward independence, which shall be won by their own effort. An idea and attitude, no doubt, Byronian. He does not accept the sacrifice of Mickiewicz offering himself up to suffering "for the millions."

To Mickiewicz's *Forefathers' Eve,* Słowacki opposes his *Kor-*

[4] *Ibid.*

dian, an ultraromantic drama with great depth of psychological analysis. It is based in some measure on the story of a Polish conspiracy hatched during the holidays of the coronation of Nicholas I in Warsaw, a story that was half true and half imagined by the poet. The hero of the drama is "a child of the century," a young aristocrat, permeated with all his epoch could furnish him, in a certain degree bowed down under the burden of superabundant richness of sentiment and intellect. This super-abundance of sensitivity and of cerebral labor is in perpetual contradiction with the consciousness of the futility of the existence that fate had bestowed on him. The feeling of emptiness and insufficiency torments Kordian's soul, and nothing can solace this deep heartfelt pain; action is indispensable, but it cannot be the resultant of a personal decision, for all the dreams and all the desires of Kordian are contradictory:

A hundred desires in me, a hundred feelings, a hundred withered leaves . . .
Each stronger puff of wind arouses crowds!
The goal of feelings?—'t is to fade; the voice of feelings?—'t is noises
Without the harmony of sounds . . . O that the thunderbolt might burst over me,
That mid the crowd of thoughts it light one truly great!

We have there a beautiful development of de Vigny's character of Stello, a development which is all the more complicated in that the sentiment of national duty only augments Kordian's inner trouble by the very fact that in his subconscious it is precisely that sentiment which absorbs him despite everything else. The poet makes Kordian pass through a number of stages; he seeks certainty and so finds nothing but doubt.

His point of departure is love; love was to become a frame guaranteeing the purity of his impulses and his dreams, it was to stimulate him to activity; but the impossibility of winning the heart of Laura reveals to him the sterility of this sentiment; the void becomes only greater, and Kordian flees Laura.

By this evasion he is fleeing from life; Kordian approaches death, to which he beckons with a Wertherian gesture. The blow misses; escaped from death, Kordian plunges himself anew into the real world. Everywhere, however, deception comes to stigmatize his hopes . . . In London he perceives nothing but man's lying and humiliation; and London is after all the summit of European culture.

Finally, he finds peace and a semblance of happiness again in poetry:

Shakespeare! O magnificent spirit, you constructed an edifice
Greater than that of God: I should prefer a black cloud
Over my eyes and to look at the world only through your eyes, Shakespeare!

All the same, poetry cannot fill up his existence and his search continues. If chaste and pure love has not given him happiness, will sensuality and lust, perhaps, give him oblivion of himself and his constant agonies? Laura is replaced by Violet; failure cannot be avoided, and he soon tires.[5] Little by little, by a process of elimination, Kordian comes face to face with that which will be confirmed in his consciousness as the goal of his life; this goal is the motherland, work for her, work inspired by a strong religious faith.

But here again his heart crashes grievously into a hard and unforeseen obstacle. Kordian would like to begin by appealing to the conscience of humanity, which he hopes to arouse and animate on behalf of his country's cause. Whom shall he address, if not the man who is Christ's vicar here below and, as such, protects the oppressed and defends the truth, represents in the

[5] For this passage, see J. Kleiner, *Juljusz Słowacki*, Warsaw, 1920, Vol. I, pp. 290-293.

midst of a wholly materialistic and utilitarian world the idea of evangelical love? So he goes to see the Pope. The conception of this scene is beautifully ironic. Listen to it:

Vatican. Salon, hung in damasks. The Pope, shod in golden slippers, is seated. Beside him, on a golden tripod, is his tiara, and on the tiara a parrot with scarlet collar. The Swiss who opens the door to admit Kordian shouts:

THE SWISS: Count Kordian, a Pole.

THE POPE: I salute the descendant of the Sobieskis. *(Extends his hand. Kordian kneels and kisses the Pope's hand.)* Does Poland still ever receive the grace of Heaven? I am saying a prayer to call down Grace on that blessed country, for the Czar, like an angel with an olive-branch, cherishes quite sincere intentions toward the Catholic religion; we must sing Hosanna . . .

THE PARROT *(in a thin and raucous voice)*: Miserere!

KORDIAN: I present you, Sire, with a holy relic: a handful of earth from the country where ten thousand children, old men, and women were massacred . . . These martyrs did not receive their Eucharistic bread before their death . . . Deposit this handful of earth where you hide the precious presents of the Czars, and give me in exchange one single tear . . .

THE PARROT: Lacrima Christi! . . .

THE POPE *(smiling at the parrot and gesturing at him with his hand-kerchief)*: Go away, you Luther you, go away. Well, my son of Polonia, have you seen St. Peter's dome, the circus, the Pantheon? I advise you, go on Sunday and listen to the Choir at the Basilica. For a new chorister has just arrived from Africa, the Dey of Fez sent him to me. Tomorrow I shall give my benediction to Rome and to the world from my eminence. You shall see whole peoples prostrate themselves with humility. Let the Poles pray, venerate the Czar, and believe . . .

KORDIAN: But no one is blessing the handful of blood-soaked earth . . . What can I say?

THE PARROT: De profundis clamavi, clamavi!

THE POPE *(wishing to hide his confusion by laughter and chasing out the parrot)*: Get away, little devil! From the tiara he goes off to the crozier! Vile bird. I am quite prepared to believe that it is Luther's soul doing penance in this parrot; it's full of conjunctions, this little bird: "ergo, forasmuch as, because." Once, hidden behind a curtain, he struck up a discussion with the Cardinal President of the Curia. It seemed to the Cardinal that his questions were being answered by a well-equipped doctor; the parrot cleaned his feathers, and the Cardinal tore his hair and resorted to tears. Finally the parrot slew him with his Hebrew by shouting, "Pappe satan, pappe satan, aleppe . . ."

Stupid little thing! Thus does God sometimes approve the overthrow of the Goliaths of the mind by the devil . . . Well, my son, go with God, and may your people destroy the germs of Jacobin fire . . . Let it take into its hands the psalter, the hoe, and the plough!

KORDIAN *(throwing the handful of earth into the air):* I throw to the four winds the ashes of the martyrs . . . I shall come back to my country with soiled mouth.

THE POPE: I shall be the first to hurl my malediction at the defeated Poles. Let Faith stretch forth its branches like the olive, and may the people live under its shade!

THE PARROT: Alleluia!

Kordian goes out.[6]

This scene recalls the *Dialogue inconnu* from A. de Vigny's *Servitude et Grandeur militaires*—except that the situation in Vigny is quite different. Bonaparte demonstrates to his prisoner, the noble and courageous Pope Pius VII, the absolute weakness of the Church before the triumphant Caesar, he makes him weep; a tear "glided rapidly down the livid and desiccated cheek of Pius VII." To Vigny that tear appeared to be "the last adieu of dying Christianity abandoning the earth to egoism and chance."

Pope Pius VII still wept; Pope Gregory XVI no longer knew how to weep. In vain does Kordian ask of him "one single tear, one single tear" in exchange for the holy relic he had brought him. Słowacki's pessimism, then, is further advanced than that of Vigny; the Church has lost not only its authority but also its Christian virtue; it no longer has a heart. In that, the Polish poet antedates Dostoevski: the conversation of those three personages —Pope Gregory XVI, Kordian, and the parrot—could be a sketch for the *Legend of the Grand Inquisitor,* in which the Rus-

[6] Cf. Słowacki, *Kordian,* Act II.

sian "Goliath of the spirit" reveals the imprisonment of the
Catholic Church by materialism and utilitarianism. Słowacki's
theme survives: the heart of the popes is dried up, it no longer
knows the tears of pity which the Saviour dropped when He beheld
the suffering of men, the earth is henceforth "abandoned to
egoism and chance."

So Kordian has been once more disgraced; for Słowacki, that
was only a question of demonstration and polemic. Mickiewicz
believed that in order to succeed it was necessary to unite the
Polish problem to Catholicism, the patriotic cause to the religious
cause. Słowacki strives to demonstrate that this hope is illusory
—patriotism was not to be separated from its religious base,
that was an axiom as irreducible for Słowacki as it was for
Mickiewicz, but for him this religious base had to be sought not
at Rome but elsewhere. Where? On the top of Mont Blanc! Which
means that man finds his religious inspiration through God's
cognition in the universe, in nature.[7] The idea is reminiscent of
Rousseau: "See the spectacle of nature," we read in *Emile*,
"listen to the inner voice . . . If no one had listened to anything
but what God said to man's heart, there would never have been
more than one religion on the earth."

All the Romantics, by the way, were faithful to this motto.
Lamartine, Byron, Lermontov, Mickiewicz himself, Słowacki
most of all—unlike Vigny, who for his part turned away from
God as well as from nature.[8] On Mont Blanc, Kordian understood his proper calling and that of his country: Poland must
become the Winkelried of the peoples,[9] the knight who will open

[7] Cf. Kleiner, *op. cit.*, pp. 294-297.

[8] Cf. W. Lednicki, *Alfred de Vigny* (Z historji pesymizmu religijnego), Warsaw,
1923, *op. cit.*, pp. 13-21.

[9] This is the explanation of the poet himself: "He (Winkelried) was formerly
the head of the free Swiss. In battle he embraced his enemies' pikes in his two
arms, plunged them into his heart, and thus cleared the way for his soldiers,"
(Kordian, Act III, Sc. IV). (The battle given by the Swiss to the Austrians at
Sempach in 1386.)

the door to the revolutionary currents of the peoples. Thus armed, he rushes to Poland.

If the first two acts of Słowacki's drama are attached to Mickiewicz's *Forefathers' Eve*, Goethe's *Faust*, and Byron's *Manfred*, the third act comes back in a way to the subject of Stefan Garczyński's poem, *The History of Wacław*, and the procedure of Hugo in *Hernani*; it also contains reminiscences of *Stello*.[10] The plot unfolds in the third act. Kordian, a young officer, is the man who eggs on the conspirators to decide upon murdering the Czar at Warsaw, and it is he who voluntarily offers himself as executor of that decision.

The moment arrives for the accomplishment of the act. Kordian is at the threshold of the Czar's bed chamber, and there his impotence to commit the murder triumphs, it is repugnant to him to do it. It was he who during the session of the conspirators had found all the arguments necessary to justify the crime.

He had opposed the plots of the old chairman, who wanted no clandestine struggle. The noble old man urged swords instead of daggers and open and loyal action, as it is fitting for Poles to act. He outlined the frightful disaster to which the crime must lead by engendering other crimes; after the Czar, he said, his wife and children and brothers would necessarily perish. What an immense responsibility before Europe! How would Poland differ from Antony, who had shown Europe Caesar's bloody cloak and incited the whole world to vengeance . . .

Kordian contradicted all that; he reasoned with perspicacious precision and rashly assigned all the responsibilities, he pretended to be himself willing to assume a great part of them. On the balance of justice which his reasoning had erected, he placed the crimes of the Czars and the martyrdom of Poland, and the weight was great enough to counterbalance murder. Reason

[10] Kleiner, *op. cit.*, pp. 303-311.

approved the act; it appeared just and legitimate. But see the sudden change when the hour of vengeance rings! Kordian is incapable of executing his decision.

Hamletism, it has been said—Hamletism which the poet voluntarily exposed in order to bring up Mickiewicz's Konrad and raise against him his Kordian, a weakly being impotent to lift the blade of action, capable of struggling only by means of useless words and vain threats. Such was, it has been said, Słowacki's exact intention, a satirical intention which, once realized, was to demonstrate to Poland what was really represented by the heroism of the generation of 1830.[11]

To that have been added other presumptions. *Kordian* is a work of psychological analysis; it is a study of fear; it contains, besides, some personal reminiscences: the poet has not forgotten how in the era of the insurrection fear had made him quit the country and live far from the trenches and fields of battle.[12]

For us to stop there would be, I think, to limit our view, to diminish the importance of *Kordian,* and, consequently, to undervalue it. Does the moral element really play no role at all in this drama? Would it be absolutely impossible to get anything else out of *Kordian* than satirical ill-humor and the examination of pathological nervousness? Does not this drama suggest to us the (doubtless Pascalian) idea that the conscience of man is not always governed by the rules of algebra, that the heart does not always approve what reason counsels, that mathematical equations do not trace the lines of the conduct of the conscience; that what appears equitable to reason is not necessarily so to conscience? So we could reply to those who hold the "psychological" and "satirical" thesis by saying this: the impotence of Kordian to commit the act of murder cannot be considered only as proof

[11] See J. Ujejski, in J. Słowacki: *Kordian,* "Biblioteka Narodowa," Kraków, 1925.
[12] *Ibid.*

of his weakness, it is not just to see in this sentiment of repugnance for murder a debility that must necessarily compromise the
hero and show that he has no real aptitude for heroism.

To reason thus is, in a way, to follow the path of Dostoevski,
who had by means of his Raskolnikov indicated the road to crime
justified by an individual conscience: Raskolnikov's conscience
was degenerate or simply savage. Raskolnikov was chastened;
the crime, however, was committed, the criminal act duplicated
the inner decision. Is that heroism?

The greatness of the catastrophe in Słowacki's drama is affirmed by the very fact of this moral slavery of his hero, who had
had only the illusion of having emancipated himself, of being released from the power of the precepts of morality. He never forgot
them, and his conscience could not be rid of the yoke of that slavery. This catastrophe is deeply pathetic, and Kordian is never
greater, perhaps, than at the moment when, tormented by the
hallucinations and fearsome visions that his imagination called up
before him, he sinks down on the threshold of the door leading to
the Czar's bedchamber. Never greater, I say, than at this moment
of moral victory, realized with the help of the moral instinct acting
in his subconscious. And *there* lies Słowacki's generous and moving optimism, which illumines the gloom of the subconscious to
show us that man is, deep down, good, that his physical organ-
ism, one might say, is capable of making gestures of forgiveness
that no logic could justify.

Kordian's fright before the murder anticipates, so to speak,
the alarm of Lady Macbeth washing her hands: and both the one
and the other are in the region of the subconscious, and both the
one and the other are provoked by vigilant moral instinct.

I have before me a charming tale by Kellermann: *Among the
Saints*. It is the story of some madmen in a mental hospital. They
commit all kinds of incoherent acts which manifest their absolute

madness. But at the bottom of each one of these acts the writer has been able to find the goodness which stands out as the essential element; this element governs their line of conduct in what would be called, in normal men, an unprecedented manner. And that is comforting; in it consists the sweetest caress that poetry can make to man. Słowacki gives us confidence in ourselves, he suggests to us this idea of such beauty and attractiveness, that it is goodness that is the prime matter of the human soul, that the happiness of man as well as that of a whole nation cannot be founded on another's suffering or on crime, and that no one but God can mete out responsibility. If it were otherwise, crime would breed only more crime, and the world would perish under the avalanche: repugnance to crime, and the gestures of sublime pardon—or of resignation—or even simply of indifference—are perhaps the most efficacious obstacles that a generous heart can place in the way of crime. Kordian showed it to us: he was an example for the Poles; they cherished and adored his soldier's uniform which led them to battle; they took swords and never sought daggers. In that, Słowacki's drama is profoundly national. In that the role of this "uprooted" has been significant and great.

2. *The Undivine Comedy*

There is no reason to insist, on this occasion, upon too many biographical details, and we cannot be ambitious of tracing a complete biography of the author of the *Comedy*. Only *some* facts, and *some* traits, must suffice us.

Let us note here that Zygmunt Krasiński belonged to the great Polish aristocracy. His mother was a Princess Radziwiłł, a descendant of one of the most illustrious families in Poland, related to European dynasties and royalty, and his father, Count Wincenty Krasiński, offspring of an old Polish house, had been a

brilliant general in the Napoleonic army, who had gone on all the
Emperor's campaigns, who had been commander of the Light
Horse of Somo Sierra, brigadier general, head of Polish legions
under General Dąbrowski, the man who had had the great honor
of accompanying to Poland the remains of Prince Joseph Poniatowski after his death at the Battle of Leipzig. He was a Lovelace,
a brilliant talker of Gascon humor and Gallic temperament, educated, lover of literature, unsteady, very brave, opportunistic in
political affairs, loyalist and legitimist; a Pole who, after Napoleon's fall, had gone over to the service of Alexander I,
and who during and after the Polish Insurrection of 1830-31 had
rejoined Nicholas I!

His family life had not been harmonious—it was a bad marriage; his wife, much older than he, had not found happiness in
this *mariage de raison*. So the poet passed his childhood in an
atmosphere of conflicts and misunderstandings. He lived his youth
in the atmosphere of the general's grave dissension from Polish
national and political movements. He suffered profoundly from
it; he was even a direct victim of it, undergoing offenses and
insults from his comrades in high school for taking an attitude of
solidarity with his father. This loyalty toward the general was
based only on attachment and the spirit of filial obedience. The
poet disapproved of his father's political opinions—in his inner-
most heart he profoundly disapproved of them.

He was a sickly child, he suffered from bad eyes and bad lungs,
which obliged his father—who adored his son—to send him
abroad for all kinds of cares and cures. Therefore he spent whole
years in Austria, Switzerland, and Italy.

He was a precocious child; his poetical genius and, simply,
his genius, were so early revealed in him that in Paris in 1816,
at the age of four (he had been born there in 1812), he astonished and even amazed Elizabeth, Empress of Russia, by his

replies, as unforeseen as they were witty. He received an excellent education (his father was a well-lettered man)—and met many famous personalities in the general's house in Warsaw and abroad—at Geneva, Vienna, Florence, and Rome, the great intellectual centers of Europe at that time. Among the men of mark with whom Krasiński was in close contact were Mickiewicz and Słowacki: both of them left an ineffaceable impression on him.

A great friendship united him to a distinguished Englishman, Henry Reeve, with whom for many years he had a very rich exchange of letters and of ideas. He began his poetical career very early with Walter-Scottish novels, studies of a more or less philosophical character, and poems. Suddenly, after his stay in St. Petersburg, in 1832-33—that is, at the age of twenty to twenty-one, he wrote his *Comedy!* That must be unique in the history of literature. There is something almost supernatural in the fact that the *Comedy* is the work of a boy of twenty, but it is quite true.

After the *Comedy* he wrote another drama, *Irydion,* which is likewise one of the greatest masterpieces of Polish literature. Then he published poems of a philosophical and religious nature in which he elaborated a philosophy of history and laid the foundations of Polish romantic messianism. He published "occasional" and erotic poems of less value; Krasiński was a poet whose poetical expression was always inadequate to his means as a thinker and great master of prose.

In connection with the greatest novel, the greatest sentimental story of his life, which had morally detached him from his delightful wife *(née* Countess Branicka) and subjected him profoundly to the famous Countess Delphine Potocka, he worked at poems which were to be a philosophy of love. But it is above all his correspondence with Countess Potocka that retains importance as a document that is profoundly human and tragic and sounds the depths of passion and feeling.

He took up the theme of the *Comedy* again in a work called the *Unfinished Poem* and published political articles, taking the position of a writer who was essentially Catholic and conservative but always very brilliant, very European, very Western. He was an implacable enemy of Russian despotism and imperialism, and some of his pages on these subjects evince a penetration which often appears singularly clairvoyant—today, it must be said, prophetic.

Of all his works the greatest and most beautiful is the *Comedy*. It has been many times translated into Russian, Czech, French, English, German, Italian. It has seen all the greatest stages of the European theater. Writers like Lord Lytton and Chesterton in England have paid it the greatest homage. Monica Gardner has published a fine monograph on it. Dostoevski and Blok, in Russia, must be considered in his debt. In Poland, poets and writers like Sienkiewicz, Kasprowicz, Wyspiański, Żeromski, and Berent are among his disciples. His *Irydion* imposed on the Polish nation the concept of Christian resignation and charity, called to replace the spirit of vengeance and hatred for one's enemies; and thus he set on high the flight of Polish thought, providing it with a beautiful and elegant rhythm. That was in accord, too, with the ideas of Mickiewicz and Słowacki. His best Polish commentators and biographers were Stanisław Tarnowski, J. Klaczko, B. Chlebowski, M. Zdziechowski, and above all Juljusz Kleiner.

The *Undivine Comedy* is one of the most beautiful masterpieces of Polish poetic genius and at the same time represents one of the vastest enterprises in European Romanticism.

What strikes us in this romantic drama is in the first place the variety and complexity of the problems the poet puts to us. What is yet more striking perhaps is the "algebraic" conciseness, the virile sobriety, astonishing for an author aged twenty-one, the extreme laconicism of expression, the daring of the symbolism of what we are wont to call the *form* of the poetic work. Divided into four acts, the *Comedy* is composed of a long series of short scenes, of dialogues shortened to the last mathematical degree. It is a series of philosophical signs and formulae—at once analytical and synthetic—which possess symbolic sense and value of superior richness.

Before our eyes pass scenes of family life, scenes connected with the intimate life of the hero, Count Henry; then scenes in the hospital, revealing his wife's illness and at the same time presaging universal evil (a kind of index of world catastrophe); then the scenes where the child appears; then finally the scenes representing the revolutionary movement, its leaders and the populace, the scenes where the old world is laid bare, the meeting of the two leaders of the opposite camps, the battle, and the denouement, with the appearance of Christ in the sky.

This richness of content shut up in abstract symbolical formulae of crystalline purity, in which the concrete and tangible substance of life receive a general, universal value, suggests a comparison of the *Comedy* with Calderon's *Theater of the World.*

But—there are also the prefaces, the lyrical introductions to each act.

The *Comedy* is written in prose, and yet we call it a "poetical" work. It *is,* in the higher sense of the word. It is a "Summa," a "mystery." It is a modernized antique tragedy, and its modernization gives us a presentiment of expressionism. The classic element is betrayed in the prefaces, in their role in connection with the acts which they precede; it is in the "play" of these prefaces and theatrical scenes that the classic element appears. The prefaces are written in the most beautiful Polish prose, in a style highly poetic, grave, solemn—maintained in the style of "high poetry." They are lyrical. They are a lyric suggestion of what is going to go on on the stage; and the action, the scenes which follow, the characters which appear against the background of those vast prophecies, of those fatidical presentiments, of that "Dionysiac" *melos* (to use the formula of Nietzsche) become the neat and lucid vision, the "Apollonian" vision, the plastic realization of the dream and of presentiment. One would compare them then, to the play of the chorus and the actors of Greek tragedy, the "notices" of Homer indicating the stages of epic narration in the *Iliad*.

The *Comedy* is a romantic drama; its "philosophy," its poetic structure, its interconnections, and its literary tendencies prove it. It is an universalist "mystery-play," a representation of the eternal struggle of good and evil; in that, the *Comedy* continues the tradition of *Faust*, of Byron's "mysteries," of the *Forefathers' Eve of* Mickiewicz, and of the works of many, many other French, Polish, German, and Spanish poets. It is a romantic drama also in the sense that its metaphysics and its mysticism are revealed in the introduction of "spirits"—angels and demons who take part in the struggle of good and evil in the bosom of the human soul.

It is a Dantesque and Shakespearean drama, thus once again romantic; Dante was, along with Shakespeare, an object of especial adulation on the part of the Romantics. This last element appears not only in the title—which was able to suggest his own title to Balzac, through his Polish connections—but also in the composition: we have, in Krasiński's structure, "the Inferno," "Purgatory," and a suggestion, a presentiment, of "Paradiso," we also have Dante's "tourism," with its guide through the different circles of the Inferno and Purgatory. But just what does this "tourism" of Dante represent—this journey which lasts, as we know, exactly one week, this excursion which conducts the poet into the depths of the Inferno and onto the summit of Paradise? It is a journey, like *Hamlet,* through the human heart, it is a story of its falls and its uplifts, it is a "Last Judgment" on the human personality. It is in the same Dantesque sense that Krasiński's *Comedy* is likewise a "Last Judgment" and a drama on the human person in the widest acceptance of the term.

It is a romantic drama by reason of its manifest but intentional "fragmentarism" acting as a function of the famous romantic conception of *irony.* No poetic work—for a Romantic—can be adequate to the poet's prophetic vision of the reality that is superior, true, existing behind the veil of the "practical" reality that is common, vulgar, concrete, tangible to our senses. In the moments of his poetic inspiration—and that romantic cult of poetic inspiration has found its best expression in the celebrated *Improvisation* of Mickiewicz—the poet, in these moments when the God of inspiration touches him, becomes a clairvoyant, a prophet who sees all and understands all, who contemplates from the peaks of his "ascent," of his poetic "elevation," that veritable, transcendent, "Platonic," metaphysical reality of which our own is only an ill-made and sadly ordinary shadow. But once the instant of inspiration is ended, the poet's vision becomes only a memory which he vainly attempts to reproduce by the inadequate and insufficient means of art; these means are inadequate because they belong to "empiric" reality, to "sensual" reality—inferior to the metaphysical truth which the poet has known thanks to the heights of his inspiration.

The poet is aware of his irrefutable and irremediable weakness and insufficiency, he knows that his work is not capable of representing the true world; that is why he takes an ironic attitude in regard to his art and to himself, and on the other hand renounces the attempt to give a complete formula of his vision of the world: he operates with suggestions, he intentionally introduces fragmentarism. Such is the *Third Part* of Mickiewicz's *Forefathers' Eve*, a romantic drama par excellence.

In the same order of philosophical and aesthetic ideas and conceptions are the works of the German Romantics, who can be considered the founders of the concept of romantic irony and fragmentarism—expressions of the metaphysical idealism of the German romantic school. We may note that Sterne had already prepared the way for the development of these ideas.

But Krasiński—and this was due to his precocious philosophical intuition—went still further. Some of his reflections on these subjects show him to be a thinker who preceded Schopenhauer, Bergson, Dostoevski, and Tolstoy. Here is one of those meditations on art which assured him the place we have just assigned him in the evolution of philosophical and aesthetic ideas: ". . . a painting," he says in a letter written in 1833, "a statue, a word, a sign—it is always the same thing: an instant of life arrested in its passage and immediately struck into immobility and death. Man can express himself only by inanimate things. Each one of these expressions, therefore, is a falsity, as it is charged with representing life while being itself a corpse . . ."[13] As is well known, this dilemma was the principal object of the philosophy of Henri Bergson, prepared by the intuitivism of Schopenhauer and the irrationalism of Dostoevski and Tolstoy.

On the other hand, however, Krasiński, the "Polish Vigny," poet-thinker and poet-philosopher, was a child of the century, which meant that the categorical imperative of the heart, the "Rousseauistic Charter" of sentimental irrationalism which all Europe, in opposition to the Age of Enlightenment, had from that time on recognized and accepted, became for him an irrefutable gospel.

[13] *Correspondance de Sigismond Krasiński et de Henry Reeve,* Paris, Delagrave, Vols. I-II, 1902.

That Rousseauism, that imperative of the heart—the only source of true human wisdom—Krasiński had found in Mickiewicz's *Ode to Youth,* which had established the superiority of the man who was "wise through passion, wise through exaltation," and who had opposed to the "magnifying-glass of the scholar" the "wisdom of the heart," to the egoism of the parasite the altruism of the man of action, to the indifferent cruelty of the Wisdom of God *(Improvisation)* the love and goodness of man. The *Comedy,* then, is a drama of the human heart, and it is in this that its universal significance first of all consists. It is a refutation of individual egoism as well as of social egoism.

But the *Comedy* is equally a drama anent the poet. The preface to the first act, the first act itself, Count Henry—hero of the work —his wife, their son Orcio, all that is directly attached to the problem of the poet, poetry, and the role of the poet and of poetry in human life.

And yet, as appears in Krasiński's text, his *Comedy* is a refutation of the poet and of poetry. The *Comedy* is a condemnation of the unlucky gift that the Muses bring man; poets and poetry sow only disaster, and although revealing the beautiful and the good, are not the beautiful and the good. There we have a postulate which by no means conforms to the classical cult of the poet established by Romanticism in every country; neither Goethe, nor certainly A. de Vigny, nor Pushkin, nor even Mickiewicz, nor Byron had ever attacked the poet. Quite the contrary, the romantic poet had become a sort of prophet, of clairvoyant, of priest, of magician, and his priesthood continued to exist down to the time of the Parnassians and the Symbolists.

Krasiński expresses his ideas on the subject very neatly in one of his letters: ". . . Art is but the truth of truth, the sentiment of sentiment, and not sentiment itself. There are ineffable delights for the artist, but he is also destined to suffer more than anyone

else in the world. True, his egoism is sublime, but it is still egoism
. . . He will never know what is truly love for a woman, for to
him he is all . . . He loves his masterpieces but he loves nothing
else . . . He comes into the midst of men like Cain bearing a curse
on his forehead . . ." (April 4, 1833.)[14] A little earlier, in January
of the same year, he was writing as follows: ". . . Imagination
without heart is equivalent to Satan himself . . ." We have here
the program—*in nuce*—of the first preface and the first act of
the *Comedy*.

Although this refutation of the poet and this judgment so severely pronounced on poetry appear here as a very personal
gesture of thought (in a certain measure that is so, given the
circumstances in which Krasiński lived himself and in which he
worked out this system of ideas), there are here easily decipher-
able romantic elements. It is a Byronism, but it is Polish Byronism: Byron's poetry was interpreted among us in the sense of a
poetry of action, *par excellence*. It is the formula of Mickiewicz
which appeared in his brilliant study on the poetry of Byron and
Goethe, written in the period of the poet's youth as well as in his
course on Slavic literature given at the Collège de France. This
interpretation—Polish *par excellence*—conforms, it must be admitted, to the life of the English poet, to the fact of the intimate
union which existed between that life and his poetry, it conforms
to the sentiments expressed in Byron's last poem:

> 'Tis time this heart should be unmoved,
> Since others it hath ceased to move . . .

But there is not only Byron; there is also *Don Quixote*, that
marvelous book on enthusiasm, idealism, on the human heart;
that "modern" novel which became, for Schlegel and for Tieck,
the never-surpassed model of "total" art, the complete and

[14] See *Correspondance*, etc.

definitive history of the conflict that exists between the ideal and the reality, between poetry and life, the book on which the romantic conceptions of Irony were, in great measure, based; the book that Heine had so admired . . . And let us bear in mind that Krasiński was a disciple of the German Romantics, whose cult for Cervantes and Calderon could not be foreign to him. Besides —very soon, a little bit later, his great friend Juljusz Słowacki devoted himself with great zeal to his translation of Calderon's *Prince Constant.*

Thus, only a poetry of action, a poetry representing moral action, is worthy of recognition as true, really great poetry. Krasiński does not admit "poetic speculation." ". . . First of all," he said in a letter of the same year, 1833, "we reject the positive, we live the life of the pure spirit; that cannot last long. Man must be reconstituted, his soul must be amalgamated with his body, and if this transformation operates in the individual it will operate in poetry also . . . he (the poet) will be *par excellence* a man, he will understand his brothers, and sometimes he will turn to the higher world as one turns to the memory of a lover or the presentiment of felicity . . ." (April 7, 1933.)[15] A year before, meditating on the lot of the men of his time, he averred that men ". . . must become conscious beings . . . that up till now they were (in his imagination when he was conceiving his drama) poetic beings—now they must become moral beings . . ."[16] (June 21, 1832, and January 23, 1833.) The idea of sacrifice for someone else was gradually and little by little added to the concept of his drama. That is how, finally, he reached the conclusion that the work of thought must be in the center, in the middle, with its analytical role placing it between vague presentiment and the lucid conviction that gives the feeling of truth.

[15] *Ibid.*
[16] *Ibid.*

On the other hand it would not be well to neglect another striking and quite significant detail: the curse the poet put on poetry as a destructive element of life is justified in the *Comedy* by the fact that the victims of this mysterious but so maleficent power are just those beings who are morally the most beautiful and innocent: the mother, that madonna of goodness and charity, and the son Orcio, who become the holocaust. Poetry, of which Count Henry is the messenger in their life, destroys them and kills them, especially the woman. There, one might say, is a reminiscence of Ophelia, and at the same time a prophetic preamble to Turgenev's charming and penetrating stories in which the great master of the Russian novel revealed the metaphysical role of poetry in human life and the tragic mysticism of that role. The greatest disasters of human life are sometimes due to the unlucky and maleficent prestige of poetry, which invades innocent souls and exploits their charity; here, it is true, we are not too far from either *Eloa* by Alfred de Vigny or from its replica, Lermontov's *Demon*, or from *Faust*. But no one before Krasiński had succeeded in demonstrating that mysterious phenomenon of our existence with the same lucidity of mind and with the same severe clairvoyance.

But the *Comedy* is also a domestic drama; and here, once more, Krasiński outstrips his epoch and takes the attitude of disavowing romantic individualism and openly disapproving all the abuses of those who in following only the commands of their egoism, considered as a stamp and as a privilege of the superior being which is in their eyes the elect of the Muses, lead to suffering, to unhappiness, and to disaster those who depend on their whims.

The young poet, in some scenes of really exceptional conciseness, traces the tragic destinies of the domestic drama—of the drama between husband and wife—which unfolds in the first act of the *Comedy*. This attitude is neither classical nor typical for a Romantic—the frenzies of Romanticism are made to submit, in the moral judgment of the author, to the ideological prestige of the family hearth and the moral prestige of the wife. In this sense the first title of the *Comedy*, absolutely Balzacian *(avant la lettre)*— *Commedia Umana*—appears quite justified. Especially so, as the essential personages in the drama are surrounded by a crowd of men and women who represent, thanks to the surprising economy of Krasiński's descriptive means, a true synthesis of the society of his time.

But in this domestic drama, which by the way is developed within the first act, it is especially the marriage, and it is the husband—Count Henry, presented in the first phase of his life— and wife who occupy the foreground of the stage, becoming the living bands of the action. This couple is symbolic in its essence. It appeared in Polish poetry for the first time, and at a moment when even in universal poetry the problem of the alleged incompatibility of the "higher" nature of the artist and the "flat," "bourgeois" forms that family life had taken on after the French Revolution, which had restored the prestige of the family hearth, had not yet arisen. This couple moved Poland deeply and has been seen again since the *Comedy*, under the pen of novelists like Sienkiewicz and Prus as well as dramatists like Wyspiański.

It is above all the glory of the martyr, the agony of woman, which created the special moral prestige of this drama and which made it a powerful projection of skepticism and criticism; its rays penetrated into the very depth of that primordial cell which is marriage and the family hearth in the social order, while revealing the menace sheltered in what the poet had called "imagination without heart." Here we face problems which will be developed much later in Europe, at the moment when the criticism of Romanticism will become a rigorously repressive judgment—we mean, at the moment of the appearance of *Madame Bovary*.

The *Comedy* is a drama of the child. In some lines of the preface to the second act, in some scenes where little Orcio appears, the poet has sounded out an infinitely fine and delicate depth in the child's heart, scrutinized all the remote corners and touched all the abysses. In this sense the *Comedy* can be placed beside *Cuore* of de Amicis, the poems of Lermontov, Tolstoy's *Childhood*, the stories of Daudet; and Krasiński's little Orcio belongs to the pathetic group of the children of Holy Writ, the children of Dostoevski and Dickens, that group in which we may see beside him the children of Prus and that truly unique angel, the little Litka of Sienkiewicz's *The Połanieckis*. The only difference is that Orcio, with mystical clairvoyance, understands the latent meaning of the cataclysm of which he, the sick blind boy, is a passive witness, while Litka, nailed to her bed by disease, weaves in her soul like a garland of flowers the destinies she devotes to the happiness of the two beings whom she loves and has decided to reunite.

The *Comedy* is a social and religious drama, it is a drama on revolution and on Christ, and it is here, in this plane, that the chief meaning of this work lies, it is here that the greatness of its poetical attestation of the present and the import of its prophetic significance come into view. If it is today, above all, that Krasiński's comedy appears to our eyes in all the splendor of its hitherto latent revelation, it is because, as drama attached to the idea of an overthrow of the universal order, it definitely discloses its transcendent meaning in the climate of a cataclysm, in the atmosphere of the hurricanes of the history, in the face of the dissolution of entire worlds which collapse and fall apart.

In this sense the last scene of the first act, which takes us into a madhouse, is especially compelling:

THE WIFE *(who has gone mad)*: He does not know what he is saying, but I am going to declare to you what would have happened if God were to go mad *(she takes her husband by the hand)*. All the worlds fly high and low, every man and every worm cries, 'I am God,' and one after the other they perish, the sun and the stars die out . . . Christ will no longer save us, he has taken his cross in his hands and hurled it into the abyss. Hear how that cross, the hope of millions of men, breaks into bits striking against the stars, it shivers into pieces, its bits fall lower and lower . . . Nothing is left but dust . . .

The *Comedy* was finished in the autumn of 1833; the first reflections on the work date from 1832, when the poet, after the Polish Insurrection of 1830-31, found himself forced by his father, General Krasiński (adversary of that Insurrection), to go to St. Petersburg in 1832-33 and, what was more, to be presented to Emperor Nicholas I.

Europe had just undergone a series of political and social shocks and commotions. The French Revolution of 1830, the Belgian Revolution of 1830-31 . . . In England the Reform Bill (June 7, 1832) was to give rise to threatening movements among the people, and Krasiński's intimate English friend—the celebrated Henry Reeve—reported all the events to him with very great care; he predicted a revolution.

Riots occurred in Lyon, and Krasiński observed them attentively from Switzerland, where he was before and during the Polish Insurrection. In Paris, Saint-Simonism was in full swing: *Le Globe* was full of speeches and articles by Enfantin, Bazard, Rodrigues, Barrault. These articles, speeches, and sermons preached a new religion with a new God—the God of Humanity; hailed the wrecking of thrones and the ruin of the family; announced a new religion, a new politics, a new morality, a new society. Humanity appeared divided into two camps, those who work and those who are idle. The idle had all the privileges, the others were only victims. That must change. A new aristocracy—formed of representatives of science, of the arts, of industry, and of the Saint-Simonian clergy—must rise up. The emancipation of Woman was promulgated; the equality of mind and matter, labor as the moral basis of power, the cult of free love—these are the "slogans" which the poet found in the *Globe* and in other publications. Two young workwomen whom he had met one day at Ferney had haughtily replied to him that all was finished for the "rich," and that the revolution was going to put an end to "their abuses."

Such was the practical, concrete, experimental side of the problem of revolution with which the young poet was preoccupied. Let us add to these facts, again, that he did not take part in the Polish Insurrection of 1830-31, despite his great desire to join the Polish troops—all because of the irrefutable prohibition of his father, who considered the movement as perilous for the country and as an emanation of the revolutionary and "Jacobin" clubs.

The poet suffered doubly: first, because of his own desertion, and then because of the martyrdom through which his country was going after the Insurrection had been liquidated by Nicholas I. Little by little the suffering of Poland and his own suffering took on a symbolic and universal meaning in the poet's soul; this essentially moral theme—for the Polish Insurrection had become for him a dilemma of the moral order—presided, so to speak, at the discussions with Reeve on European events and in the poet's reading. These meditations of the poet on events took on, in their turn, a more and more general meaning; for him they became symptoms of the termination of one phase of history. It was in this order of ideas that this social and political drama was conceived.

The finale of the drama—that ultimate end, where all is consummated, the vision of Christ which ends the drama—the idea of
such a conclusion had come to the poet from the impression which
the Coliseum, with its humble cross in the center, had given him:
the cross dominating everything—the glories of the past, battles
to exhaustion, human misery, worlds in ruin . . .

However, we have not yet exhausted the content of this social
and political drama. There is one special element in it which
makes it a distinct work, and which at the same time places the
Comedy at the head of a whole line of masterpieces belonging to
European poetry of the nineteenth and twentieth centuries. We
have in mind the "religionization" of revolution, the mystical side
and the metaphysical meaning of revolution which Krasiński
revealed so splendidly in the final scene of his *Comedy,* to which
we have just alluded. That mystical and metaphysical element has
two facets here: on one hand, it is the apocalyptic attitude of the
poet vis-à-vis revolution, accompanied by a kind of obsession. On
the other hand we are struck by the effort to Christianize revolution and its conquests.

Krasiński was not alone on these avenues of historical and
philosophical thought. The problem of the theodicy of revolution,
of the "religionization," was a matter of deep preoccupation to
the European minds of that era. Without citing Joseph de Maistre,
with his glorification of the martyr, it will be enough to note that
Krasiński had certainly read and studied Schiller, Schelling,
the Schlegels, Hegel, but above all Ballanche, Guizot, Cousin, de
Gerando, Quinet, Jean Paul Richter and through the mediation of
Reeve he later drew near to the English, in particular to Carlyle.

The century continued to reflect upon this problem; the year
1847 alone saw the appearance of Lamartine's *Histoire des
Girondins,* an apologia of the Revolution ("holy and necessary"),
Louis Blanc's *Histoire de la Révolution,* Michelet's *Histoire de la*

Révolution—which gives a mystical interpretation to the Revolution—and so on. Then comes Renan, who, dazzled by Michelet, will proclaim that the Revolution is going "more and more to religionification" and will compare the Revolution of 1789 to the revolution that Christianity wrought in the world—without saying that his *Life of Jesus* gives us the conception of the Kingdom of God as the coming of the poor into their rightful reward. Well before him, Lamennais, Montalembert, Lacordaire, and Mickiewicz preach the same charity and undertake the bold design of "Christianizing" the Church . . .

In 1844 Mickiewicz says in one of his lectures at the Collège de France:

"The common people are those who suffer, those who languish, those who are free in spirit and who do not come with ready-made bundles of systems . . . These classes—the upper layer in the Church—have abandoned the Church; they are not willing to suffer, they have always done all they could to evade suffering and they have shut themselves up in books, in theology and in doctrines. Each of us knows that it is much easier to believe and to make arguments than to tell the truth sincerely and to suffer in its defense. Force breeds only suffering . . . He therefore who desires to be a creator in art or indeed a leader in politics must necessarily identify himself with the spirit of the masses who suffer and languish while awaiting the future. What then must be the suffering of those who represent the Church? It is indescribable grief—what Saint-Martin called prophetic agony, it is quite different from the torments of the artist or indeed from individual suffering: it is a grief which one man feels for millions. He who is not preoccupied with his own salvation is incapable of feeling such suffering."

In 1848 he cries to Pope Pius IX during an audience at the Vatican, in a moment of supreme emotion: "Do you know that

the spirit of God now dwells in the shirts of the workers of
Paris?" And Lamennais: "Christ restored freedom on earth."
... "The cry of the poor man rises to God, but reaches not the ear
of man."[17]

But all that came after the *Comedy;* it was indeed Krasiński who
was first to pose the problem of Christ and Revolution, and this
courageous act was of immense poetic import, for it is possible
to establish a tradition of this thought: after the *Comedy* we see
the rise of the poems of Tyutchev in Russia, Wyspiański and
Kasprowicz in Poland, Victor Hugo, Leconte de Lisle, Villiers
de L'Isle-Adam in France, the *Legend of the Grand Inquisitor*
by Dostoevski, Bely's *Resurrection of Christ,* and finally *The
Twelve* of Alexander Blok in Russia . . .

It would be truly difficult not to cite here two texts belonging
to this singular poetical tradition.

Here is the first. In 1903, or a little later, our great poet and
playwright Stanisław Wyspiański sketched the following plan of
a drama he proposed to write:

Castel Sant' Angelo. The workers' revolution has already invaded
all the old world, it has scattered all the kings and all the aristocrats. The
latter have fled hither with the head of the Church. The revolutionaries,
at the head of whom is a young leader, besiege the castle and keep on
attacking it. Despite the insistence of the conversatives, the Pope does not
let the order be given to fire on the besiegers. Finally he yields and orders
the cannon used. The assailants scale the walls, led by their chief. He
appears before the Pope; his face is that of Christ.[18]

The other is Blok's *Twelve:*

> They come thus, with ordered step,
> Behind them, the famished dog;
> Before them, bearing the bloody flag,

---

[17] See M. Handelsman, *op. cit.,* p. 105.
[18] See W. Feldman, *Współczesna Literatura Polska, 1863-1923,* 7th ed., pp. 290-
291; and V. Lednicki, *Christ et Révolution dans la Poésie Russe et Polonaise,*
"Mélanges Jules Legras," Paris, 1939.

Invisible in the tempest,
Invulnerable to the bullets,
Dominating the hurricane with his tender bearing, glitter
In a glitter of snowy pearls,
Crowned with white roses,
Before them advances Our Lord Christ.

In Kasprowicz, the red flag of revolution appeared as a remnant of the Cross. Tyutchev has the "Face of God" shining over the water which "will come to cover all the horizon"— "When the world will hear the last hour sound." It will be also the "immaculate surplice of Christ which will come to heal the wounds" and the "scars of blows and a thousand cruelties" and will aid the souls devoured and the hearts shattered by corruption . . .

Leconte de Lisle, Hugo, Dostoevski, Villiers de l'Isle-Adam make Christ appear face to face with the Pope or with the "Grand Inquisitor" in order to show that Christ is with the people, with the poor, with the, rebels. Dostoevski says once that if there has to be a choice between Truth and Christ, and if Christ were not Truth, he would choose Christ . . .

What is striking in this poetical tradition inaugurated by Krasiński's *Comedy* is, first of all, the feeling of cosmic disorder that the Revolution brings, but that feeling—apocalyptic in its essence—is accompanied by another: that this terrible play of the elements, the chaos, the general confusion of things, the disaster terminating an era (the wreck of the old world), and inaugurating a new era, this universal cataclysm, is bursting forth under the auspices of Christ.

There is even more—an obsession, as I have already said. All these writers and poets feel themselves, despite everything and against everything, attracted by this power, as elemental as it is unwonted. They were convinced—Krasiński, at any rate, as we shall see presently—in the depth of their souls that revolution represented only a work of destruction, and it attracted them all the same. It frightened them, but they yielded to its suggestion. They adopted this state of mind in an apocalyptic faith that the reign of God would be established on the rubbish of the old world destroyed by revolution. Aside from that, it is also striking that the effort to Christianize Revolution and its conquests comes from those who in fact belong to neither one of the two hostile camps. These ranks are in the center, in the middle of the combat, although they have all been formed by the old world and represent the disinterested thought, of itself full of altruism, generosity, and condescension, of the intellectual élite, always and above all *organically, fatally* pacific. Such is the ontology of these neutral layers facing the "cosmic chaos" unchained by revolution.

This ontology has nothing in common, it goes without saying, with Bolshevistic or Nazistic ideology—both equal and adequate in the absolute negation of Christian morality, of immanent and transcendent morality. It must be considered to be precisely *pity* which made Christ appear in the works of the poets cited here: they understood that this meant to create not only a theodicy for revolution, but a moral protection for those who stood in greatest need of it: for the rebels become persecutors.

It is in this sense that this system of moral and social ideas is flagrantly opposed, as I once said,[19] to Nietzsche—to his *Antichrist*, to that consecration *avant la lettre*, to that *annunciation* of the Bolshevistic or Nazistic *Weltanschauung*. "This toleration," we read in the first chapter of the *Antichrist*, "and this *breadth* of heart, which pardons all because it 'understands' all, is for us something like a sirocco . . ." "I am making sure to say," con-

[19] *Christ et Révolution*, etc.

tinues Nietzsche, "what I think of the Germans . . . Did not Kant see in the French Revolution the passage of the inorganic form of the state to the *organic* form? Did he not wonder whether there existed an event which was unexplainable otherwise than by a moral aptitude of humanity, so that through this event would be demonstrated once for all the 'trend of humanity toward the good'? Kant's answer: It is the Revolution! Instinct which is mistaken in all things, instinct against nature, German decadence in the guise of philosophy, that is Kant!" . . . "To protect the instinct of life, it would be necessary in fact to find out some means of striking a blow at an accumulation of pity in order to burst it . . . Nothing is more unhealthy in the midst of our unhealthy modernity than Christian pity . . ."

Here we have already entered into the domain of the interpretation of the *Comedy*.

We may use here several sources: in the first place the work itself, in the second place what the author has said elsewhere on the subject of his work and in relation to the problems to which he gave value in his work, and, finally, what has been said by those who have studied the *Comedy*.

Let us begin with those texts of Krasiński that do not belong to the *Comedy*.

In his letters to Reeve, the poet somewhat exalted the duty of the aristocracy to take an attitude of stoical heroism in the class struggle. "I repeat," he said, like Hugo, speaking of the antichrist, "he will come . . ." And he added: "In the name of Jesus we are suffering, and, when we are forced to it, we shall fight. At the moment of combat we will be aided by the strength of the barbarian or the gentleman who was our first father. Then, when we shall have perished, let them arrange the earth to their humor, free for them; and I do think that a day will come when love will capture it again. For God is justice and beauty, the universe is harmonic, and I am immortal . . ."[20]

Here is a still more important text: "We are born and we live in night which has followed the sunset and precedes the dawn. The night can indeed be lit by some bloody and fleeting meteor; but long before the rise of another sun we shall all have disappeared from the scene. Now, call forth the shade of Attila the Hun, who without doubt was one of the men whose movement prepared European civilization, and ask him whether he foresaw the coming of General Washington. Take two men linked still more intimately than the Hun and the General, take Luther and Danton: the first never suspected the second. God alone can live in all ages; a man can live only in one. So I think that they who wish to rise above the vague instinct of the future, an instinct common to us all, those who pretend to explain, describe, coordinate that future, are nothing but knaves and fools. *Risum non teneatis, amici.* For, I repeat, we are born in the twilight of night; now, the glooms of night thicken around us, and, when our bones have rotted, then will come the dawn . . ."[21]

In another letter, in that in which he makes Reeve a detailed exposition of his *Comedy*, after recounting the development of the action and explaining the characters as well as the meaning of the conflict and cited the last scene almost textually, he adds: "He (Pancras) has seen the cross; and his work has appeared false to him. He is vanquished at the moment of his victory; his edifice is smashed, and he dies repeating the last words of Julian the Apostate."[22] One would say, then, that the poet makes a refutation finally of the leader of the Revolution and that consequently he is undertaking the defense of the opposing camp?

In another letter (February 5, 1833) he expresses himself just

[20] See *Correspondance*, etc., Vol. II, pp. 28-29.
[21] *Ibid.*, pp. 16-17.
[22] *Ibid.*, p. 59.

as unequivocally: "God forgive me for having arrived at a conclusion that is degrading for humanity: it is that the masses have only appetites and never use reason, that man is everything—men are nothing . . ." "Men have begun to live in order to live—they live because they live and not because they work . . ."[23]

Finally, in 1834, when the *Comedy* had already been finished, his pessimism became still more acute (Letter to his friend Gaszyński) : "With what men do you wish to organize the Republic in France?" With the merchants who reign, and the workmen who labor in the factories? For he sees no one else on this earth . . . Both are far from being willing to make any sacrifice. "The first are greedy and cruel because they possess; the others, greedy, passionate, and cruel—because they suffer." He sees only two possible systems—despotism or anarchy. He foresees destruction. "Our civilization is coming to its end; the time is near when new crimes will come to punish the old crimes and denounce themselves before the face of God—I know that they will create nothing, that they will construct nothing—they will pass on like Attila's horse."[24]

The problem of the interpretation of the *Comedy* became particularly difficult thanks to the fact that Krasiński worked from 1838 to 1852 at another work, entitled *Unfinished Poem*, which took up the same subject again. It is evident that the poet's ideas had evolved, had changed, and that his own conception of the *Comedy* was modified. The fact of adding to it a new work treating the same subject represents a rehandling of it.

We must not let ourselves be guided by the *Unfinished Poem* when we try to interpret the *Comedy*—that is an essential point. The *Comedy* is a "finished poem," and Krasiński himself can no longer change anything whatsoever in it. We must take into

[23] *Ibid.*
[24] See Stanisław Tarnowski, *Zygmunt Krasiński,* Kraków, 1893, p. 74.

account here also a very significant aesthetic phenomenon: that is, the intrinsic independence of the finished artistic work. It represents a world that is closed and by itself, and even the author of the work is no longer the master there once his labor is accomplished.

We know many facts which attest this independence—even the independence of the characters. We know that Prince Andrey Bolkonski, in *War and Peace,* survived the Battle of Austerlitz, which was contrary to the first design of the author; he began a life in the novel which had become independent of Tolstoy's will. We know that when Thackeray was questioned about his characters, he sent his interlocutors back to his characters, claiming that the latter knew much more about it than he. Mauriac dwelt on the same problem. We know, for example, that Jules Romains' characters are much more intelligent than the author of *Men of Good Will* . . .

The *Comedy* had its own meaning, which Krasiński himself would not be able to define in formulae and abstract words . . . One of the first interpreters of Krasiński's work was Mickiewicz. He did it in his course on Slavic Literature at the Collège de France. He dwelt especially on the explanation of the final, and incidentally the most important, scene of the *Comedy.* "The end of this drama is sublime," said Mickiewicz. "I know nothing comparable. It is that truth was neither in the camp of the Count nor in that of Pancras; it was above them; it appeared in order to damn them. Pancras, after doubting everything, is troubled and finally recognizes that he has been only an instrument of destruction. It is then that he perceives on a cloud a sign invisible to all but himself; and at the moment when he recognizes it he falls dead, pronouncing the famous words of the Roman Emperor who tried in vain to destroy Christianity, and who, dying, exclaimed, 'Thou hast conquered, O Galilean!' Therefore, it is to the glory of the Galilean that this drama is really consecrated. The author has been accused from two sides: some have seen nothing else in his work but the expression of violent hatred for the ideas of progress: for he has exaggerated to caricature the language of modern reformers and heightened the character of their adversaries; the others have blamed what there seemed to be of irreligion in the spectacle of triumphant evil. But the truth is that this poem is merely the cry of despair of a man of genius who recognizes the greatness and difficulty of social questions and who, unfortunately, did not raise himself to a height from which he could glimpse the solution of them . . ."[25]

It would seem that the accusations cited by Mickiewicz, as well as his own reservations, are unjust. Attentive examination of the work itself suggests several corrections in Mickiewicz's exposé as well as in the commentaries on Krasiński.

In the first place, Krasiński in no wise appeared in his work like a man who felt a "violent hatred for the ideas of progress." The scenes which pertain to the "circles" of the Revolution—to use Dante's term—are not scenes of the Inferno—it is, rather, Purgatorio . . . These scenes are signs, algebraic formulae of everything Krasiński could have read in the *Globe*. We have there an exceedingly exact reproduction of Saint-Simonism. Let us note here, however, one thing: that from the purely Christian point of view, progress is, as has been said, an anti-Christian idea, in the sense that it establishes an inequality of souls toward the Lord, toward the Last Judgment—it admits only death to innumerable preceding generations . . . The idea of perpetual progress conceives life and history as having no end, as infinite, and the Infinite is not a Christian concept: the philosophy of history such as is revealed in the Christian idea foresees an end. The *Undivine Comedy* suggests this idea of the end.

[25] Adam Mickiewicz: *Les Slaves*, Paris, 1914, pp. 91-93.

On the other hand, the poet certainly did not exalt the character of the enemies of Revolution. In this sense, the first scenes of the fourth act are extremely striking. The poet throws into relief the vulgar platitude, the cowardly opportunism, the spiritual emptiness of the nobles assembled in the trenches of the Holy-Trinity. There, all is rottenness, all is lost—save money. When the noble ceases to be "noble," when he loses the sentiment of honor and the consciousness of his moral superiority, his reason for being no longer exists.

These aristocrats assembled at the Holy-Trinity are ready to make an alliance with the devil if it should be necessary, to commit all possible base acts, in order to save their privileges and their money. It is an alliance of capital with knavery, fraud, and cowardice. It is not a war for ideas and for a clear program, for an ideology, for a religion, for a moral charter—it is a war for one's hide. The poet shows that everyone has arrived inwardly at his moral finish, if only because he has lost all faculty for heroism. He demonstrates it not only in the scenes of the first act, where each of the aristocrats is ready to surrender and ready to betray the common cause. Besides, for them there is no common cause! He shows it in the scene of the meeting of the two leaders, when Pancras goes round to all the Count's family portraits and reawakens the memories of the past, unveils all the abuses, cruelties, frauds, adulteries, debauches, usurpations, which have made up the content of their life . . . Therefore, there is nothing of that to be saved—not even the past!

On the other hand, in the scenes of Revolution we perceive the wives of aristocrats, princesses and countesses, who have deserted the aristocracy, who have abandoned their husbands and joined the Revolution . . .

So there is nothing of that to be saved—not even the past! That is the true, the veritable "Inferno"; it is indeed that place before which we may inscribe, "Abandon all hope, ye who enter here."

The leader of the aristocrats, Count Henry himself, is of the same opinion; in some rapid words he exchanges with his co-religionists, the i's are dotted very neatly. The Count knows very well that there is nothing there to defend; his attitude is that of a stoical skeptic, of a noble who, à la Vigny, accomplishes his "heavy task," although he knows that he will perish only for his own honor and not for a cause that could justify that struggle.

The poet pushes his disclaimer even further; in the scene where Count Henry is with his son George (Orcio), with whom he is going down into the underground of the castle, the poet causes the vision of the Last Judgment to appear before George's prophetic eyes: Count Henry is to be judged by all the sins, and all the crimes, all the abuses of his caste and all the sufferings of the oppressed.

It would be very difficult, then, to pretend that the *Comedy* is a defense of the old regime and that it represents an absolute refutation of Revolution. Of course Revolution is an evil, it brings "new crimes" and "new abuses"—we know that "the masses have only appetites"—but the poet in depicting the frightful atrocities of Revolution wishes to suggest the idea that the rebels are not really responsible . . . And in the last analysis it is they whom he would like to protect.

The problem, it seems, is more complex, and J. Klaczko, an admirable writer and literary critic of the last century who, in 1862, published in the *Revue des Deux Mondes* an article on Krasiński's *Undivine Comedy*, to which he refers as the *Infernal Comedy*, saw it more clearly. Some of the passages of this very fine study give the impression of having been written in our own day. "However it may be, it is certain, alas, that we are not yet at the end of our tribulations, and that the *Infernal Comedy* will be for a long time yet the drama of the future. The dangers that society runs will more than once make us prefer the established order to the moral order, and we catch ourselves on more than one occasion invoking the phantoms of the Middle Ages in fear of the Red Peril, to play at being sons of the Crusaders without being even children of the Cross, and to proclaim ourselves papists without being Catholic . . ."[26]

Comparing the character of Count Henry with that of Hamlet, Klaczko adds: "The hero of the Polish poet does not only recall the type invented by Shakespeare: he continues it in new and even more harrowing conditions, created by contemporary catastrophes. Certainly it is a sad thing to wish for and even to glimpse the good and to feel one's self powerless against evil; the Prince of Denmark felt terrible anguish; but it has been reserved to the man of our day to undergo a much more fearsome torment, that of aspiring toward the good, and not only of being constrained to tolerate evil but even to defend it through fear of worse, through apprehension of the abyss of nothingness. Hamlet defending the reign of imbeciles and swindlers, of Poloniuses and Osrics, Hamlet making his breast and his heart a rampart for the throne of the crowned brigand Claudius, and all that to escape from the tipsy logic of the 'grave-diggers,' who find that the highest nobility must belong to ditchers and undertakers—unquestionably the irony is bitter, satanic. It is, however, the role that is devolved on Count Henry, the combat to which the liberal man of the nineteenth century is sometimes called. The struggle is sad and deceiving in quite a different way than it was in times still near enough to our own, for in that struggle we catch ourselves lacking not only faith, but even *good faith,* and the drama becomes so much the more poignant in that, for all that it be *tragic* and *infernal,* it does none the less sometimes resemble a *comedy.*"[27]

[26] See "Revue des Deux Mondes," Paris, 1862, Vol. 37, p. 26.
[27] *Ibid.,* pp. 27-28.

As we know, Count Henry, leader of the aristocrats, is faced by Pancras, leader of the rebels, the lackeys, butchers, workmen, peasants, women of the town, the rebel mass, finally, of the proletariat. He is the spiritual leader of that movement, its organizer and inspirer, it is he who possesses the idea of reform and faith in the justice of the cause which he represents. Without him his idea will perish, for the masses "have only appetites" . . . And here is a quite significant detail, perhaps the most significant: why is the vision of Christ granted by the poet to Pancras, leader of the Revolution, and not to Count Henry, leader of the nobles?

It was the poet's grandson, Count Adam Krasiński, who very courageously opposed the Catholic criticism which had insisted that Pancras' vision, the Christ—who appeared to him menacing in the sky—must be considered as a sort of canonical repudiation cast on social revolution.

He shows in his study that the essential difference in the characteristics the poet has given of his two heroes, Count Henry and Pancras, rests in the fact that Count Henry is, independently of the catastrophe, the victim of his egoism, of his lack of faith and of his "heartlessness"; while Pancras is a man whose faith, whose fanatical belief, hope and realization of his mission assure him the attachment of the masses and make him a man of the future. Doubtless he is mistaken, he is a fanatic, but he has the gift, the essential treasure that Henry lacks: faith. And, taking up Mickiewicz's sentence, he continues: "The end of the drama is admirable, as well as the development of the feelings in the soul of the perishing leader of millions of revolutionists. The radiance of the cross crushes him, not in his body, which sinks on Leonard's shoulders, but in his conscience, in his soul; and from this combative soul, soon afterwards annihilated in its pride, rises a cry toward humanity, asking them the shadows, and toward God, invoking mercy: *Galilaee, vicisti.*"

"In the last evolution of the falling man resides a whole world of thoughts. Count Henry sought only the abyss of the darkness, he saw darkness surrounding him on all sides. Which, then, of the two, which of these two great spirits who battle to arrive at salvation, which of the two will see the resurrection accomplished? *Pancras, and he only.*"[28]

It seems to me that Count Adam Krasiński is near the truth. Let us add this too: the poet was a fervent and a practicing Catholic, he was a Catholic thinker. The fact of having precipitated Count Henry into the abyss of suicide is an irrefutable argument: Krasiński made his choice—he accorded grace and the promise of salvation to Pancras.

We have now come to the end of our exposition and, indeed, to its culminating point.

The *Comedy* is a drama on the human personality, on a generation without heart, on a world in disorder—on a moral world in disorder. It is a drama on the uprooted—on beings who have lost their moral roots, on collective life and individual life which is detached from the essential soil of all human life—love-pity and the heart. The poet replants these detached roots; some are dry and dead, nothing can save them any longer; but to others, although they are uncultivated and abandoned, there still remains the hope of revival—the "great gardener," Christ, will replant them. Everything is there. The old world must perish because it is no longer a Christian world, because it has lost its heart in abuses and in pleasures, because the class that possessed command can no longer command since it has lost its moral prestige. Krasiński casts his vote for the heart and for the Christianization of the social and political order. In that he is

[28] See *Christ et Révolution, loc. cit.*

continuing a long and beautiful tradition of Polish thought, which
since the fifteenth century, through men like Włodkowicius, and
then above all in the sixteenth and eighteenth Frycz-Modrzewski,
Staszyc, Konarski, and then our great Romantics who put the
torch into the hands of the Prus's, Sienkiewicz's and Żeromskis,
has continued to preach the Christianization of the social and
political order. That is, perhaps, the most valuable spiritual
contribution of Polish thought, elaborated in the centuries of
national suffering. Krasiński's recipe—one can discover it by
reading his masterpiece attentively, protected against preconceived ideas and prejudices—is very simple. It conforms to the
maxim of Condorcet: "It is in living for others that we live the
most for ourselves," to the words of La Bruyère: "The people have
no mind, the great have no soul; if I must choose, I choose for the
people."

Krasiński, also, chose the people: "We shall all pass," he wrote
to Reeve, "like dust, without having admired anything, loved
anything real, after having hated much . . ." *One must love,* and
in this sense the *Comedy* is not a vision but a logical and determined verdict. This verdict is applied to the world, but it applies
also to Poland. The *Comedy,* Polish in its essence, is nothing else
than the development of Mickiewicz's apothegm addressed to
the Poles, which Krasiński found in the *Book of the Polish Pilgrimage.*

If Poland today is able to die as it is dying for the Christian
principles and ideas which have always been so dear to her, it is
in great part the merit of the great poets and thinkers who have
never ceased to direct her soul toward an essentially human and
essentially religious ideal: love for the fellow man.

"The *Infernal Comedy,*" Klaczko has said, "is rather an adieu
than a welcome addressed by the poet to humanitarian inspira-

tions, it is a powerful protest against the fatal illusion of the age, which believes that it can regenerate humanity without previously regenerating man, that it can establish laws without having previously fortified the individual in the consciousness of his duties."[29]

[29] See *op. cit.*

VIII

Polish Traits

UNCONSCIOUSLY for me, I believe, my lectures have taken on a movement that is, if not chronological, at least historical. I have tried to give a general and synthetic picture of the evolution of the political and religious ideas and of the cultural and literary development of Poland from the beginning of Polish civilization to our own day.

It is evident that many facts, many works and personalities have remained outside my rapid summary of Polish civilization. I could not do otherwise—for my subject is too vast. There remain to be treated, however, two themes which represent, to tell the truth, the final goal of these meetings; they represent, too, the peaks of the historical evolution that I have tried to outline before you. These two subjects are the Polish *intelligentsia* and the modern Pole, as well as his present lot. In him we shall be studying at the same time the modern traits which result from historical evolution of the Polish character.

What is this intelligentsia? In the first place, the term itself is, from the point of view of European linguistics, a barbarism. It is difficult to establish at the present time where it comes from, Russia, or Poland. It rather seems, however, that its origin is Russian. In Russian the term has no other interpretation than that which sociology assigns to it: *intelligentsia* in Russian signifies only a social class. In Polish, *inteligencja* means intelligence, that is, faculty of the mind, and also means a social class. The term in its social acceptation was established in Poland at the same period as in Russia, in the second half of the nineteenth century. It is a class of declassed people, a class which represents a social group that is in a way supra-, extra-class. It is a *genus mixtum*, a meeting place of the declassed—of individuals who have found themselves automatically reunited in one group but who, while yet members of this new social union, are originally from other social classes such as the nobility, the bourgeoisie, the peasants, the proletariat. This class, by the very fact of the complexity of its social consistency, has never developed a clear class-consciousness; it is a group which has never known how to defend its interests—quite the contrary: almost without exception, it has always put itself at the service of other groups, by preference of the oppressed groups, the peasants and the proletariat.

If we were to let ourselves be guided by the dialectic of Marx, we should have to admit that this group has taken no part in the class-struggle, at least in the sense of the defense of its own interests. It is essentially a pacific, altruistic and non-exploiting group, at any rate from the social and economic point of view. The economic basis of the group was in the labor of the liberal professions; in Poland, then, to the intelligentsia belonged and still belong high school and university graduates, professors of universities, judges, lawyers, physicians, engineers, artists, men of letters, actors, musicians, higher state officials, diplomats— although the latter do not in general possess the indispensable qualities required for this group.

The nobility—although it became, from the end of the nineteenth century, more and more contaminated and debilitated as an independent social factor—still considered this group as a declassment and from their point of view a negative one: for the causes which in most cases brought the nobles into this class were economic. For all the others, it was positive declassment, that is, a social advancement. This meeting place of all the classes created within itself from the very beginning an atmosphere of social good will, a climate of comprehension and benevolence. The usages and forms of social life were the same as those of the gentry—the prestige of the family, the traditional respect for the parents, the authority of the father and the moral role of the mother, the external customs, ceremonious and polite; hospitality and refinement of manners. Some of those traits very sharply distinguish the Polish intelligentsia from the former Russian intelligentsia; I say former, because there is no longer any intelligentsia in Russia, in the pre-revolutionary sense of the word.

In Poland this class is perceptibly differentiated, according to the regions of Poland. In Posnania, in former German Poland, it is the bourgeois element that predominated. In Galicia—the peasant element; in Eastern Poland this class is almost entirely an emanation of the landed nobility, which while conserving its lands has been enrolled in the liberal professions, for reasons of an economic order; in central Poland we have representatives of the nobility and of the bourgeoisie. There is no doubt that it is indeed this class that has become the brain of the nation, its conscience, the human reservoir of its moral forces and its creative genius. All our great writers and poets, all our great painters, scholars, lawyers, engineers of the second half of the nineteenth century and in our time have sprung from this class; that is the class to which they have belonged independently of the historical origin of their families—such as Sienkiewicz, Orzeszkowa, Konopnicka, Prus, Żeromski—all nobles, but all belonging first to the intelligentsia; such as Kasprowicz, Reymont, Feldman, Berent, Kleiner—Polish peasants, petty bourgeois, or Jews—but all in the first place members of the intelligentsia.

It was this class which above all after the Insurrection of 1863 assumed responsibility for the political and spiritual life of the country and the nation; it took into its hands the organization of economic life; it organized the Polish state after the War of 1914. It is this class, therefore, which down to our own day is the most representative of Poland; if one wishes to become familiar with Poland, to know what Poland thinks, what she believes, how she feels and in what she places her hopes, what are her goals, how she lives—it is to this very class that one must turn. This class it is, also, which represents all the national traits; it has become a sort of synthesis, a kind of quintessence of the national soul. The Polish intellectual is really the true, veritable, imperishable type of Pole—I say imperishable: so long as Hitler's satraps do not succeed in destroying him. But it is precisely him that they assail and hunt down; it is not the peasant, and it is not the landed proprietor who at the present time is suffering the most —it is the intellectual; he is perishing surrounded by a savage pack led against him—consciously led; it is a matter of killing the mind and the soul of the nation, the salt of the Polish earth.

What are the essential traits of this class?

In the first place, modesty. The noble has entered it in the guise of a man who has lost his class, so he has necessarily had to abandon all his "defensive" characteristics—he has adapted himself to the climate of labor, of the intellectual proletarian; labor represents the constitutional principle of this class—by which I mean personal labor: a man who directs or organizes others is no longer an *inteligent*. (Architects and engineers form an exception.)

The peasant has become polished and civilized without acquiring the characteristics of the newly rich—for, indeed, in Poland this class has always been a poor class. Insolvency has always been one of the essential conditions of the life of this class: once a man has acquired great revenues he has ceased to belong to it— he has passed automatically either toward the upper bourgeoisie or toward the landed nobility.

Modesty and disinterestedness as concerns material things, yes, material disinterestedness, that is the second trait of the intelligentsia. This class did not accumulate, it stored up no reserves. For this there were two reasons. The first is that it had nothing with which to store up reserves; and the second is that it always held money in contempt. The Polish intellectual cared very little about material goods. The history of his country accustomed him to this. All the wars, all the insurrections, all the Siberias, all the prisons, all the confiscations and sequestrations, that he had known for generations taught him that there was nothing less stable than money. Besides, he earned little of it, but that little he spent freely, easily, without regret and without fear for the future. The Polish state during the period from 1919 to 1939 made great efforts to impose on the nation the habit of economy and of thrift—with good results, too. Especially in what concerns the domicile: the Poles all set to constructing little houses with the help of the State or else with the help of local organizations; the need of a home, the need of the domestic hearth, has always remained very strong in the Pole. Besides that there is a great sociability. The intellectuals, absolutely like the squires in the good old days, loved to receive, to invite, to pay visits, to take part in festival occasions. So, just as before, Christmas holidays, Easters, name-days, balls, theater, cinema, *jours fixes*—all that represented an important part of the life of the intellectual.

Journeys. The Pole adored journeys. The most modest people, even the poor, were acquainted with France, Italy, Germany,

Switzerland, often the Scandinavian countries—much less England, because of the language. The Polish intellectual spoke two foreign languages, German and French; much less, Italian, and still less, English. Only in recent times had English begun to gain some ground.

The taste for elegant clothing remained with him; I recall that foreigners often made the observation that even Poles of moderate income were always well dressed.

This class was characterized by great generosity. In proportion to his means, the Polish intellectual had always been more generous than the bourgeois or the landed proprietor; it may be that the lack of respect for money which characterizes the poor in general was of some account here.

The tradition of the insurrections had inculcated the faculty of patriotic sacrifice. The intellectual was not bellicose and did not desire war. However, in 1920, when the Bolshevik armies approached Warsaw, the whole intelligentsia enlisted immediately, without exception: nor would public opinion ever have suffered any exceptions of this nature. The present war has exemplified the same thing: it is the intellectuals who have formed the cadres of our aviation, it is the intellectuals who represent the majority in the Underground Movement.

The intelligentsia, and not only it but most of Poland, is characterized likewise by absolute material unselfishness vis-à-vis the fatherland and its needs especially in time of danger. It would never occur to any Pole to deliberate whether he might gain or lose by putting himself at the service of the fatherland in time of danger. He will sacrifice really everything—and his family will matter nothing in all that; quite the contrary, it *would* matter something to him if he were to act otherwise.

The intellectual formation of this class before 1914 was quite varied. Let us take, first, literature. Nowhere, perhaps, did litera-

ture play so important a national role as in Poland. Given the fact
that for almost a century and a half the nation had lived under
the yoke of its oppressors and that its national life had been
severely mutilated, literature became for this life a higher and
at the same time unique plane: it was there that the spiritual life
of the nation, all her creative forces, and all her moral energies
were manifested and realized. A Polish intellectual, then, is first
of all a literary man; attachment to, and familiarity with, the
national literature is even, perhaps, one of the essential characteristics of this social type. Galicia and German Poland had
undergone a great influence from Germanic culture. The Poles
of those regions all spoke excellent German, knew German
poetry (Goethe had translators in every generation), they traveled
a great deal in Austria and Germany, drank Rhenish (and Hungarian) wine, went to Karlsbad and Marienbad, to Kissingen and
to Wiesbaden, were well acquainted with Greek and Latin. The
Poles of the Eastern sections had undergone Russian influences
even while defending themselves against Russification—which,
by the way, did not take hold on these men, who were particularly
robust and immunized against that menace. They accepted the
knowledge of Russia, they read Russian and had a good idea of
Russia. Not the women—from 1830 on, they did not know one
word of Russian and maintained a deep fear of Russia. The
Insurrection of 1863 and the Russian atrocities in Wilno and elsewhere at that time strongly reinforced those sentiments.

Central Poland—the Kingdom—defended itself against Russian influence with all its might; there was only one short period,
toward the end of the nineteenth century, of efforts toward collaboration, but the intelligentsia lent itself only very badly to
that sort of thing. One single exception did exist: the collaboration of the Polish radicals and socialists with the Russian revolutionaries. To that, let us add the influence of Russian literature

(music, painting, and theater were much less important) toward the end of the nineteenth and the beginning of the twentieth centuries.

As for German influences: except for modernistic literature and painting, the Munich School, they were very weak, almost nil, in that central region.

It was France which dominated here, intellectually but not only intellectually. The Pole of the Kingdom knew French without knowing German, he read French books, he traveled to France, he went to Paris so long as he could, he studied at the Sorbonne or in Belgium, he drank Bordeaux and Burgundy, he also drank, with gusto, Fine, champagne, and chartreuse or benedictine. The theaters played French dramas, and French books were little translated, for everybody read them in French.

These foreign, heterogeneous influences, however, did not succeed in halting the movement of national and spiritual unification and union which was being systematically accomplished in all these Polish regions and provinces. This union came about with the help of two essential factors: literature, and the essential westernism of Polish cultural traditions. All the provinces read not only Mickiewicz, Krasiński, and Słowacki, but Prus, Orzeszkowa, Sienkiewicz, and, in more recent times, Konopnicka, Wyspiański, Reymont, Żeromski, Kasprowicz, Staff, and many, many others! All these regions read the books of the professors of the universities at Cracow and Lwów, of the scholars of Warsaw and Poznań, they all were familiar with Polish painters, be they from Cracow, Warsaw, or Poznań.

On the other hand, the Polish intelligentsia at this moment— the end of the nineteenth century and the start of the twentieth— followed with especial fidelity the rhythm of the artistic and intellectual life of Europe. That is, impressionism, symbolism, decadence, in the plastic arts as well as in letters, were propagated in Poland with astounding rapidity and force. This was also the period when Poland underwent suggestion from Russia—the Russian temptation subjugated Polish imaginations and produced disasters there. *Fin de siècle* in Poland was accompanied, as elsewhere in Europe, by sybaritism and bourgeois quietism. A current of collaborationism swept away Polish society—of collaborationism with Russia, in Russian Poland, and of collaborationism with Austria, in Austrian Poland. People did "business" —economic business in Russia and political business in Austria. The well-being in the Europe of the end of the nineteenth and the beginning of the twentieth centuries, the "banquet of Peace" which Mr. Ferrero has praised so in his morally peculiar books, tossed the crumbs from its feasting to Poland . . . The mass of Polish society was in a state of blissful somnolence . . . People read the Przybyszewskis and the Andreevs, the Nietzsches and the Maeterlincks, the Baudelaires and the Merezhkovskis, they translated Edgar Allan Poe, Wilde, Shaw, the Keatses, the Schnitzlers and the Hauptmanns, the Omar Khayyams, the Ibsens; they admired the Dulacs and the Aubrey Beardsleys, the Russian ballets, they went to the concerts of the Hoffmans and the Busonis; they built houses of unbelievable ugliness in the German-Austrian style of Secessionism; they sought the grand passions and the atmosphere of sin by creating it with the help of a Sibelius's *Valse Triste*, of the alcoholic "symphonies" of a Huysmans, of dramas of passion, of suicides, of all sorts of erotic and intellectual excesses . . . However, more in literature than in reality.

It was a revolt of the spirit of individualism against the monotony and flatness of bourgeois life—but quite a silly revolt . . .

The best synthesis of this life has been given by Berent, a very great writer, in his novel *Rotted Wood:* the world we see there is in a state of lamentable torment; people torture one another, in order to escape the ennui of bourgeois existence. The *Rotten-*

ness shines in the night. It was at Munich that this whole world of Polish artists, painters, and writers was located, detached from their natal soil, rooted in the cosmopolitanism of the "Lumpen-proletariat," declaiming slogans about art for art's sake, hyper-culture, *Uebermensch;* they abandoned themselves to all the drugs and all the alcohols, to terminate all this rush in the abyss of suicide, in the dark glooms of a Germano-Oriental, Russo-Teutonic Nirvana . . . It is the image of the macabre triumph of art over life and victorious "low-lifery." Here we have the image of the individualism of the decadents of the end of the nineteenth century; the "Ivory Tower" of the Romantics and the Parnassians was transformed into a bottle of cognac or Polish vodka, and man escapes from reality, not by means of the Middle Ages or even of exoticism, as the Romantics did, he rides on into unknown worlds whither he is carried by fumes of opium or erotic delirium.

In another novel, *Winter Wheat,* the same author, one of our greatest stylists by the way, our Flaubert, continues his chronicle of Polish life; only, this time the society is more mixed—the bourgeoisie and the intellectual world find themselves side by side on this stage. One would say, too, that it is truly a stage. The entire novel is the story of a single ball in Warsaw at the moment when the Russo-Japanese War breaks out. It is a dream, the nostalgia of which pines for a life that is potent, rich in passions, senti-ments, and ideas . . . Everything there is crushed under the pres-sure of low-lifery and bourgeois materialism; all is mediocrity, flabbiness, baseness . . . We are a little in the atmosphere of Wyspiański's *Wedding* and of the *Undivine Comedy.* The chariot of life is caught in sand and mud . . . Only the women are still of any worth . . . They are the one goal, too, of the desires of all these men whom we see wandering over this gripping re-volving-stage of that impressive ball in Warsaw . . . But in a life where there is no goal but woman, woman becomes man's curse and man's peril.

The *lonza leggiera* of Dante—the obsession of sensuality and desire—reigns here in full autocracy . . . The gods are no longer there, and without them, passions have become vile and low . . . We see here the somber truth of shabby, lewd life revealed and symbolized by garters, rumpled waistcoats, and evening gowns; by uncovered breasts, kisses; women who abandon themselves to passion and prurience; a sensual, unhealthy restlessness shakes this world; a mazurka unleashes elemental madness . . . Finally the Russian anthem is heard in the streets—the Russo-Japanese War is let loose. The Russian anthem becomes a rousing alarm . . . The Russian colonel who is attending the ball goes away; he takes with him a young Pole, telling him that it is better for him to perish in the trenches of a war that is not his than to rot in this life . . . under the yoke of these women . . . who are so terrible, terrible . . . that the Devil, he says, would have nothing else to do than to lay his horned head docilely on their knees . . .

Winter Wheat is a biting satire, an anti-Russian satire, which shows the vilifying and demoralizing influence of the Russian regime in Poland, of the divisive penetration of the literature of the Andreevs, Artzybashevs, Kuprins . . . It is a satire against Western influences, too, against the erotic and alcoholic manias of the German decadents whom Przybyszewski represented with veritable eloquence.

It is a satire against all those bankers, strategists in the field of affairs, of compromises with the oppressors, against the commanders-in-chief in the field of balls and dinners; it is a satire against all those usurers of the national conscience, who silently but knowingly decompose the soul of the nation . . .

In the streets can be heard revolutionary songs . . . The

Polish socialists come out of thier underground shelters . . . A new life begins . . .

And one of the characters confesses: "I believe only in those who have never trafficked with fate—in those to whom their own soul suffices for the undertaking of something . . ."

The radical populist and socialist movements become stronger and stronger, more and more energetic and active . . . It is in these surroundings that the ideas of a revolution for the independence of Poland are worked out. It is there that preparations are made, attached to the presentiment of a general European conflict; it is in these surroundings of the radical, socialist, but deeply patriotic intelligentsia that Piłsudski, gifted with astonishing intuition and clairvoyance, organizes the cadres of his future legions, which from 1914 on will fight for the independence of Poland.

A new type of Polish intellectual is crystallized more and more clearly: the intellectual sacrificing all his strength for the oppressed classes, seeking this time the universalism that union with the "humble of the earth" assures him, seeking the universalism of pity which neutralizes and reduces all the wildly, fiercely individualistic attitudes of the intellectual who had sought refuge and asylum in the theories of art for art's sake. It will be Kasprowicz, whom I have already cited, who in his *Book of the Poor* will give an example of love-pity whose surest expression will be simplicity. But above all it will be Stefan Żeromski who will become—after Skarga and Mickiewicz—the new tyrant of Polish hearts, and who will represent this new type of Polish universalism.

"Young Poland"—a school of writers and poets, representing Polish modernism—had imposed on the nation the concept that a literature was worth nothing unless it was an art. Sorel had said once that literary revolutions were always revolutions of the literary language. Tetmajer, Przybyszewski, Wyspiański have enriched the language, created a new poetical vocabulary; Kasprowicz, Żeromski, Reymont, Orkan have introduced a popular lexicon—the talk of the peasants, the mountaineers of the Tatras, a speech of artisans and workmen. Kasprowicz and Żeromski opened the gates to Old Slavonic. Przybyszewski, Staff, and Miciński were the men who represented the assimilation of foreign civilizations. Wyspiański gave a synthesis of the national soul and the historic moment—the end of the nineteenth century, at the same time that he synthesized the historic past. The entire school aimed to create a new Polish cultural type. In working out this new type, Żeromski played a role of the first order —a unique role.[1]

"J'aime d'un amour bestial et profond, méprisable et sacré, tout ce qui pousse, tout ce qu'on voit, car tout cela, laissant calme mon esprit, trouble mes yeux et mon coeur, tout: les jours, les tempêtes, les bois, les aurores, le regard et la chair des femmes . . ."[2] So wrote Guy de Maupassant. These words could be used to give a picture of the work of Żeromski—they were, in fact, quoted as a motto in Adamczewski's monograph.

Żeromski does indeed represent this kind of pantheistic universalism. He represents the union of the Polish soul with all the past, with geography, with the archaic attachment of the Pole to the glebe and to the sea—yes, to the sea, to the Baltic sea; to the mountains—to the Carpathians; to legends and history, to glories and calamities . . . His feverish and ardent love embraces the entire Polish world; there is not one thing that this "heart of hearts" has forgotten. That heart loves, but it bleeds—

---

[1] See W. Feldman, *Współczesna Literatura Polska.*

[2] ("I love with a wild and deep passion, despising and sacred, everything which grows, everything we see, because all this, leaving my spirit calm, disturbs my eyes and my heart, all: the days, the storms, the woods, the dawn, the glance and the flesh of women . . .")

it bleeds constantly; this is why Żeromski's work is so sorrowful, so tormented and so uneven . . . That heart has too much curiosity and too much memory, and that is why we behold that abuse of details, that swarming of details which are often hypertrophied and exaggerated . . . It is like an expressionistic film, where the detail overflows and absorbs . . . That heart bleeds and protests; it protests against the universal order of life. Nature —as in Vigny, whose work Żeromski had known from childhood —is cruel. Man's life is only brigandage, and it is the glorious merit of our civilization that, thanks to it, evil and unhappiness do not reach the cads and poltroons who are sheltered because ensconced in the "ivory towers" of their egoism, but it is the best and most generous who are stricken . . .

He protests against history, as in his *Ashes*, that Polish *War and Peace*, that Napoleonic epic. He tells à la Vigny, very much à la Vigny and à la Tolstoy, not only about *la majesté des souffrances humaines* but about the futility of those sufferings; history takes its victims without recompense, not only without individual recompense but without national recompense . . . All is in vain, all the acts of heroism, all the sacrifices are useless —all ends in *ashes* . . .

There is more to it than that. The *Ashes* is not a fantasy; the writer is observing sorrowfully the tragic heroism displayed for causes and aims that are infinitely inferior to the sacrifices demanded. Worse, he sees at the end of the swords of the Polish legions the injustice that those swords bring with them . . .

In the *Ashes*, as in another great novel, *Homeless People*, he has shown the heroic effort to live and exist, to fulfill one's duty without the knowledge of life's "divine truth" . . .

These are Vignesque problems and attitudes; we are in the tragic atmosphere of the *Destinées* and of *Servitude et Grandeur Militaires* . . .

All is in vain, all ends in ashes and in futile suffering . . . A generous woman loves a dastard, a churl; an enthusiastic physician contracts the disease of the patient he is tending; the impressionable and loving soul of a young girl is dragged off by love into the abyss of prostitution and crime . . .

All of Żeromski's work is filled with the lava of a powerful, even excessive eroticism. It is a stormy and scum-covered sea, but its squalls often raise problems of a higher, moral, philosophical order. A woman's hair grazes a man's forehead in a shelter while a heavy rain obliges a crowd to take cover and people are pressed against one another in the multitude . . . Desire flares up . . . The flowers, the clouds, the trees, and the dark water of the ponds were the accomplices of the guilty loves of Łukasz and Eve—but it is she alone who falls under the burden of sin and under the blows of punishment . . . Then why are not the rain, the trees, the sky, the flowers, and the sleeping waters, why are not all these mischievous accomplices of sin called before the "Last Judgment," and what will be that judgment? The problem, therefore, that the author is posing is that of free will and of temptation. We are in Eden all over again, in the Garden of Adam and Eve—only the serpent that God had concealed there under the leaves of the Tree of the Knowledge of Good and Evil has here become a gigantic serpent—all of nature, the animal and human, natural and cultivated world, in short, nature and civilization, have become the great temptation which with its gigantic serpent's coils binds the free will of man and woman . . . What will be the "Last Judgment"?

And those terrible antinomies, those disconcerting contradictions that exist between the human face and the human soul! In the crowd of his characters we see old men so beautiful that despite their sixty-five years they could seduce girls of sixteen, splendid old men with blue eyes, dreamy, gay, confident, with smiles sweet as a dream, with thick white mustaches covering the sensual lips, with graying hair, a kind of diadem on the forehead. It is the face of a president of the Republic, of a minister reading his speech, of a chief justice, or of a porter at Monte Carlo . . . But this man's soul is that of a Feodor Karamazov. Żeromski is as cruel toward his characters as a Dostoevski could be . . .

His naturalism is sometimes atrocious; he paints scenes and acts, human destinies, the cruelty and the horror of which exceed all measure . . .

But it is that very same man, Żeromski, who has taught us, on the other hand, that the black bread of suffering nourished youth by giving it power; it is he who has told us the marvelous tale to the effect that the soul could grow *physically* . . . It is he who, in his joyous universal pity—in that respect quite like St. Francis of Assisi—doted upon a poor tree destined to grow without sun, in the middle of a paved yard, a poor tree encircled in an iron hedge . . . It was he who spoke of and understood the poor birds . . . His charity sometimes makes one think of the charity of a deliciously feminine heart, it is so sweet, tender, and pardoning.

On the other hand, with what ferocious hatred, with what bitterness, did he not attack certain abject vices of his compatriots and so much the more abject, for him, in that they were uncovered by his loving heart. Among them there is one that is particularly sinister—the hatred of any higher living being, a hatred which in Poland precedes the worship of the dead . . . It is in his *Lay of the Hetman* that he gave the history of this dark vice, developed in the atmosphere of the famous Polish equality. And still, as the great Żółkiewski has said, we must love Poland although she kills us . . . And they all adored that Poland, all her great sons, without reciprocity before death . . . It was only

the mediocrities who were happy and applauded in their life-
times.

"For thirty years," as Professor Stroński said, "Żeromski's
works rushed out on Polish life like storms coming from a terribly
black cloud, lightning fell from those works . . . but they nourished that Polish earth by the rain of impressions they gave, and
now and then caused ravishing smiles of the sun and the clear blue
sky to appear . . ." Indeed, we feel here the thunderbolts of
the *Undivine Comedy*.

The essential thing for him is human happiness. To the Sorelian
enthusiasm for labor—life's only sovereign, indifferent to the
happiness of its citizens, Żeromski, Sorel's disciple, opposed the
simple statement that the triumphs of labor, of progress, were
worth nothing if they were powerless to guarantee happiness to
man—to every man.

There was in him a kind of Tolstoyan anti-occidentalism, of
the Tolstoy of *Lucerne*, a kind of revolt against the European
order—a revolt reproducing the accents of Ivan Karamazov. "I
want nothing of this world in which there are the tears of little
children . . ." In this sense, Żeromski represents "the Slavic
spirit" of Poland. His work is profoundly attached to that spirit;
it offers a spontaneous response to the rationalistic skepticism
of an Anatole France who destroys religion by his historicalism,
it is quite opposed to some Maurras or to some de Montherlant
who prefers a few Catholic bishops to the four Jews who wrote
the Gospel, and who tolerates Catholicism only to the extent
of its deviation from pure Christianity . . .

All that is in the tradition of Mickiewicz . . . One might say
that Żeromski's work in this sense is the "legend," made concrete
and realistic, a living illustration, of the legend of the "Grand
Inquisitor" . . . which, as I have noted, possesses common accents with the *Improvisation* of the author of the *Forefathers' Eve*.

Here we are still in a world where the Polish intellectual sacrifices himself completely and entirely for the humble, the poor, the worker, the suffering mass of the proletariat; he strives not for his own happiness but for that of others. And there are no limits to these sacrifices . . . When it is necessary he disregards his personal happiness, like the hero of *Homeless Men*, Dr. Judym, he disregards it in order not to "go soft" . . . One more reminiscence of Mickiewicz, this time attached to *Konrad Wallenrod*.

He will suffer no injustice. "Doctor Peter, in the story of that name, renounces his old and dearly-loved father from the moment when he learns that this father gave him his education by means of reductions year after year in the wages of workmen in the factory of which he was manager. Doctor Peter leaves his home, determined to work with blind energy; he will live in privation, to restore to the workmen the money which had been filched from them."[3]

When it is necessary, Żeromski's hero sacrifices himself. Such is the touching story of the hero of the "comedy," *My Little Quail Has Fled Away*.

"The hero, one Przełęcki, is a young scholar devoted to social work. An enthusiast himself, he gathers similar enthusiasts around him. All of them regard the work upon which they are engaged as a kind of mission. But there is among them a married woman who falls in love with the hero. And he falls in love with her. It is a deep, passionate, persuading love, but if they accept it, the work which is so dear to Przełęcki will be ruined by scandal, and a third person will suffer. For the sake of the moral values at stake Przełęcki resorts to an heroic buffoonery: he degrades himself in the eyes of the woman and in the eyes of his friends. There is a risk: will they reject him or reject the idea to which he had attached them? This risk is tragic for Przełęcki but he

[3] W. Borowy, *Żeromski*, "The Slavonic Review," 1935-36, p. 405.

wins against himself. He is condemned to an existence of insignificance and seclusion. He loses what is dearest to him; but in feeling himself a victor, he is justified."[4]

Nothing could be more gripping than the meeting of Przełęcki with the husband—who begs for his charity.

That play contains a germ of another story. And that germ is attached to it by the will of destiny. It is as if we had there a metaphysic of heroism. The scholars who appear in that comedy are almost all professors of the University of Cracow. The action takes place in the twenties of our century. Among these professors is one who is a linguist, who delivers brilliant and enthusiastic lectures on the historical grammar of the Polish language. A legend had made Żeromski's readers and spectators recognize in the figure of the professor a kind of reverent allusion toward a great scholar of Cracow, whom all Poland knew for his magnificent studies and for his fanatical devotion to science. This legend spread with such obstinate vigor that the artist who played the role of the grammarian in Warsaw was made up so as to make people think immediately of his living prototype.

I knew this professor well personally; we all held him in the greatest esteem, and at the same time in a sort of fear, a sort of impatience. The esteem was due to his immense merits. It must be said in passing that the "linguistic school" of Cracow represented a team of scholars of the first rank; in latter days the linguists of Cracow won a position in Europe which no other European linguistic milieu could dispute. Like our mathematicians and logicians of Warsaw, our linguists of Cracow were known and renowned throughout the world. The professor in question was one of the leading men of that school. His erudition, his faculty for work, were truly extraordinary; he was a fanatic. He was also a man of absolutely scientific probity: in all his

4 Borowy, *ibid.*, p. 413.

judgments, in all his opinions, he let himself be guided only by purely scientific considerations. That is why one knew that in any personal question his judgment would be characterized by the greatest possible sureness and integrity. But this man had a particularly disagreeable character, disagreeable in the sense that it was organically impossible for him to conceal his opinions, to attenuate his judgments, at least the expression of his judgments, when the latter were unfavorable. That is the reason why he caused fear: everyone was sure to hear from his mouth judgments whose aim was irrevocably that of truth, without circumspection, without the least effort to be circumspect, to spare ambition and self-love. On the other hand, there was in him a deep personal humility toward those whom he recognized as scholars "without blemish or reproach." Such was always his attitude toward our great philosopher and "scholar-poet" of the language —Jan Michał Rozwadowski. But, while savage and ferocious in his criticisms and smashing in his words of scientific anger, he was all caresses when he spoke of things or of personalities which became the object of his admiration; at such times a deliciously good smile appeared on his lips.

He was arrested by the Gestapo on November 6, 1939, with all the teaching and administrative corps of the University, and sent to the concentration camp of Oranienburg, where he was detained for three months. As you know, they underwent there the most terrible regimen, after which, as I have already related, eighteen professors died in Oranienburg and several immediately after their return to Cracow, so enfeebled had they been by their existence at Oranienburg.

I went to see him after his return, in his modest villa, situated, as it happened, in the most ravishing quarter of Cracow, on a little hill with a delightful view of the Vistula and the Wawel . . . He had changed greatly, he had grown terribly thin, his hair was

shaven, he coughed every instant. But in his eyes I recognized the
same energy and the same will, which glittered through the glass
of his very thick lenses: he was myopic.

Fearfully, with a constricted feeling in my heart, I asked him:
"Was it terrible?"

The voice we knew so well, always snappish and dry—but
which had suddenly become to me, I know not why, so dear,
unique, immensely precious, that I stifled sobs in my throat—
replied to me:

"Yes, it was harsh—but, you see, I held out, and I don't feel
bad . . ." And then he changed the conversation . . . It was a
trait that was general for all. They did not want to tell; in them
there was the shyness of the man who had undergone mad degrada-
tions, horrible defilement of his human dignity . . . they did not
want to talk about it . . . I immediately caught this trait in
him as well, and that made me shudder inwardly even more.

"You know," he told me, "that we were able to organize lectures there, during the first three weeks—later the Germans for-
bade it . . . Everyone gave lectures on different subjects, of
course . . . And, as always, there were good ones and bad
ones . . ." Here he began to list the speakers and pass them in
review, for all the world as he had been accustomed to doing
before . . . He did not spare even those who had died in the
camp . . . When it came the turn of one of our greatest masters
of the history of Polish literature—and it was a friend of my
host, and he had died in Oranienburg—I heard the following
observation: "Well yes, he spoke too, he treated the history of
the literary life of Warsaw at the end of the nineteenth century;
it was good, it was vivid, but—well, you can imagine, you are
familiar with his style,—anecdotes, reminiscences, *Kleinmalerei.*"
And he said, "One day we had a lecture from Mr. ————
whom you know. It was very weak. You know me too, so you

will foresee that I did not hide my opinion from him. Well, and can you guess what he replied to me? He said, 'I did not have time to prepare my talk.' . . . He did not have time! I did not refrain," he continued, "from telling him what I thought of him: 'How is this—no time! You know of course that in this terrible cold, in this snowy mud that we have in the barracks, in this stench—no one can sleep, or even close an eye; and yet you tell me that you didn't have time to prepare your talk . . .' "

I am not capable of translating into words the stupor, the admiration, the enthusiasm which this man roused and kindled in my heart. I felt crushed; I was there like a poor earthworm contemplating a star . . . That man, shaven like a prisoner, casting his glance through his glasses that glittered in the twilight which was coming from the snow-covered plain into the room, that man who was physically weak, bent with age and with the torture itself, coughing, but sweetly and tenderly smiling at every scientific idea that pleased him, appeared before my dazzled eyes as the perfect example of what I should like here to call the heroism, the holy asceticism, of science . . . Its living representative, before my eyes, was this—"knight errant" of science. I thought also, at that moment, I do not know why, about *My Little Quail Has Fled Away* . . .

I have tried in my exposition to present all the most essential stages and the most important factors in the historical evolution of Polish civilization, as well as the most salient traits of Polish mentality and character.

These factors, stages, and traits are: Roman Christianization, Latin spirit, Western messianism, individualism, powerful traditions of liberalism in politics and of tolerance in religion; patriotism; therefore, in sum, the alliance of nationalist and universalistic conceptions in the soul of Poland. I have treated

Mickiewicz as a symbolical figure; his life and work represent some elements, the significance of which is in fact very essential for the entire nation. To be noted among these: the power of spiritual factors in man's life, the prestige of this power; the dynamic element—that development, that continual progress of the personality, its incessant march toward more and more exalted goals—the gradual stages of which were individualism, nationalism, universalism; the desire, the moral necessity, to find a higher, religious justification (in the broadest sense of the term "religious") for the national catastrophe; the capacity for sacrifice, in short. Those are some of the traits, and gestures of the soul, that symbolize the march of all Poland in its history.

I have tried to make it understood that modern Poland represents a synthesis and a symbiosis of all that history has been able to develop in it and trace on it—the memory of Poland's glories in the sixteenth century, the picturesque, the suavity of the follies of the eighteenth, the capacity for unlimited, absolute sacrifice which appeared in the Poles in time of misfortune, the profound remembrance of catastrophes lived through, the devotion to causes of a higher, supranational order, the profound attachment to the West.

There comes to my memory a very just observation on that phenomenon which I find in one of the most beautiful books about Poland at war—in the book of an English lady who has gracefully hidden her name under the verse of Mickiewicz: *My name is million.*

In recounting her impressions of Warsaw, the author of this deeply penetrating book admits that when she arrived in the capital of Poland, after London and Paris and even Berlin she felt disappointed: Warsaw appeared to her like a city which had not yet attained all the elegance of modern urbanism, it produced a mediocre impression after the immense and magnificent cities

like Paris and London . . . One really felt one's self on the
borders of Europe, we read in that book.

And yet, after a week, this Englishwoman felt and understood,
as she herself neatly says, that this capital was becoming in her
eyes not only like the *last* European capital *but the most European
of all!* In a certain sense, in the plane of the metaphysics of history, it is really so . . . Warsaw is more European and more
Western than any other city, because its soul is imbued with a
peculiarly deep and indestructible attachment to Europe, because
that soul is the soul of a missionary city. One always felt there
a particular tension of Europeanism: the West had become there
an ideal which was to be attained, to be cultivated, and to be
defended all at the same time.

Let us take another example, also English, I mean Polono-
English, Joseph Conrad: We, rather our tragic fate, gave him to
England, and he is much more devoted to the West than any
purely English writer could be. It might be that his *Patna*
is a symbolic picture of Poland, and that in his imagination
Poland lay in her glorious past as a silent wounded creature; that
his Western messianism was more Polish than English; that his
constant readiness, developed in him by his experience of the
sea, readiness for fight against the elemental powers of Nature,
was a symbol and a sign of his own and Poland's readiness to
fight against the inhuman powers of history.

In fact, it is *"la Pologne tout entière à sa 'prose' attachée."*
But there is also another trait peculiar to the Pole: that of intrinsic
idealism, which contains something of the spirit of gambling, the
acceptance of risk, Pascal's "wager," so to speak, the courage
to stake it all on one throw, courage which represents an emanation of profound faith in the final triumph of the "just cause."

In politics, as in love, the Pole is always ready to make the
magnanimous gesture of sacrificing everything, of "wagering his

whole fortune," by betting on that card of idealism . . . And in spite of the fact that sympathy, good will, and love leave him, just like a fickle and faithless waltzer, he is always ready to continue the "waltz" . . . Need I recapitulate once more all our waltzes with Europe, which destiny has so many times interrupted, and each time in so terribly agonizing a fashion?

Poland did her best during the last years of her independence, won back after the War of 1914, in order to regain all that the Partitions had caused her to lose . . . You cannot imagine the really fantastic labor which that country performed during those twenty years, in all fields of her life. Everything was made over anew; we were compelled to build stations, schools, hospitals, bridges, telegraphs, farms, houses; we had to organize ministries, to form an army, above all to establish primary, secondary, and higher education; several scores of thousands of schools were set up, hundreds of lyceums and secondary schools, more than twenty universities and schools of technology, arts, mines, were set going. Libraries, museums and collections were re-established; we had to struggle for the restoration of all that Russia and the other co-partitioning countries had carried away and confiscated—a Herculean labor in this field was accomplished . . . Intellectual, artistic, and literary life was taken up again . . . The cities were embellished, new quarters took birth in Warsaw, Cracow, Lwów, Wilno . . . Beautiful agricultural accomplishments, breeding of horses, of cows, of pigs, became the glory of Poland's economic life . . . Industrialization was developed . . . Finally Gdynia, which in a few years was built and became the first port of the Baltic . . .

Scientific life developed in many directions; our railroads became admirably punctual and comfortable . . .

In short, the entire life represented a labor that was hard but accomplished with enthusiasm; it was the sacrifice of the whole nation looking toward one single goal, that of making up for lost time, that of attaining as quickly as possible the level of the West. The entire nation wished for only one thing: peace, it was deeply devoted to peace . . . It desired collaboration with its neighbors and above all with the democracies . . . England, France, and the United States . . .

Poland committed faults, as all nations and all countries have committed them. But her faults—which anyway were connected only with her internal life, with the problem of the minorities in the first place—were the result of the general political climate in Europe after Versailles. In that climate only *certain* plants could grow and develop; others, often the best, the finest, perished . . . Let us not forget, either, the Hitlerite and Communistic propaganda. The former sowed discord between Poles and Jews, the latter between Poles and Ukrainians . . . The Germans, too, penetrated everywhere with their money and their agents . . .

But it was only restricted groups of the nation who let themselves be seduced by that propaganda . . . And these groups made more noise than real evil.

The purpose of this book has been to give the picture of the Polish historical, cultural and political tradition, which presents a guaranty for the future development of Poland. The last twenty years of Polish independence gave a dualistic picture of Poland's capacity of self-government. Poles know well how enormous were the achievements of the nation during those twenty years in every field of life, especially if we consider the geo-political situation of Poland between the two wars. On the other hand, we Poles also know that the political regime established in Poland in 1926 has been an object of severe criticism from the outside—but also from the inside. This regime, to the tendency of which I have made some allusions in my book, was connected with some Polish political currents which appeared in the sixteenth century, later on at the end of the eighteenth century, and finally among the representatives of the historical School of Cracow. The aim of these currents was the strengthening of the executive power in order to limit the traditional Polish individualism and liberalism, which, as we know, developed in the course of Polish history into a sort of hypertrophy. This regime was also connected with the *étatismes* which had arisen around Poland and which menaced her existence. The architects of this political organization were trying to adapt themselves and the country to this political climate in order to consolidate the strength of the state as such. From a certain point of view this realistic conception could even appear justifiable, but it never agreed with the Polish temper and character as they had been formed by history; it was not possible to change in fifteen years centuries of habits and customs.

What was striking was that, practically, this regime had only the appearance of a real dictatorship, but, as a matter of fact, it was rather a semi-dictatorial mode of rule. The best proof of this may be found in the fact that when, for instance, in 1930, the leaders of the Polish opposition (whose political descendants now head the Polish Government in London) were arrested, forty-four professors of the University of Cracow signed a protest against this arbitrary act of Piłsudski. This protest was followed by hundreds of others. It had a great moral effect and importance. And, despite the fact that these protests were published in the newspapers, nothing happened to those who signed them. It would be hard to imagine the possibility of such public acts of disapproval under the real modern dictatorships that we have known.

I am not trying to excuse or to defend this order of things; I am simply trying to explain its causes. From our Polish point of view, the most distressing feature was that the Polish state, for the sake of its security, was trying to re-educate, rebuild, transform the Polish historical type, engraved in the imagination and memory of the whole world as a man fighting "for your freedom and for ours," as a classic representative of tolerance, democracy, pacifism, liberalism, incarnated in great Polish historical figures, such as Rector Włodkowicius, Chancellor Jan Zamoyski, Frycz-Modrzewski, King Jan Sobieski, Kościuszko, Pułaski, Prince Józef Poniatowski, and Mickiewicz, who were all our "ambassadors to the United States of Humanity." The new type was to become a sort of matter-of-fact businessman, sacrificing universal values for temporary national achievements, as great as they sometimes were, and subjugated to the state.[5] A distressing feature was also the fact that the Jagiellonian idea of unions and federations, which had been for centuries so creative and effective and which had inspired Piłsudski, was not applied to the solution of our minorities problem. And of course I need not stress the fact that I do not have in mind any dream about the restoration of the Jagiellonian Commonwealth, for which we were too weak, but simply our domestic affairs. For this again we were not alone responsible, although our responsibility was great since we were the masters. But this, too, was a result of our geo-political situation and of our lack of any real help from the Western democracies.

The members of the regime established in 1926 were recruited, for the most part, from people who had spent their youth in the army and who remained in it. For that reason, they were people

[5] It should be noted in this connection that the greatest responsibility for promoting a nationalistic attitude lay with the so-called National Democrats who, in spite of some positive achievements, by their methods of action and propaganda contributed, with the help of the National Radicals, to the deterioration of political mores in the country. I hope that the National Democrats will change their attitude in the restored Poland. (About the history of Polish Political Parties see Wilhelm Feldman, *Dzieje Polskiej Myśli Politycznej*, Vols. I-II, Kraków, 1913; about the present parties—the excellent book of R. L. Buell: *Poland Key to Europe*, A. Knopf, New York, 1941.

who did not participate in the organic work of Polish society; they had no close ties with any social, economic, or cultural groups, and their isolation made of them ideal representatives of the interests of the state, in some way even opposed to the interests of the nation. In developing their statist program they were trying to monopolize the political life of the country and to concentrate the political, legislative and executive power in the hands of one party, which was meant to become the political soul of the nation. There was much naïve imitativeness in these tendencies, which, from the purely political point of view, exhausted the nation and fostered opportunism in public life. The prize of what was given to the nation was the "Great Power" concept which was constantly being imposed on her and which she in a realistic attitude, accepted with a somewhat ironic skepticism.

It should be stressed that the moral prestige of these leaders was connected with the suggestive figure of Piłsudski, who became the symbol of the recovery of Polish independence and of the fight for it, in which his collaborators had taken an active part. It was also reinforced by the fact that they did, at any rate, possess organizational and administrative ability. However, as an imitative system, opposed to the indomitable Polish spirit of independence and legalism, the regime never succeeded in becoming a real dictatorship, and the life in Poland, even for the minorities, was certainly a freer one than in the neighboring totalitarian states. Finally, I must again stress the fact that Poland had to reorganize her independent life after one hundred and twenty-five years of dismemberment and oppression, and that her task was suddenly interrupted before she had been able to overcome the exterior and interior difficulties that beset her.

And besides, where are those countries which have not committed faults and errors? On the other hand, it would seem that in this war Poland has conducted herself with truly very great elegance, with invincible courage. She was the first country which had the courage and determination to oppose Hitler with arms. No one came to her aid . . . She fought for six weeks. Need I recall Warsaw? Poland received a stab in the back, and the dagger was wielded by Russia. After the Polish campaign the Poles have continued a fierce struggle outside Poland. An army of two hundred and ten thousand men was formed. It represents one of the most compelling phenomena of this war. Two hundred thousand men escaped from Poland occupied by the Germans and the Russians! Polish aviators have fought in England for England—and how they fought! Polish divisions fought in France . . . The Polish marine has also taken part and continues to take part in the maritime war . . . The Polish army was everywhere, in Narvik as well as in Tobruk . . . It now fights in Italy . . . And the Polish divisions on the Russian front! . . .

A very powerful underground movement has been organized in Poland itself, organized in an almost unbelievable way with astonishing ramifications, with fantastic means of communication: London communicates with Warsaw in forty-eight hours! In Poland, no Quislings, no Armistice, no collaboration.

On the other hand, the miseries and the horrors of the German and Russian occupation . . . unspeakable . . . Millions deported to Germany, about one million deported to Russia . . . The Poles treated like slaves, exterminated, persecuted . . . In spite of that, this same Poland, bleeding, decapitated, decimated, stretched forth her hand to Russia . . . You know the end of that story . . .

Nor should we forget the initiative taken by Sikorski on the subject of the federation of the countries of Central Europe— proof of political wisdom, proof that the great peaceful and constructive traditions of the Jagiellons are still alive in Polish minds . . .

So this nation, as it appears today, is not a bad product of history; it represents traits whose moral value ought not to create suspicions and doubts; it represents in addition an imperishable, inexhaustible will to live . . . It is a nation at once old and young; the catastrophes through which it has lived did not succeed in weakening or degrading its spirit—on the contrary, they gave it new moral vigor and augmented its forces and its means of resistance.

Still to be known now is, what will be Poland's destiny this time? As a Pole and as an intrinsic, absolute, unreserved European, as a Pole and as a European in soul and body, I declare, I affirm, and I attest that in the soul of the whole Polish nation the cause of Poland appears once more as indissolubly attached to something greater than Poland herself—to Europe, to something still greater than Europe—to the ideal of justice. That is what we Poles understand and at this moment consider axiomatic. This interpretation of history gives us faith and reinforces it at the same time. Despite and against all the propaganda directed against us and so unjust to us, we have a firm hope that the "just cause" cannot be betrayed. We believe that if it were to be so, a general disaster would be inevitable. It is no wild and obstinate Polonocentricity which makes us think in this way; a "historiosophy" of wider character invites us thither. "Just causes" are peculiar in that their defeats are always followed, sooner or later, by the *divergence* of the "unjust causes" which collaborate and triumph in accord only for a very short time . . . And it is in this divergence that the Nemesis of history, the threat of vengeance, lies hidden.

Geography and history made Poland a factor which for almost

ten centuries assured peace and order in that part of the world. Every attempt to eliminate that factor has immediately made Poland a focus of general infection, a source of conflicts; Poland has become a battlefield of Europe, and war and disorder have spread in that part of the world, fatally degenerating into general catastrophe—history has shown us this on several occasions . . .[6]

I am speaking here not only as a Pole and European but in the quality of an idealist who is convinced and sure in his faith, an idealist who, in spite of everything and against everything, has never ceased to believe in the final triumph of the "just cause," and who for that reason continues to keep his optimism and regards with confidence the future of Poland, of Europe, and of the whole world. Because Poland is a principle, a part, a fragment of a system of principles for which this war is being waged.

Let me repeat once more: this is not Polonocentricity, it is a faith that finally the hour will come when the "inhuman forces" of history will be vanquished forever, it is a faith that the "divine forces of history" are not, and cannot be, "inhuman."

In a reconstituted democratic Poland—possible only within a reconstituted democratic Europe—it is to be hoped that the historical ideals of Poland will again assert themselves.

[6] See R. H. Lord, *op. cit.*, pp. 3-5.

Bibliography

1. History and Some Special Topics

D'ABERNON, VISCOUNT: *The eighteenth decisive battle of the world*, London, 1931.
ASKENAZY, SZYMON: *Dantzig and Poland*, London, 1922.
BAIN, R. NISBET: *The last King of Poland and his contemporaries*, London, 1909.
BOSWELL, A. BRUCE: *Poland and the Poles*, London, 1919.
BOYD, LOUISE A.: *Polish Countrysides*, New York, 1937.
BRANDES, GEORGE: *Poland, a study of the land, people and literature*, London, 1904.
"Bulletin of the Polish Institute of Arts and Sciences in America," New York, 1942—
The Cambridge History of Poland, Cambridge, 1941—
CHOŁONIEWSKI, ANTONI: *The Spirit of Polish History*, New York, 1918.
COLEMAN, A. P.: *The Polish Insurrection of 1863*, New York, 1934.
DALTON, HERMANN: *John A. Lasco*, A contribution to the history of the Reformation in Poland, Germany and England, London, 1896.
DYBOSKI, ROMAN: *Outlines of Polish History*, London, 1931.
DYBOSKI, ROMAN: *Poland*, London, 1933.
For Your Freedom and Ours, Polish Progressive Spirit Through the Centuries, New York, 1943.
FOX, PAUL: *The Reformation in Poland; Some Social and Economic Aspects*, Baltimore, 1924.
GARDNER, MONICA: *Queen Jadwiga of Poland*, London, 1934.
GARDNER, MONICA: *Kościuszko, a biography*, London, 1942.
GARDNER, MONICA: *Poland, a study in national idealism*, London, 1915.
GÓRKA, O. L.: *Outline of Polish History*, London, 1942.
GÓRSKI, KONRAD: *Aspects of the Polish Reformation: Unitarian thought in 16th and 17th century Poland*, "The Slavonic and East European Review," Vol. 9, pp. 598-611.
HAIMAN, M.: *The Fall of Poland in Contemporary American Opinion*, Chicago, 1935.
HAIMAN, MIECISLAUS: *Kościuszko in the American Revolution*, New York, 1943.
HALECKI, OSCAR: *A History of Poland*, New York, 1943.
HARLEY, J. M.: *Great Britain and the Polish Insurrection of 1863*, "The Slavonic and East European Review," Vol. 16, pp. 155-167, 425-438.
HUMPHREY, GRACE: *Poland the Unexplored*, Indianapolis, 1931.
KELLOG, CHARLOTTE: *Jadwiga, Poland's Great Queen*, New York, 1931.
KUKIEL, M.: *The Polish-Soviet Campaign of 1920*, "The Slavonic and East European Review," Vol. 7, pp. 48-65.

LEDNICKI, WACŁAW: *Poland and the Slavophile Idea,* "The Slavonic and East European Review," Vol. 7, pp. 128-140, 649-662.

LEDNICKI, WACŁAW: *Russian-Polish Relations* (Their historical, cultural and political background), Chicago, 1944.

LEWAK, A.: *The Polish Rising of 1830,* "The Slavonic and East European Review," Vol. 9, pp. 350-360.

MACHRAY, ROBERT: *Poland 1914-1931,* London, 1932.

MACHRAY, ROBERT: *The Poland of Pilsudski,* London, 1937.

MASON, VIOLET: *The Land of the Rainbow: Poland and her people,* London, 1941.

MORTON, L. B.: *Sobieski, King of Poland,* London, 1932.

NEWMAN, BERNARD: *The Story of Poland,* London, 1940.

PADEREWSKI, I.: *Memoires,* New York, 1939.

PANETH, PHILIP: *Is Poland Lost?* London, 1939.

PHILLIPS, CHARLES: *The New Poland,* New York, 1923.

PIŁSUDSKI, JOSEPH: *The Memories of a Polish Revolutionary Soldier,* New York, 1931.

Polish encyclopedia (Publication of the Polish National Committee of America), Vols. 1-3, Geneva, 1922-1926.

"Polish Facts and Figures," published by the Polish Government Information Center, New York, 1944—

"The Polish Review," London, 1917-1918.

"The Polish Review," New York, 1941—

RETINGER, J. H.: *All about Poland,* London, 1940.

ROSE, W. J.: *Poland,* London, 1939.

ROSE, W. J.: *Slavonic Cities, Warsaw,* "The Slavonic and East European Review," Vol. 17, pp. 416-428.

ROSE, W. J.: *Stanislas Konarski, reformer of education in XVIII century Poland,* London, 1929.

SIKORSKI, W.: *Poland's defences,* "The Slavonic and East European Review," Vol. 17, pp. 343-355.

SLOCOMBE, GEORGE: *A History of Poland,* London, 1939.

SULIMIRSKI, TADEUSZ: *Poland and Germany* (Past and Future), London and Edinburgh, 1943.

SUPER, PAUL: *The Polish Tradition,* London, 1940.

SZERUDA, JAN: *The Protestant Churches of Poland,* "The Slavonic and East European Review," Vol. 16, pp. 616-628.

THOMAS, WM. J., and ZNANIECKI, F.: *Polish Peasant in Europe and America,* New York, 1927.

VOIGT, F. A.: *Poland, Russia and Great Britain,* "The Nineteenth Century and After," Vol. 133, pp. 241-259.

VOIGT, F. A.: *Poland,* "The Nineteenth Century and After," Vol. 135, pp. 49-63.

WALISZEWSKI, KAZIMIERZ: *Marysieńka; Marie de la Grange d'Arquien, Queen of Poland and wife of Sobieski,* London, 1898.

WEYERS, DR. J.: *Poland and Russia,* London, 1943.

WINTER, NEVIN O.: *Poland of To-Day and Yesterday,* Boston, 1913.

2. LITERATURE AND ARTS

BOROWY, WACŁAW: *Kasprowicz,* "The Slavonic and East European Review," Vol. 10, pp. 28-41.

BOROWY, WACŁAW: *Reymont,* "The Slavonic and East European Review," Vol. 16, pp. 439-448.

BOROWY, WACŁAW: *Fifteen Years of Polish Literature,* "The Slavonic and East European Review," Vol. 12, pp. 670-690.

CHLEBOWSKI, BRONISŁAW: *Contemporary Polish Literature,* "Russian Review," London, Vol. 2, pp. 95-113.

COLEMAN, A. P.: *Mickiewicz and Northern Balladry,* "The Slavonic and East European Review," Vol. 20, pp. 173-184.

COLEMAN, A. P., and COLEMAN, N. M.: *Adam Mickiewicz in English,* New York, 1940.

DOBRZYCKI, J.: *Old Cracow,* Glasgow, 1941.

DYBOSKI, ROMAN: *Periods of Polish Literary History,* Oxford, 1924.

FORST-BATTAGLIA, O.: *The Polish Novel of To-day,* "The Slavonic and East European Review," Vol. 15, pp. 663-674.

GARDNER, MONICA M.: *Adam Mickiewicz, the national poet of Poland,* London, 1911.

GARDNER, MONICA M.: *The Anonymous poet of Poland; Zygmunt Krasiński,* Cambridge, 1919.

GARDNER, MONICA M.: *The patriot novelist of Poland, Henryk Sienkiewicz,* London, 1926.

GARDNER, MONICA M.: *The Polish rising in the Dramas of Wyspiański,* "The Slavonic and East European Review," Vol. 9, pp. 361-374.

HUMPHREY, G.: *Come with me through Warsaw,* Warsaw, 1934.

HUMPHREY, G.: *Come with me through Krakow,* Krakow, 1934.

KRIDL, MANFRED: *Wacław Berent,* "The Slavonic and East European Review," Vol. XX, pp. 401-404.

KRZYŻANOWSKI, JULIAN: *Polish Romantic Literature,* London, 1930.

KRZYŻANOWSKI, JULIAN: *Bolesław Prus,* "The Slavonic and East European Review," Vol. 9, pp. 695-707.

KRZYŻANOWSKI, JULIAN: *Przybyszewski,* "The Slavonic and East European Review," Vol. 6, pp. 420.

LECHOŃ, JAN: *Polish Literature,* N. Y., 1943.

LEDNICKI, WACŁAW: *Marian Zdziechowski,* "The Slavonic and East European Review," Vol. XX, pp. 407-411.

LEPSZY, LEONARD: *Cracow, the royal capital of ancient Poland; its history and antiquities,* New York, 1912.

LEWITT AND HIM: *Polish Panorama,* London, 1941.

MANNING, C. A.: *The great past of Poland,* "Art and Archeology," (May, 1928), pp. 211-230.

PRZYPKOWSKI, J.: *Warsaw,* Glasgow, 1941.

RETINGER, J.: *Conrad and his contemporaries,* London, 1941.

ROSE, W. J.: *The Poets of Young Poland,* "The Slavonic and East European Review," Vol. 20, pp. 185-199.

SREBRNY, STANISŁAW, *Wyspiański,* "The Slavonic and East European Review," Vol. 2, pp. 359-380.

WALAUX, MARGUERITE: *The National Music of Poland; The Character and Sources,* London, 1917.

ZAWACKI, EDMUND: *The Utopianism of Stefan Żeromski,* "The Slavonic and East European Review," Vol. 21, pp. 96-113.

ZIELIŃSKI, TADEUSZ: *The Peasant in Polish Literature,* "The Slavonic and East European Review," Vol. 1, pp. 584-597, Vol. 2, pp. 85-100.

For special research and translations from Polish into English see: *Polish Literature in English Translation.* A bibliography with a list of books about Poland and the Poles, compiled by E. E. Ledbetter, published under the auspices of the Polish National Alliance, New York, 1932, and *What to Read about Poland,* compiled by J. M. Baxter, Scottish-Polish Society Publications; No. 3, Edinburgh and London, 1942.

Index*

Adamczewski, Stanisław, critic, 297
Aesop, 93
Aksakov, S. T., 185
Alembert, J. d', 11
Alexander I of Russia, 116, 162, 169, 173, 224, 228, 253
Alexander II of Russia, 21
Amicis, E. de, 265
Ancelot, J. A. P. F., 174
Andreev, L., 293, 295
Andriolli, M. E., painter, 133
Ankwicz, H. Mlle., 189
Ariosto, L., 97, 202
Aristotle, 49, 56, 64, 99
Artzybashev, M., Russian novelist, 295
Askenazy, Szymon, historian, 27, 112
Attila, 274, 275
Aubigné, Agrippa d', 38
Axentowicz, Teodor, painter, 110

Bach, J. S., 110
Ballanche, P. S., 185, 217, 268
Balzac, H. d', 264
Balzer, Oswald, historian, 112
Barbier, H. A., 213
Barcewicz, Stanisław, violinist, 111
Barrault, E., 266
Barthélemy, A. M., 220
Batory, Stefan, King of Poland, 53, 66, 78, 89, 102, 162
Baudelaire, C., 293

Baudouin de Courtenay, Jan, scholar, 112
Bazard, St. A., 266
Beardsley, S. A., 293
Bellay, J. du, 97
Bely, A. (Bugaev), Russian poet, 197, 270
Bem, Józef, General, patriot, 225
Benkendorf, A. Kh., Russian general, 175
Béranger, P. J. de, 213, 215
Berent, W., novelist, 123, 255, 288, 293
Berga, A., 71, 74
Bergson, H., 259
Bernacki, Ludwik, scholar, 112
Bernardin de Saint-Pierre, J. H., 140
Bestuzhev, A. A., Russian writer, 170
Bèze, Théodore de, 38
Bibesco, M. L., Princess, 133
Bielski, Marcin, chronicler, 92, 98
Biernat of Lublin, humanist, 93
Bilbasov, V. A., Russian historian, 142
Bismarck, O., Prince von, 18, 21, 22, 218
Blanc, L., 268
Blok, A., Russian poet, 197, 198, 201, 255, 270
Bobola, Wojciech, nobleman, 137
Bobrzyński, Michał, historian, 20, 24, 25, 26, 27, 105, 112
Boehme, J., 204

* This index does not include names mentioned in the Bibliography.

321

NOTE FROM AUTHOR

THE passage on page 210 beginning with the words "It was a new Homer etc.", containing a comparison of Mickiewicz with Homer, is repeated from memory. It is a comparison which the late Professor S. Kolaczkowski used in one of his studies on the Polish poet.

5- 8
11- 3